HAPPINESS IS FREE

And It's Easier Than You Think

BOOKS 1 THROUGH 5

The Greatest Secret Edition

Lester Levenson
& Hale Dwoskin

Sedona Press

Sedona Press, a division of
Sedona Training Associates

2000 Plymouth Road, Suite 300
Minnetonka, Minnesota 55305

888-282-5656 (US and Canada)
1-952-767-9822

Mail@Sedona.com
www.Sedona.com

"The Sedona Method'" is a registered trademark owned by
Sedona Training Associates

ISBN: 978-0-9719334-9-1

Library of Congress Control Number: 2020919826

In loving memory of Lester Levenson

and

*To all seekers and finders of the ultimate happiness everywhere
and Sedona Method graduates worldwide*

Contents

Acknowledgments

from Hale Dwoskin

I would like to thank the following people for making this book possible: My loving wife, Amy Edwards; all Sedona Method graduates worldwide; all the teachers who have influenced our work, including Ramana Maharshi, Nisargadatta Maharaj, and Robert Adams; and all the Sedona Training Associates staff.

Foreword

*With the deepest love and gratitude
to the legendary Lester Levenson*

Lester Levenson was a man who discovered the Ultimate Happiness that is available to each of us. His journey started in 1952, when his doctor told him he had very little time to live due to his damaged heart. And Lester's heart was not the only issue; he had been living with many health problems, including depression, migraine headaches, gastrointestinal imbalances, jaundice, an enlarged liver, kidney stones, spleen trouble, hyperacidity, and ulcers that had perforated his stomach and formed lesions. Upon hearing the news from the doctor that he would die any day, Lester went home. For the first few days he was terrified of dying. Then, he decided that if he was going to die, he would at least reflect back on his life and work out why he had rarely been happy. This began a process that was to become the journey of his life.

Lester searched back through all the memories from his life and looked for the times when he was actually the happiest. To his amazement, what he found was that it was not when he was loved that he was happy. It was when *he loved* that he was at his happiest. With this revelation, Lester took his unhappy memories one at a time, and loved each one, causing any suppressed negative emotions around the memory to be released. With each negative emotion that was released, Lester discovered that hundreds, thousands, tens of thousands, and even hundreds of thousands of negative thoughts were released at the same time. From following this process, and from several other profound realizations, all the negativity was gone from his body, his heart condition spontaneously resolved itself, and one by one every disease and affliction in his body disappeared. Even more miraculous than the healing of every affliction in his body, Lester became enlightened. And all of this happened in just a three-month period!

Lester lived for another forty-two years in continuous peace and joy. He was the living proof of what takes place in a diseased body when the light of the truth penetrates it. Lester used to say that "disease in the body is disease in the mind."

Lester has been an inspiration to thousands upon thousands of people, and his teachings have continued to inspire and free many from suffering well after the death of his form in 1994. Lester called his practice of releasing negative emotions the Sedona Method. And in the early 1990s Lester passed his teachings to one of his students, Hale Dwoskin, who is featured in both *The Secret* and *The Greatest Secret*.

One of my most treasured books that changed my life is Lester's *Keys to the Ultimate Freedom.* It features Lester's words and insights drawn from decades of his teachings, and it is the only book that sits on my bedside table. Unfortunately the book has been out of print for a long time, but Hale Dwoskin has taken all of Lester's teachings from *Keys to the Ultimate Freedom* and put them in this new book, along with many of the releasing methods from the Sedona Method. You have the best of Lester's teachings and his methods in this one book, and if freedom and joy are what you seek, I couldn't recommend this book more. I used the Sedona Method occasionally over a ten-year period and found enormous benefit from it. Then, when I met my teacher—who was a student of Lester Levenson's—four years ago, Lester's releasing methods became a crucial part of my everyday life and my awakening.

I remind myself often that Lester was just like you and me, and yet he discovered his true Self and became fully enlightened in just three months. It didn't take him lifetimes or even decades to awaken, making his story nothing short of inspirational. It means we can follow in Lester's footsteps and in a very short time be totally free of any suffering and be in lasting joy and happiness. Let's say "yes" to that!

Rhonda Byrne
author of *The Secret* and *The Greatest Secret*

What Is Happiness?

Hale Dwoskin

Happiness is your natural state. It is totally independent of whatever you have, be, or do, yet it improves all that you experience. It makes it all more enjoyable, precious, and easier. Happiness really is who you are, and you can experience this for yourself by looking openly and honestly at your own direct experience.

If you are in doubt that this is possible for you, that is okay. I encourage you to believe nothing that you read in this book until you can prove it for yourself. But I promise you that what this book points to is really possible for you. I have the absolute conviction that you can uncover your ultimate happiness and live it in every moment. This conviction is based on my own direct experience over more than four decades of working with the teachings of the late Lester Levenson, my friend, mentor, and the coauthor of this book, and then sharing his teachings with hundreds of thousands of people around the world.

Quite simply put, happiness is you being your Self. Not the limited self that you pretend to be most of the time, but the unlimited Self that you are and have always been. This is the Self that is always effortlessly present before, during, and after everything else that appears in your experience. You are the radiant yet changeless background that allows for everything else to exist, even in a tumultuous world.

For most of us, this is not our living experience. We have covered over our Beingness with thoughts, feelings, and beliefs to the contrary. We now spend most of our time bolstering the illusions that we have created for ourselves, leaving very little time for the inner reflection that can set us free from this totally self-imposed and artificial sense of limitation.

It takes tremendous energy to maintain the illusion that unlimited Beingness is actually limited to the particular body-mind that you call yourself. No wonder we are so exhausted most of the time. We have unlimited energy available to us, but instead of using this energy for good or to discover who we truly are, we use this energy to convince ourselves and others around us that we are limited—that we have personal problems.

Lester used to say that extricating ourselves from this situation in which we all find ourselves is either "simple or impossible." It is simple when we allow it to be easy. We can allow our energy to flow inward toward self-discovery and for loving acceptance of what is. It is impossible when we force our energy to flow outward. We fight against the world of our own creation and try to prove to everyone, including ourselves, that our world and its problems are real.

Are you ready to make it simple? You probably are if you were attracted to reading this book. This book is designed to guide you experientially to rediscover your ultimate happiness by uncovering the real unlimited you.

As you read this book and work with the material, you will have a direct experience of Lester's teaching style. This is significant, because it is something that very few people were lucky enough to experience during the last twenty years of his life.

This book contains thirty-five "sessions" with Lester that were sent out as weekly lessons before the creation of the Sedona Method. They helped his students dive more deeply into his teachings.

He worked with people on a one-to-one basis and in small groups, teaching sessions very much like those you will experience in this book. About 1974, with the help of some of his closest students, he summarized his teaching into a do-it-yourself system that we now call the Sedona Method and the process we refer to as releasing or letting go.

He did this to take himself out of the teaching loop. No matter how often he protested to the contrary, his students would attribute their gains and realizations to him because they felt so elevated in his presence. He wanted everyone to know that they could discover just what he had on their own without needing an external teacher.

Before Lester died, he asked me to continue his work and find ways to make the experience of letting go more powerful, direct, and more readily available. When he turned over his teachings to me before he died there was one way of letting go—deciding to drop the feeling. As I continued to work with people, four more ways were developed. They are welcoming what is, diving into the core, welcoming opposing polarities, and the Awareness-based group of questions we call the 5th Way—Free Way. I have added "Releasing Explorations" at the end of each session to expose you to all of the ways of letting go that we teach. I hope you will find the combination of the sessions and releasing explorations liberating, enlightening, and even fun.

Lester's sessions were first published in 1993 under the title *Keys to the Ultimate Freedom: Thoughts and Talks on Personal Transformation* and then in 2001 as *Happiness Is Free: And It's Easier Than You Think,* a five-book series. It only included two ways of letting go because at the time those were the main ways we taught releasing. The other ways of letting go were in their infancy. We decided to update the book and rerelease it now with all of the ways of letting go in celebration of Rhonda Byrne's book *The Greatest Secret.*

I urge you to treat this book as an opportunity to discover your true nature and uncover your innate happiness, peace, and joy. You can benefit from this book even if you only read it casually. But if you dedicate yourself to using it to the fullest, the results you can achieve will astound you.

About Lester's Language

Hale Dwoskin

Lester had a unique way of using the English language. I have purposely preserved his style of communication, because I've noticed that when you read or listen to any teacher in his or her own vernacular, the words have more of an import than when they have been heavily edited. My intention here is to give you the feel of having been present as Lester's talks unfolded, so that you can be as open as possible to his deepest message.

Lester came to this unique communication style for several reasons. His realization came quickly and spontaneously without him following any particular teacher or discipline or even having done any reading or studying of the path. So, he had no language that adequately expressed what he was experiencing and what he wanted to share with others. As a result, he looked in existing spiritual books from both the East and the West to try to find a suitable language that would best communicate his amazing discoveries. From the East, he was attracted to the teachings and writings of Ramana Maharshi and Paramahansa Yogananda. From the West, he drew upon the Bible, especially the New Testament. You will probably notice the influence of these sources in his writing. Occasionally he even slips into Old English to express himself.

Most of the Lester material in this book comes from talks that took place in the 1960s and early 1970s. Therefore, he often uses a vernacular that was more appropriate for that era. You will notice that his reference to current events and statistics, like population figures, are also reflective of that same time period.

In addition, Lester had difficulty grounding himself in time. He saw time as a self-imposed limitation or merely a concept. He would refer to things as happening yesterday that happened ten or twenty years earlier, and things that were about to happen that have yet to occur. He always seemed to be factually accurate and yet frequently was not able to place his perceptions in the appropriate time period.

Lester also did not believe in the limitation of space, so the words *here* and *there* often had the same meaning to him. He would often refer to getting "there" when referring to Beingness when he really meant "here." Or "going free" when he knew there was nowhere to go. He also used language this way because he was wanting to communicate to people where they were. Most people believe that Beingness is apart from where they are now; that's why they go looking for it. The "there" that Lester referred to when speaking of Beingness is closer than your breath.

Lester also learned his instructing style from an old school that uses imperatives heavily. He often used the charged words *should, have to, must,* and *only.* These words were used by Lester to wake people up by using a little extra force. If you notice that these words stir up resistance in you, this in normal. These words tend to do that in most of us. Allow yourself to let go of the resistance as best you can and be open to the underlying message.

He also saw himself as a cheerleader for Truth, so he tended to use language designed to inspire and motivate us toward greater dedication to exploration and letting go.

Lester saw everyone as Beingness not their bodies. However, his language reflected the bias in the vernacular of the 1960s and he described God and master as "he" even though he saw no distinction between "he" and "she."

I loved being with Lester and I feel so fortunate and blessed that I was given this great gift. It was not just his words that inspired. It was his living presence and unshakable peace and joy. Please allow yourself to tune into the silence in between the words as best you can so you can be this presence of Awareness that we all share.

Please keep these points in mind as you read the sessions so you can allow yourself to remain as open as possible to his message without getting lost in how it is being communicated.

Lester's Story

Hale Dwoskin

I met Lester Levenson in 1976. Back then I was an ardent, although confused seeker who had gone to many trainings and seminars led by teachers from both the East and the West. I had studied various body-centered disciplines, including yoga, tai chi, and shiatsu. I had actively participated in various courses, including Erhard Seminars Training (EST), Actualism, Theta Healing Seminars, and rebirthing. I had many nice experiences at these seminars and heard and understood—at least intellectually—many useful concepts. Still I felt incomplete. I longed for a simple and powerful answer to some important, yet vexing questions like: "What is my life's purpose?" "What is Truth?" and "Who am I?"

Much of what I had heard and experienced only added to my questioning. No one seemed to have truly satisfying answers or have truly satisfied themselves about what their true nature was or what the ultimate Truth was. There was also a strong, almost universal belief that growing was hard work and required baring your soul and reliving painful, unresolved issues. However, that all changed during a very fortunate encounter with a remarkable man.

I met Lester at a seminar that I had organized for a well-known speaker, which Lester attended as the seminar leader's guest. That day, a group of us went out to lunch together, where Lester's presence immediately struck me as special. He was in total peace and equal mindedness, very comfortable with himself. He was unassuming and easy to talk to and treated everyone as his friend—even me, a complete stranger. It was obvious that he had ended his search by discovering the answers I'd been seeking. I knew I had to find out more.

When I asked Lester what he did, he invited me to a seminar that was being held the next weekend. All he would tell me about it was that "a group of people is going to sit around a table and release." I wasn't sure what that meant, but I knew if it could even point me in the direction of the qualities of which Lester was the living embodiment, I definitely wanted it. I took a leap of faith and signed up on the spot.

Almost overnight I knew that I had found what I was looking for. Deep inside I knew that this process of releasing and Lester's teachings were what I had been born to do and share with the world.

Before his passing in 1994, Lester passed all his teachings and copyrights to me and asked me to continue his work and dream of helping the world find a way to be free of suffering. Lester told me that I would expand this work and make it easier and more powerful, and to this day I have never wavered.

Now I would love to share Lester's story with you. It is told in his own words.

I was born July 19, 1909, in Elizabeth, New Jersey, into a middle-class family as a very shy person. I tried to do things the way they were supposed to be done—doing the right thing, getting a good education, and being the best in my field. My natural inclination was toward science, especially the science of the world, and of man himself. I graduated from Rutgers University in 1931 as a physicist, after which I worked twenty-some years in physics and engineering. In physics, I worked in research and development on measuring instruments and automatic control, connected with Brown Instrument Co., which later became a subsidiary of Honeywell. And in the engineering field, I worked as a mechanical engineer, an electrical engineer, a construction engineer, a heating and venting engineer, and a marine engineer—actually, fourteen different fields.

I also went into various businesses, including restaurants, lumber, building, and oil, intertwined with engineering, wanting to make money, wanting to make it in the world. At that time, I did not know what I now know—that what I was seeking was actually the answers to life itself. Nothing that I had worked at would give me that answer, and as the years went by, I became heavy with depression and with sickness.

By 1952, I had been through constant illness—I even had jaundice three or so times a year. I had an enlarged liver, kidney stones, spleen trouble, hyper- and hypo-acidity, ulcers that perforated and formed lesions, and to top it off, I had at least ten years of migraine headaches. This all culminated in 1952 when I had my second coronary thrombosis.

After the second coronary, I was told I would not live much longer—that I might die any day and shouldn't make the effort to take so much as a step unless I necessarily had to. I was extremely fearful of dying, but I said to myself, "You're still breathing, Lester—there is still a chance." So I sat down and began thinking on an "around the clock" basis. Having lived forty-two or so years, and having reached the end of the line without happiness, without health, I realized that all the knowledge I had accumulated was of no avail. I had studied Watson's behaviorism in the 30s and Freud's in the late 30s and early 40s. I had studied the philosophies. I had studied logic. I studied economics. I studied all the major fields of man, and with all that knowledge there, I was at the end of the line. This made me realize that the accumulated knowledge of man was of no use.

So I decided to start from scratch. Forget all that knowledge. Begin from point zero and see what you can pick up. So, I posed the questions, "What am I?" "What is this World?" "What is my relationship to it?" "What is Mind?" "What is Intelligence?" "What is Happiness?"

I began by asking myself, "What do I want out of life?" And the answer was happiness. Investigating further, I went into the moment when I was feeling happiest. I discovered something which to me was startling at the time. It was when I was loving that I was happiest. That happiness equated to my capacity to love rather than to being loved. That was a starting point.

I began correcting all my thoughts and feelings in that direction from that of wanting to be loved, to that of loving. And in that process, I discovered another major thing that kind of shocked me. I saw that I wanted to change this entire world, and that was the cause of my ulcers—or one of the major causes. In realizing how much I wanted to change things in this world, I saw how it made me a slave of this world, I made the decision to reverse that. And in the process of following out these two directions—actually unloading all the subconscious concepts and pressures in those directions—I discovered I was getting happier, freer, lighter, and feeling better in general.

As I saw this direction was good, I made the decision that if a slice of pie tasted this good, I wanted the whole pie. And I decided not to let go of this direction until I got that entire pie of happiness, and with it the answer to, "What am I? What is this life, and what is my relationship to it?" This decision allowed me, as I claim, to get the answer to life itself in a matter of only three months. I believe if I can do it, anyone can do it if they have that much "want to."

In that three-month period, all the ailments I had in my physical body corrected. All my miseries dropped away. And I ended up in a place in which I was happy all the time, without sorrow. Not that the world stopped pushing against me, it continued—but I was at a place where I could resolve things almost immediately. Having cleared out the negative fears, all the negative "I cannots," I would focus right on the answer to every problem, and get it very quickly. And so, my whole life turned around from being depressed and sick, to being happy all the time, and being in perfect health all the time.

One of the things that happened in this process was my identification with others. I saw that we are all related, we are all interconnected, each mind is like a radio broadcasting and receiving station; that we are all tuned into each other unconsciously—that we are just not aware of it. As a lot of the suppressed energies are let out, this becomes obvious to us and once we identify with everyone else it is just natural that we want everyone else to discover what we have discovered. That life was meant to be beautiful . . . meant to be happy all the time with no sorrow. And to be with perfect health. And so after reaching that high point of understanding in 1952, I have wanted to help others to discover what I had discovered.

I was deeply moved by Lester's story because it offered hope for all of us who may not have had the good fortune to have an ideal life. Lester was able to discover his true nature in a relatively short time and despite extreme adversity. If he could do it, I knew that I could too.

In the following section Lester expands on his actual realization.

I was at the end of my rope. I was told not to take a step unless I absolutely had to because there was a possibility that I could drop dead at any moment.

This was a terrible, shocking thing, suddenly to be told that I couldn't be active anymore, having been so active all my life. It was a horrible thing. An intense fear of dying overwhelmed me, the fear that I might drop dead any minute. This stayed with me for days. I went through a real, horrible, low, spinning period there, in the grip of intense fear of dying or of being a cripple for the rest of my life in that I wouldn't be able to be active. I felt that life would not be worthwhile any more.

This caused me to conclude with determination, "Either I get the answers, or I'll take me off this earth. No heart attack will do it!" I had a nice easy way to do it too. I had morphine the doctors gave me for my kidney stone attacks.

After several days of this intense fear of dying, I suddenly realized, "Well, I'm still alive. As long as I'm alive there's hope. As long as I'm alive, maybe I can get out of this. What do I do?"

Well, I was always a smart boy, always made the honor roll. Even got myself a four-year scholarship to Rutgers University at a time when scholarships were very rare through competitive examinations. But what does this avail me? Nothing! Here I am with all this brilliance, as miserable and scared as can be.

Then I said, "Lester, you were not only not smart, you were dumb! Dumb! Dumb! There's something wrong in your intellect. With all your knowledge, you've come to this bottom end! Drop all this knowledge you've so studiously picked up on philosophy, psychology, social science, and economics! It is of no avail! Start from scratch. Begin all over again your search for the answers.

And with an extreme desperation and intense wanting out—not wanting to die, I began to question, "What am I? What is this world? What is my relationship to it? What do I want from it?"

"Happiness."

"Well, what is happiness?"

"Being loved."

"But I am loved. I know several very desirable girls with beauty, charm, and intellect who want me. And I have the esteem of my friends. Yet, I'm miserable!"

I sensed that the closest thing related to happiness was love. So I began reviewing and reliving my past love affairs, looking at the points where the little happiness that I had were. I began to pull up and dissect all my high moments of loving. Suddenly, I got an inkling that it was when I was loving that I had the highest feeling!

I remembered one evening, a beautiful balmy evening in the mountains when I was camping with my girlfriend. We were both lying on the grass, both looking up at the sky, and I had my arm around her. The nirvana, the perfection of the height of happiness was right there. I was feeling how great is love for my girlfriend! How wonderful is knowing all this nature! How perfect a setting!

Then I saw that it was my loving her that was the cause of this happiness! Not the beauty of the setting or being with my girlfriend.

Then I immediately turned to the other side. Boy it was great when she loved me! I remembered the moment when publicly this beautiful, charming girl told the world that she approved of Lester, she loved Lester—and I could feel that nice feeling of approval. But I sensed that it was not as great as what I had just discovered. It was not a lasting feeling. It was just for the moment. In order for me to have that feeling continuously, she had to continue saying that.

So, this momentary ego approval was not as great as the feeling of loving her! As long as I was loving her, I felt so happy. But when she loved me, there were only moments of happiness when she gave me approval.

Days of further cogitation gradually revealed to me that this was correct! I was happier when I loved her than I was when I got that momentary ego-satisfaction when she loved me. Her loving me was a momentary pleasure that needed constant showing and proving on her part, while my loving her was a constant happiness, as long as I was loving her.

I concluded that my happiness equated to my loving! If I could increase my loving, then I could increase my happiness! This was the first inkling I had as to what brings about happiness. And it was a tremendous thing because I hadn't had happiness. And I said, "Gee, if this is the key to happiness, I've got the greatest!" Even the hope of getting more and more happiness was a tremendous thing, because this was the number one thing I wanted—happiness.

That started me on weeks and weeks of reviewing my past love affairs. I dug up from the past, incident after incident when I thought I was loving, and I discovered that I was being nice to my girlfriends, trying to get them to love me, and that that was selfish. That was not really love. That was just wanting my ego bolstered!

I kept reviewing incidents from the past, and where I saw that I was not loving, I would change that feeling to loving that person. Instead of wanting them to do something for me, I would change it to my wanting to do something for them. I kept this up until I couldn't find any more incidents to work on.

This insight on love, seeing that happiness was determined by my capacity to love, was a tremendous insight. It began to free me, and any bit of freedom when you're plagued feels so good. I knew that I was in the right direction. I had gotten hold of a link of the chain of happiness and was determined not to let go until I had the entire chain.

I felt a greater freedom. There was an easier concentration of my mind because of it. And I began to look better at my mind. What is my mind? What is intelligence?

Suddenly, a picture flashed of amusement park bumper cars that are difficult to steer so that they continually bump into each other. They all get their electrical energy from the wire screen above the cars through a pole coming down to every car.

The power above was symbolic of the overall intelligence and energy of the universe coming down the pole to me and everyone else, and to the degree we step on the gas, do we use it? Each driver of the cars is taking the amount of energy and intelligence that he wants from that wire, but he steers his car blindly and bumps into other cars, and bumps and bumps.

I saw that if I chose to, I could take more and more of that overall intelligence.

And so I dug into that. I began to examine thinking and its relationship to what was happening. And it was revealed that everything that was happening had a prior thought behind it and that I never before related the thought and the happening because of the element of time between the two.

When I saw that everything that was happening to me had a thought of it before it happened, I realized that if I could grab hold of this, I could consciously determine everything that was happening to me!

And above all, I saw that I was responsible for everything that had happened to me, formerly thinking that the world was abusing me! I saw that my whole past life, and all that tremendous effort to make money and in the end, failing, was due only to my thinking!

This was a tremendous piece of freedom, to think that I was not a victim of this world, that it lay within my power to arrange the world the way I wanted it to be, that rather than being an effect of it, I could now be a cause over it and arrange it the way I would like it to be!

That was a tremendous realization, a tremendous feeling of freedom!

I was so ill when I started my searching; I had one foot in the grave. And when I saw that my thinking was cause for what was happening to me, I immediately saw my body from my chin down to my toes as perfect. And instantly, I knew it was perfect! I knew the lesions and adhesions of my intestine due to perforated ulcers were undone. I knew everything within me was in perfect running order.

And it was.

Discovering that my happiness equated to my loving, discovering that my thinking was the cause of things happening to me in my life gave me more and more freedom. Freedom from unconscious compulsions that I had to work, I had to make money, and I had to have girls. Freedom in the feeling that I was now able to determine my destiny, I was now able to control my world, I was now able to arrange my environment to suit me. This new freedom lightened my internal burden so greatly that I felt that I had no need to do anything.

Plus, the new happiness I was experiencing was so great! I was experiencing a joy that I had never known existed. I had never dreamed happiness could be so great.

I determined "If this is so great, I'm not going to let go of it until I carry it all the way!" I had no idea how joyous a person could be.

So, I began digging further on how to extend this joy. I began further changing my attitudes on love. I would imagine the girl I wanted most marrying one of my friends, or the boy I would want her to marry least, and then enjoy their enjoying each other. To me, this was the extreme in loving, and if I could achieve it, it would give me more of this wonderful thing that I was experiencing.

And so I worked on it. I took a particular fellow, Burl, and a particular girl, and I wouldn't let go until I could really feel the joy of their enjoying each other.

Then I knew I had it—or almost had it.

Then later on, I had further tests of this in talking to people who were opposing me no end when I was trying to help them. I would consciously feel the greatest love for them when they were attacking me. And the joy of loving them was so wonderful, I would, without any thought, thank them so profusely for having given me the opportunity of talking with them, that it threw them into a dither.

But I really felt that. I thanked them from the bottom of my heart for having given me the opportunity of loving them when they were making it as difficult as they possibly could. I didn't express that to them. I just thanked them for the opportunity of having been able to talk with them.

That I was able to do this was good news to me because, like other things, I was able to carry loving to the extreme. I could love people who were opposing me.

And I would not stop until I could see the end of the line of this happiness I was getting. I would go higher and higher and higher and say, "Oh, my gosh, there can be nothing higher than this!" But I would try. And I would go higher. Then I would say, "Oh, there can't be anything higher than this!" But I would try, and go higher! And then say, "Oh, there can't be anything happier than this!" until I realized there was no limit to happiness!

I would get incapacitated. I could look at my body, and I couldn't move it I was so top-heavy with ecstasy and joy. I was actually incapacitated. I would do this for hours, going higher and higher and then I would have to work for hours to keep coming down and down and down until I could start being the body again in order to operate it.

Contemplating the source of intelligence and energy, I discovered that energy, as well as intelligence was available in unlimited amounts, and that it came simply by my freeing myself from all compulsions, inhibitions, entanglements, hang-ups. I saw that I had dammed up this energy, this power, and all I had to do was pry loose the logs of the dam which were my compulsions and hang-ups—and that was what I did. As I let go of these things, I was removing logs and allowing this infinite energy to flow, just like a water dam flows if you pull the logs out, one by one. The more logs you pull out, the greater the flow. All I needed to do was to remove these logs and let the infinite power and energy flow.

Seeing this, the power that was right behind my mind was allowed to flow through like it had never flowed before. There were times when I'd get this realization of what I am that would put so much energy into me, I would just jump up in the air from my chair. I would go right straight out the front door, and I would start walking and walking and walking, for hours at a time—sometimes for days at a time! I just felt as though my body would not contain it, that I had to walk or run some of it off. I remember walking the streets of New York City in the wee hours of the morning, just walking at a very good pace, and not being able to do anything otherwise! I had to expend some of that energy. It was so tremendous.

I saw that the source of all this energy, of all intelligence was basically harmonious, and that harmony was the rule of the universe. And that was why the planets were not colliding, and that was why the sun rose every day, and that was why everything functioned.

When I started my search, I was a very convinced and absolute materialist. The only thing that was real was that which you could feel and touch. My understanding of the world was as solid as concrete. And when some of these revelations came to me that the world was just a result of my mind, that thinking determined all matter, that matter had no intelligence, and that our intelligence determined all matter and everything about it. When I saw that the solidity that I formerly had was only a thought itself, my nice, solid, concrete foundations began to crack. Twenty years of buildup began to tumble.

And my body shook, and shook so much; I just shook for days. I shook just like a nervous old person. I knew that the concrete view I had had of the world was never going to be again.

But it didn't drop away gracefully, with ease. For days, I actually shook, until I think I shook the whole thing loose.

Then, my view was just the opposite of what it had been months previously, that the real solid thing was not the physical world, was not my mind, but something, which was much greater. The very essence, the very Beingness of me was the reality. It had no limits, it was eternal, and all the things that I saw before were the least of me, rather than the all of me. The all of me was by Beingness.

I saw that the only limitations I had were the ones that I accepted. So, wanting to know what am I? And looking for this unlimited Being that I had had an inkling of, I got insight of this tremendous unlimited Being that I am.

And on seeing that, I right there and then realized, "Well, I'm not this limited body and I thought I was! I am not this mind with its limitations that I thought I was!"

And I undid all body limitation, and almost all mind limitation, just by saying, "I am not it! Finished! Done! Period! That's it!" I so declared.

It was obvious to me that I wasn't that body and mind that I had thought I was. I just saw that's all! It's simple when you see it.

I let go of identifying with this body. And when I did that, I saw that my Beingness was all Beingness. That Beingness is like one grand ocean. It's not chopped up into parts called drops of bodies. It's all one ocean.

This caused me to identify with every being, every person and even every atom in this universe. Then you are finished forever with separation and all the hellishness that's caused only by separation.

Then you can no more be fooled by the apparent limitations of the world. You see them as a dream, as an appearance, because you know that your very own Beingness has no limits.

In reality, the only thing that is, is Beingness. That is the real, changeless substance behind everything.

Everything of life itself was open to me, the total understanding of it. It is simply that we are infinite beings, over which we have superimposed concepts of limitation (the logs of the dam). And we are smarting under these limitations that we accept for ourselves as though they are real, because they are opposed to our basic nature of total freedom.

Life before and after my realization was at two different extremes. Before, it was just extreme depression, intense misery, and sickness. After, it was a happiness and serenity that's indescribable. Life became so beautiful and so harmonious that all day, every day, everything would fall perfectly into line.

As I would drive through New York City, I would rarely hit a red light. When I would go to park my car, people sometimes two or three people would stop and even step into the street to help direct me into a parking space. There were times when taxicab drivers would see me looking for a parking space and would give up their space for me. And after they did, they couldn't understand why they had done it. There they were, double-parked!

Even policemen who were parked would move out and give me their parking place. And again, after they did, they couldn't understand why. But I knew they felt good in doing so. And they would continue to help me.

If I went into a store, the salesman would happily go out of his way to help me. Or, if I would order something in a restaurant and then change my mind, the waitress would bring what I wanted, even though I hadn't told her.

Actually everyone moves to serve you as you just float around. When you are in tune and you have a thought, every atom in the universe moves to fulfill your thought. And this is true.

Being in harmony is such a delightful, delectable state, not because things are coming your way, but because of the feeling of God-in-operation. It's a tremendous feeling; you just can't imagine how great it is. It is such a delight when you're in tune, in harmony—you see God everywhere! You're watching God in operation. And that is what you enjoy, rather than the time, the incident, the happening. His operation is the ultimate.

When we get in tune, our capacity to love is so extreme that we love everyone with an extreme intensity that makes living the most delightful it could ever be.

When I found the explanation above, I was deeply moved. As I worked to put this book together, I knew it was important for you to be exposed to it as well so you could appreciate the point of view from which Lester did his teaching.

Lester dedicated the rest of his life, from 1952 through his death in 1994, as he put it, to "helping the rest of him discover what he had discovered." He joyously lived for others without any sense of sacrifice, tirelessly working to help them to discover their true nature or at least let go of their suffering.

The Basic Goal
and Ways to Attainment

Lester Levenson

That which every one of us is looking for in this world is exactly the same thing. Every Being, even the animal, is looking for it. And what is it that we are all looking for? Happiness with no sorrow! A continuous state of happiness with no taint whatsoever of sorrow. Now, if this is the goal, why is it the goal? The reason why it is the goal is because imperturbable happiness is our very basic nature! And what is imperturbable happiness? Complete and total freedom—and that is freedom to do or not to do anything and everything. This is the real natural state, before we encumber it with limitations.

Why is it that most of us do not have this continuous happiness with no sorrow? There is only one reason: being this infinite Being, we have done away with this happiness by thinking, "I am an individual, separate from the all, " and thereby we have assumed limitation. To make myself separate from the all, I must set up a means to accomplish this. The means is my mind, and, with my mind, I create my body and the external world. Then I proceed, looking for the all in the external world, creating more and more thoughts and matter until the thoughts and matter have me so involved that I have forgotten my real identity as the infinite Beingness that I am.

The original thought of, "I am separate from the All" necessarily creates a feeling of lack and loneliness. I am only satisfied when I am the All. Seeking fulfillment of desire in the world therefore cannot undo the lack, as lack is not there in the first place; lack is assumed in my mind. Our totality is in our Beingness only, and we go on and on trying to satisfy desire externally, and we never, never succeed. If we could succeed, we would be able to satisfy desire, and, therefore, all desire would disappear!

The real purpose of being here on this earth is to learn, or to re-remember, our original natural state of totality of Beingness, which allows imperturbability with complete freedom and no limitation. Once we are led to see that this is our natural state, then we begin to let go of all the limitations.

The prime, the very first, limitation is the feeling, "I am an individual separate from the All." Eliminate that and you eliminate all loneliness, all limitation.

To say this in another way, "God is all! Let go and let God be. It is not I but the Father who worketh through me." We must let go of the ego sense, which is the original sense of our separation—from the All—and allow our natural Being to just be, and then everything will fall perfectly into line. However, even after this idea is accepted, we do not find it easy to accomplish. We don't find it easy because of habits that have been established since the beginning of time. And, for some reason, we like these habits, and so we continue them. We call them subconsciously directed behavior, and we go on and on and on behaving automatically, as though we are a victim of our subconscious mind.

Now, the subconscious mind is only that part of the mind that we refuse to look at. When our desire for freedom is strong enough, we will dig up these subconscious habits, look at them and begin to let go of them.

There is no growing into the natural Being that you are. That Being is whole and perfect, here and now. There is only letting go of the concepts to the contrary—that you have limitations, that you have troubles. Anyone who says, "I have trouble," has it in his mind. That is the only place where it is, because you can't see or conceive of anything anywhere else but in your mind. Whatever you look at, whatever you hear, whatever you sense, is in and through your mind. That is where everything is. Change your thinkingness and you change your world for you. Do this and you have the proof!

So, the way to freedom—the path—is simple, but the method of undoing the limitations is not easy because of habit. We need a very strong desire to begin to let go of these habits. Without that strong desire, there is no growth. This desire must be stronger than the desire for the world—to control the external world or to have its approval.

The world as you now see it is really an imagination. When you see the Truth, the world turns out to be a dream, a fiction in your mind. First you will see it as a dream, and then you will see it as a dream that never really was. It is exactly as what happens with a night dream. While you are in the night dream, you have a body. There are other bodies, there is action, interaction, there is good and there is bad. And so long as you remain in that night dream, everything there is real to you. When you awaken from the night dream, you say, "My gosh, it was just a dream! It never really happened! This dream was all in my mind!" And in exactly the same manner you will awaken from this dream called the waking state. You come to see that it was only a fiction of your imagination; it was only a dream. And then you let go of it—lock, stock, and barrel, and what is left over is the infinite you! Then you are called fully realized, totally free.

Actually, we are fully realized all the time. We are fully realized Beings saying that we are not. So, all we do is let go of "we are not," and what is left over is the fully realized and free Being that we are.

Are there any questions on what I've said so far? No? Then everyone understands this, at least intellectually.

All right, if you understand this intellectually, and you are not able to use it, it is because you are not looking at yourself honestly, truthfully, with a deep desire to let go of your limitations. You have set up in your subconscious mind all the things you will not look at, and they have culminated as inhibiting and compulsive feelings. It is necessary that you release all the inhibiting and compulsive feelings. You are now run by them, you are a victim of them. By releasing them, your mind quiets, and you become free. Therefore, undo these limiting feelings and thoughts, quiet the mind and this infinite Being that you are becomes self-obvious. Then you see that you never were subjected to that mind, that body, and from that moment on, the mind and body have no influence upon you. You then determine for the body as you would a puppet, and it has no more effect upon you than a puppet would.

So, the very best method of all methods is to quiet the mind by releasing all subconscious feelings and thoughts, and there remains the Being that you are.

"What am I?" is the final question that everyone answers, so why not begin with the final question? If you can, all good, all wonderful. But there are very few of us who are capable of using this method of just holding on to "What am I?" We have gotten ourselves so habituated with subconscious thoughts and feelings that we cannot let go of them; therefore, we need other methods, other aids. The other major methods from the East are called Jnana Yoga, Raja or Kriya Yoga, Bhakti Yoga and Karma Yoga. The path that is best for you is the one that you like best.

Each path includes all the other paths. The only difference is the emphasis. If we are intellectual, we emphasize the Jnana path, the path of intellect and wisdom. If we are of devotional nature, we emphasize the Bhakti path of love and devotion to God. If we like to be of service to mankind, we use the Karma Yoga path. Each path leads to the quieting of the mind, enough so that we may see the infinite Being that we are.

Since all the above paths aim to achieve the quieting of the mind, why not go directly to the mind itself? That would be direct and practical and the most efficient of methods. If we examine the mind, we will discover that it is simply the totality of all our thoughts, conscious and subconscious, and that all our past thoughts on particular things have culminated in feelings. The feeling now motivates the thoughts. If our thoughts are motivated by our feelings, all we need to do is release our feelings, the motivators of the thoughts. Then our mind will be quiet. When the mind is quieted, the infinite Being that we are is what is left over and is self-obvious. Simple, is it not?

Following the above, there fell into place a simple method that anyone can understand and use. It is called the Sedona Method, and information about it is available to anyone who will write for it.

Let us now take a look at this so-called apparency: the world. The

24

world is only an imagination that we created mentally. It is not external, but in reality is within us, within our mind. Someday you will discover that you created the entire universe that you see. Creation began by first creating what we call a mind. The mind then imagined the world. Thus we created our mind, which is a composite of all our thoughts and feelings, conscious and subconscious, and in which is our world.

Every little thing that happens to each and every one of us is created in our thinking. We mentally set up a thing called time that makes it even more difficult to see the creation process, because we think now and the effect of that thought happens much later. But the only creator there is is mind, your mind. Is God a creator? Yes, because you are. Thou are That! You set up a mind and, through the mind, create.

It is necessary and good to discover that everything happening to us is caused by our feeling and thinking. Everything that happens to us is created first in our thought. When you discover that you created your trouble, then you realize that you can create anything you desire and will create only good things.

After you discover that there is nothing that you cannot create, you are still not satisfied. The reason is that you have separated yourself from your infinite Beingness, your Oneness, and only upon recognizing and being your infinite Beingness are you perfectly satisfied. So if there are any problems that remain, they only remain because you are holding on to them in your thought. The moment you let go of them, they are gone! If you tell me that isn't so for you, that isn't true. The truth is you are still holding on to them, telling me that it doesn't work. Trying to get rid of a problem is holding on to it. Anything we try to get rid of, we are holding in mind and thereby sustaining it. So, the only way to correct a problem is to let go of it. See not the *problem, see only what you want.* If you would only from this moment on see what you want, that is all that you would get. But you hold in mind the things you do not want. You struggle to eliminate the things you don't want, thereby sustaining them. So, it is necessary to let go of the negative and put in the positive if you want a positive, happy life.

This subject cannot be learned intellectually; it cannot be learned in the mind, because Truth is perceived just behind the mind. We can use the mind to release the mind so that by getting it quieter we can see behind the mind. If it were possible to get this subject through the mind intellectually, all we would need to do is to read the books on it and we would have it. But it doesn't work that way. We have to concentrate in order to seek our Self that is just behind the mind. Turn the mind back upon the mind to release the mind, and then you may go beyond the mind to your Self. To understand, each one must experience it, realize it, make it real by going to the place just behind the mind and perceiving it there, and then you know and know that you know. Then you operate intuitively, from the realm of all-knowingness.

Now, the very highest state is simply Beingness, and if we could only be, just be, we could see our Infinity. We would see that we are the All. We would be in a perfectly satiated, permanent, changeless state. And this state is not a nothingness, it is not a boredom, it is an Allness, an Everythingness, a total satiation that is eternal. You will never, never lose your individuality. The feeling "I" as you use it to mean your individuality will never, ever leave you. It expands. What happens as you discover what you are is that you begin to see that others are you, that you are me, that there is only one, that you are now and always have been that one and glorious infinite Being.

This next segment of this chapter and all the Sedona Method releasing explorations at the end of each session in this book are from Hale Dwoskin.

Releasing Explorations by Hale Dwoskin

You are already unlimited Beingness. You are that now and have always been, and every path or technique is designed only to make you, as Lester often put it, "self-obvious to yourself." Lester also often asked, "How long should it take for an unlimited being to discover their unlimitedness?" It does not need to take any time whatsoever, because you already are Awareness.

You can discover this for yourself by simply checking your own direct experience. In this moment, if you focus on your current experience of yourself simply check, "Are you that or are you that which is aware?" Be sure to do this with your heart as opposed to your head as best you can. You may find that this instantly stills the mind and reveals that self-radiant Awareness that you are. If that happens, just simply rest as that effortless Awareness. It may stir up the thoughts and feelings that are resisting this direct looking at Self.

If the mind does generate resistance, simply allow or welcome it and repeat the same question. As you do this, you will find the mind surrendering more and more until it has become quiet enough for you to remain at rest. This question is from a part of the Sedona Method we call the 5th Way. We will be exploring parts of this process throughout the book; some will be labeled as the 5th Way and some will not.

Problems and
How They Resolve

Lester Levenson

D o you want me to talk, or do you want to ask questions? I guess I could start with telling you my impressions of what has happened to you since I was here last year.

We seem to have greater, more intense problems. This is for all in general, not anyone in particular. This intensification of problems makes it appear as though we are going backward, but it isn't true. We have risen to the state where we can better express ourselves outwardly. We are expressing our problems out in the world more rather than holding them dormant in the subconscious mind. When we are apathetic, it's difficult for us to express, and it's difficult for us outwardly to act. So our problems remain unresolved, swirling around in our subconscious mind. They don't come out and materialize in the world and make a solution possible.

When we begin to move a step above the apathetic state, we begin to acquire more capability of action in the world. Then our problems manifest outwardly in the world, and it seems as though the world is falling in on us. But it's actually a state of growth to move up from the apathetic state into the beginnings of the doingness state. This is the state of apathetic-doingness. When we come into this apathetic-doingness state, we begin to do—with apathetic, agitated tendencies—and therefore we're somewhat destructive, even to ourselves. We become outwardly or expressively destructive to the world and to ourselves; we seem to have more problems and things seem worse. We think we're going backward, but we're actually moving ahead, because apathetic-doingness is higher than apathetic non-doingness.

Now, the step above apathetic-doingness is one of doingness in which we are equally constructive and destructive. Move up another step and we move into the doingness-beingness state where we're big doers and where we are only constructive. When we step up from there, we go into the beingness state: we don't have to do, we only just be, we only just are.

The world today is in a state of apathetic-doingness. It has moved up into this state and therefore has bigger problems. Although this appears otherwise, it is progress, a step forward from stage 1 to stage 2.

The foregoing stages of growth are set out in the following chart.

Stages of Growth

INACTION 1. Apathy: Inaction, due to apathy, with resentments, hostilities and fear to express for fear of retaliation. A subjectively destructive state.

2. Apathetic-doingness: Beginnings of action, having enough will to express outwardly. A beginning of an outwardly active but destructive state.

ACTION 3. Doingness: Action that moves us out of stage 1 toward the equilibrium of stage 5. Here one is equally constructive and destructive to oneself and to the world.

4. Doingness-beingness: Energetic doingness with calmness; much outward action, all constructive to oneself, the world and the universe.

INACTION 5. Beingness: Inaction due to serenity; the ability to just be; witnessing, watching, allowing and accepting the world and universe as it is.

Q: Is this the world in general, or is it just the people on the path who are caught up in this?

Lester: It's both. We are all involved in this. You see it expressed in the race issue, the revolt against the establishment, juvenile delinquency, Vietnam, Africa. It's prevalent everywhere today. It is part of the world growth (stage 2).

Q: Is this because people are more developed to cope with the world?

Lester: They're more developed, not to cope with the worldly problems but to do something about them. The way they're trying to cope with them is a destructive way. Problems could be solved by discussions, and should be. However, the state the world is in, one of apathetic-doingness, is a step forward from the lower state of pure apathy with no doingness. The world today is in a slow state of Beingness (stage 2). It's a materialistic age.

About AD 1700, we came out of the lowest state, a period of physical, animal sensuality wherein we lived only to satiate our appetites. You know what the Dark Ages were. We're now in the second period wherein we can enjoy the finer, more cultural things, and we're still having the growing pains of getting out of the first into the second. But the second is not a highly spiritual state. It's the period where, in the world, we advance scientifically. The third period begins the era of knowing that this is a mental world and that we are all related. We are more loving to one another and we stop fighting each other. The fourth period is the state in which man knows fully his Beingness in God, that his and everyone's Beingness is God. He knows he is a free, unlimited being.

These four periods are the Iron, Bronze, Silver and Golden Ages the ancient Greeks spoke of. (The fifth stage is really beyond this world although it is accomplished in this world.) However, at any time, whenever anyone chooses, they may move into the highest state. We don't have to stay at the level that the world is in, and those of us who are on the path are moving up out of this general level. Aren't we lucky?

Q: Even with our problems?

Lester: Yes. To people in the world, everything seems hopeless. They feel helpless, but we know the way out. No matter how much the world hurts us, we know there's a way out. We have hope and a direction.

And what is the way out? Not looking to the world for happiness, but looking to the place where happiness is, right within us, within our own consciousness. Unlimited joy is our natural, inherent state. We have, through ignorance, undone it by imposing concepts of limitations: I need this, I need him, I need her, and if I don't get what I want, I am hurt, I have trouble. Growth is only letting go of these concepts of lack and limitation, or, on the positive side, going within and seeing this unlimited Being that we are.

Any time we have trouble, any time we have a problem, we are being the limited ego. We are trying to express the Self through the limited ego, and it's too small; we get squeezed, and it hurts. So, if there is a problem, the thing to do is to ask yourself, "What am I doing? Wherein am I demanding with ego motivation?" If the answer comes, if you see how, ego-wise, you're causing this so-called problem, you will pull the causative thought up from the subconscious into the conscious. Once it is conscious, you will naturally let go of it.

If you don't let go of it, the reason why is that the cause, the thought that initiated the difficulty, remains subconscious. So, either we make the thought conscious and let go of it, or— and this is the higher and the better way—we know strongly enough that we are the Self.

Knowing that we are the perfect Self, that we are not this limited body and mind, all problems immediately resolve. It sounds quite indicting when I say any problem, any trouble, is ego motivated, but that, you'll find, is true. When you be just your Self, there is no problem, there is nothing that does not fall into line perfectly, harmoniously, with no effort. The more ego motivated you are, the more difficult it is to accomplish something, the less is the harmony and the greater is the misery. It is really as simple as I'm putting it.

What is not easy is to let go of the wrong habit of insisting upon being an ego. This habit is strong. It has been deeply ingrained over thousands of years. We are now letting go of it, but we don't let go of it easily because the habit has been there for such a long, long time. However, the moment we choose to let go of it, we can. If we say we can't let go, it's because we really don't want to. The desire to let go isn't strong enough.

Do I make this too simple? You know why I'm addressing you,

because I know you've had quite a lot of this. You have probably heard it presented in complicated ways, with a lot of things added to it that make it more difficult to see. But once we accept it and see the simplicity of it, all we need to do is affect it. And no one can do it for us. We have to do it ourselves.

Q: I have a friend who has problems. She's Catholic and very pious. When things get blackest and she has no more hope and is at the bottom, at that very moment, something happens so that everything turns out right.

Lester: Do you know why she must reach bottom?

Q: Well, she has faith and she knows that—

Lester: No, she doesn't have faith, and she is not pious. This is her trouble. You see, faith would cause her to let go and let God—being pious, being humble and surrendering, would cause the same thing. Outwardly, she's the way you say, but inwardly she's the way I'm saying. You see, she tries herself to control everything, and that's not letting go and letting God.

Q: She prays.

Lester: Yes, she prays, but she wants it the way she wants it. She's found out that her praying for it doesn't help her. If you surrender, you don't have to pray. You've got to let go and let God. When does she let go and let God? When she herself can't do anything anymore, she lets go. In the extreme, she lets go—and the moment one lets go, everything resolves itself. Can you see that? When things reach the extreme, she feels, "Oh, there's nothing I can do," and that's when she lets go and lets God. If you can show her this point, she'll see it, most likely, and then be more consciously able to use it.

Q: I keep trying to tell her that she must be confident.

Lester: Conviction, which is stronger than faith—absolute conviction of God—that will do it! Let go and let God and then everything straightens out. But when we try to do it, we have trouble.

Q: When you say, "Let go and let God," does that mean that you should work strictly on inspiration, or should you just sit back and let things happen?

Lester: Have the feeling of "letting things happen." To accomplish this, we have to let the ego-sense go. The ego is the feeling, "I am an individual, Lester, and I have a body and I do things." That's wrong. I have to get Lester out of the way and let God or Self operate. When this is achieved, you'll sort of *float* through things, and there will be no effort. If there is effort, there is ego.

Of course, now you're going to have to use some effort, because you're not starting off as the realized Self. You see, only when this girl goes to the extreme does she let go of the sense of doership and then things happen effortlessly. That's letting go and letting God!

Professing faith, professing all these things, doesn't do it—actually having them does it. The fact that she has troubles is proof that she doesn't have the conviction of God, because God is All. God is perfect, and if God is All and God is perfect, *everything* must be perfect and that leaves no place for imperfection or troubles. If you take that attitude, so be it! It is the feeling that I am not the doer, and that I let go and let it happen.

Q: I can't tell when I'm ego.

Lester: When there's no effort, there's no ego. The more the effort the more the ego.

Q: When the effort is extreme, you have to more or less go the other way, anyway.

Lester: Yes. I'm trying to give you a method of knowing whether it's ego or not. The more the effort the greater the ego. However, you're going to use effort until you're fully realized. Now, there will be times when you'll use no effort, and everything will fall perfectly into line for you. At these times, you'll be your Self.

Q: But doesn't this type of thing make you indolent, so that you don't do any action? Is it that you shouldn't try to do anything? That's what I don't understand.

Lester: Indolence is an action, a negative action. It is the act of holding yourself from moving. It is impossible now for you to be actionless. To achieve the actionless state, you should try to let go of your ego more and more, because now you can't do it totally. If you could, you'd be fully realized. But if you keep letting go of the ego, you will eventually drop it and then be the witness rather than the doer. Does that make sense? Be not the doer. Let it happen. Have the feeling, It's God's world, whatever is happening, so let him!

Q: How do we get rid of problems?

Lester: The moment you say, "I have a problem," you are stuck—you are making it real! You can't get rid of the problem, because you are making it real. You've got it.

Q: So, if when we have problems, we say, "There is no problem at all," will they vanish then?

Lester: No. If you say, "There is no problem," they won't vanish, because you're saying, "There is no *problem*." You're mentally holding the problem in mind and therefore sustaining it. Erase the problem from your mind. Know that everything is *perfect*—then the problem is necessarily nonexistent.

Q: I think that way, that everything is really perfect.

Lester: If you really do, then everything must be.

Q: How easy it would be if we understood this from the beginning.

Lester: Yes. You see, naturally, life should be totally effortless. There is no effort in life whatsoever when we are just being our natural Self. But we're trying to be a limited ego—that takes effort. It takes effort to be limited when your natural state is unlimited. The more you try to be limited, the more effort it takes.

To be your unlimited Self takes no effort. Just like your friend: when she gets to the extreme, she lets go and everything straightens out, with no effort. All the time she tries and tries, things get worse and worse. But when she gives up and lets go, things resolve.

Q: Well, she had to go out and look for a job. She had to go to an agent, she just couldn't sit down and wait.

Lester: I say all she had to do was to *let go and let God*. Then, even if she had locked herself in a chamber somewhere, the things would have come to her. You don't sit down and wait, you don't do anything. Just let go of the sense of doership. You just *know* that everything is perfect, and then the slightest thought you have will come into being quickly. There's no limitation on God, the Self. Whatever you think will have to come into being if you let go, because you're invoking your infinite power—God, your Self. Nothing can stop it!

Q: But at the same time you have to struggle to get some action.

Lester: No, I said just the opposite. I said lock yourself in a chamber and padlock it, and if you will do what I'm saying, you'll find that what you want will be effected. It *has* to be. Nothing can stop it! Omnipotence is invoked!

Q: What is prayer for? What does praying mean?

Lester: Praying is for those who need praying. When you know what you know, to whom are you praying? If you are That, why do you have to pray to It? Praying admits duality: "I" pray to "God." Maintain your Oneness!

However, when one does pray, it is best to pray for one thing only: more wisdom so that you eliminate all need for any prayer, for any asking. It all depends on one's state of understanding. Most people in the world today need to pray. But prayer admits duality— God is "out there." And we should know that God is within. Even though Jesus said, "The kingdom of God is within," we still look for God without, and he's not out there. He's only within. He turns out to be our very own Beingness.

The "I" of us, with nothing added to it, is the God we seek. When you say, "I am something," that isn't It, or "I and something," that too isn't God. But just pure "I" and only "I," that is God. That is why it is said that God is closer than flesh. It is "I," and how close is "I"? It's closer than flesh. It is God, your very own Self!

Q: That's a very good feeling.

Lester: Yes, because it's reminding you of what you know subconsciously, that you are that Self. Just hold on to the word "I" only, "I, I, I, I," and you'll become more exhilarated. Try it when you're alone. Just "I, I, I," and not, "I am a body, I am a mind," but, "I, I, I," that feeling of Being. I think the word that describes God better than any other single word is "Beingness." God is all Beingness. We are all Beingness pretending we're a tiny part of it, a limited body-mind. When you look within, you'll see that you are all Beingness. Beingness is God! Beingness is also Awareness, consciousness. They are the same thing. Later on, you'll see them as identical, Beingness and consciousness. So, be your Self, and there never will be a problem.

Seeing a problem in the world is trying to be a limited ego-body-mind. If you think you have a problem, you do. If you'll just accept that *God is all*, God is perfect, that that's all there is *and look* at perfection, then that's all you'll ever meet with!

Q: Then we have to wipe out the word *problem*.

Lester: Yes. You have to wipe out the words *problem, can't, don't, won't*—all negative words. In the future, when man is in a state of harmony, all these words will disappear.

Q: As you progress more on the path, so *many* things seem so much more superficial. I don't know if that's progress, or if I'm becoming indifferent to the world around me.

Lester: Well, that is progress— being indifferent, that is, nonattached.

Q: I really couldn't care less about politics or all these things that at one time seemed so important. Is that bad?

Lester: How does it feel?

Q: I haven't analyzed the feeling. I've just seen that all these people think that what they're doing is so important. Maybe *I'm* wrong in that I don't feel that way.

Lester: No, you are right. The higher you go, the more you see the perfection, and therefore the less you see problems. The more one sees problems, the lower one is. What you're talking about is problems. The people who see them want you to see the way they see and will tell you that you're wrong. This is one thing you must be on guard against. As you grow, those who are not up to you will try to pull you down to where they are. Let them think you are wrong. You know you are right! Don't argue. It's fruitless.

Q: I find that people try to make me feel selfish because I feel that way. I don't know whether that's true or not. That is why I wanted to discuss it.

Lester: It's this way: When you don't think the way they think, they call you selfish. Just check it out. No, it's not how much you recognize a problem that shows unselfishness. It's how much you see that there is no problem and help others see that there is only perfection that shows unselfishness. This way you offer help; you're very constructive and unselfish.

Q: Just do everything with a desire to help, and that is love?

Lester: Yes. Just feel love—you don't necessarily have to do. Love and your thoughts are positive. Thought is far more powerful than action. It's the basis of and effects action. It is the initiator. It comes before and determines action. A realized being sitting in a cave somewhere all by himself is doing more good for the world than organizations of action. He is aiding everyone, as his help is being subconsciously received by all.

Now we're back to what we were talking about before: the bottom state is *inaction*, the middle state is *action*, and the top state is *inaction*. The bottom state is one of apathetic inertia. It's destructive. It just wants to stop everything, actually destroy everything.

The top state lets everything be just the way it is, because everything is perfect, and one in this state powerfully projects this mentally to everyone. The middle state is the action state that moves you from the bottom toward the top state of equilibrium and tranquility. As you move up, those who are not as far along as you are will try to pull you down to where they are.

Q: So, it's sort of a proving ground, or a testing, to see how much those things bother you.

Lester: Yes. It bests your conviction. Where is your conviction if you go with them? If you go with them your tendency is to believe more the way they do.

Q: Which is easier, I know.

Lester: No, try it. If you think it's easier, just go their way, and you'll have more misery, as they do.

Q: Sometimes it's easier just to be one of the mob.

Lester: Desire for ego approval makes it seem easier. You'll find out otherwise. You've been one of the mob, haven't you? You've been like them. It's not easy. No, the right way is easier. Do you see that? The right way is letting go and letting God and then everything falls into line perfectly—no effort. But when I have to do it, it's not God, it's me—the ego—wanting to do, to change things, correct this world and so forth.

Q: Would a mantra or something like that be the best thing to remember when these things come up that way?

Lester: Affirmations are always good. A mantra is an affirmation that's repeated again and again. Do whatever will help you to do and be what you think you should do and be.

Q: That's what I don't know.

Lester: To seek who and what you are, to know your Self, is the very best thing to do and be. There've been moments when you've let go and felt your real Self. How does it feel?

Q: Marvelous! Could I have it all the time?

Lester: Yes, certainly. Stay that way, that's all. Be what you are! You're infinite, omniscient, omnipotent, right here and now. *Be That!* Stop being this limited, miserable, little ego.

Q: Well, I have the same problem he has, and I thought I was becoming indifferent.

Lester: Yes, you're becoming indifferent to the negativity, and what's wrong with that? What is politics? It's a mechanism of force and control. In a society where everyone loves everyone, do you need politics? If you want to help the world, help yourself grow, and you'll do far more than you could by being involved in politics. The more you're capable of loving, the more you're helping the world. Parliaments cannot right the world, but enough people loving can.

The president of the United States must necessarily represent the sum total consciousness, the sum total thinkingness, of all the people of the United States added together. The world out there is only our collective consciousness. Principle, divine law supersedes manmade law. Consciousness, thinkingness, determines everything. *If we don't like what's happening to us in the world*, all we have to do is change our consciousness and the world out there *changes for us!*

Q: But doesn't this sort of thing take a great deal of courage many times? Sometimes I don't really have the guts to be able to do the things I want to do.

Lester: All right, why don't you have the guts?

Q: I don't know.

Lester: Ego. You want approval from them. You're seeking their approval; you want to go the way they want you to go.

Q: It isn't that I want their approval, I don't want their *dis*approval.

Lester: Well, isn't that the same thing?

Q: I remember you said last time that when you resolve a problem, it doesn't come up again, and it's true. But then you get new ones. When you have solved something within your own mind, and you know that you have come up a step on the ladder, it doesn't present itself again, which is a great help, but then there are always new problems.

Lester: There's no end to problems in the world. You go on and on forever and ever solving problems in the world, and you'll have more and more. As long as you are conscious of problems, they exist. Only when you discover the real you are there no problems. What you do is put your hand in a fire and say, "Ouch, it's hot! My hand is burning! Boy, do I have a problem!" That's all.

When you see that *you* are doing it, you stop. If you have a problem, you're putting your hand into a problem and yelling, "It hurts!" and acting as though you're not putting your hand into it. You act as though you are not doing it, but you are. That problem is in your consciousness. It's in your mind. Change your mind, change your consciousness, and immediately that problem is no more. Try it and you'll see that it's so.

Q: Last year, when we were all meeting together, we were higher and we had fewer problems.

Lester: That's the prime purpose of coming together as a group. You're reminded and supported in your direction. You're with people who are striving in that same direction. You are moving opposite to the way the world is moving. You need positive company as much as possible. And when you are by yourself, stop being what you are not—a limited body and mind—and just be what you are—an *infinite,* totally free, grand and glorious being, whole and complete.

Releasing Explorations by Hale Dwoskin

Look within yourself and see if you are willing to live in a world without problems. If there is any hesitancy, it is probably because, without realizing it, you want to create problems in your life. We do this because as long as we think we are a limited body-mind, we feel like we need be like everyone else and to have a purpose in life. We are afraid if there were no problems, there would be no need for us. And in a way we are right. We are not our limited body-mind-ego that thrives on creating and then solving problems in order to justify its existence. The less we are invested in limitation, the less we need to create problems to resolve, and the less we even see problems in the world. As Lester repeatedly said, "See the perfection where the seeming imperfection seems to be."

Another way to look at this is: If the One is the only doer and the One is perfect, how can there be a problem? We only perceive problems when we feel like it is "me" who is doing, as opposed to resting in the knowing that "It is not I but the father who worketh through me." The more you accept this without holding back, the less you will see problems even if everyone around you does.

You can also discover this by seeing if you can actually find a "doer" in this moment. You will find actions but if you are open, you will see that the sense of a personal doer is a mental projection based on memory. It is not based on direct experience. Seeing that you are not the doer has a positive effect on those around you because you are also holding the perfection for them and seeing them as their being-ness as opposed to a limited body-mind.

You can also explore this by asking yourself, "What frustrated ego desire is causing this problem?" If you allow yourself to be truly open to see yourself clearly, you will see the ego desire. If it does not let go spontaneously, simply ask yourself, "Could I let go of wanting that?"

Also, if you notice that at times you would rather fit in than be the Awareness that you are, you can ask yourself, "Would I rather fit in or would I rather be free?" This will probably cause you to drop your wanting love and be stronger in your desire for freedom. If there is a hesitation, just ask yourself, "Could I welcome that?" "Could I let that go?" "Would I?" "When?" And just decide to drop this desire.

The following is an exploration of the most simple form of letting go that will help you with the above exploration and throughout this book and, of course, in every part of your life.

The Basic Releasing Questions

> *What am I feeling?*
> *Could I welcome / allow that feeling?*
> *Could I let it go?*
> *Would I let it go?*
> *When?*

These are the five basic releasing questions that serve as the foundation of the Sedona Method. Here is how to apply them on your own. Experiment with asking the questions both in the first person and in the third person and find which one works best for you.

Step 1: Focus on an issue that you would like to feel better about, and then allow yourself to feel whatever you are feeling in this moment. Ask yourself, *What is my feeling about this topic?* This doesn't have to be a strong feeling. In fact, you can even check on how you feel about this book and what you want to get from it.

Step 2: Welcome the feeling, as well as any sensations, sounds, thoughts, and pictures that arise with the feeling, and allow whatever you are experiencing to be here as fully or as best you can. Ask yourself, *Could I allow myself to welcome this feeling?*

This instruction may seem simplistic, but it needs to be. Most of us live in our thoughts, pictures, and stories about the past and the future, rather than being aware of how we actually feel in this moment. The only time that we can actually do anything about the way we feel (and, for that matter, about our businesses or our lives) is *now*. You don't need to wait for a feeling to be strong or to have a label before you let it go. In fact, if you are feeling numb, flat, blank, cut off, or empty inside, those are feelings that can be let go just as easily as more recognizable ones. Simply do the best you can.

Step 3: Ask yourself, *Could I let this feeling go?* This question is merely asking you if it is possible to take this action. "Yes" or "no" are both acceptable answers. You will often let go even if you answer "no." As best you can, answer the question that you choose with a minimum of thought, staying away from second-guessing yourself or getting into an internal debate about the merits of that action or its consequences. All the questions used in this process are deliberately simple. They are not important in and of themselves but are designed to point you to the experience of letting go, to the experience of stopping holding on. Go on to Step 4 no matter how you answer this question.

Step 4: No matter which question you started with, ask yourself this simple question: *Would I?* In other words: Am I willing to let go? Again, stay away from debate as best you can. Also remember that you are always doing this process for yourself, for the purpose of gaining your own freedom and clarity. It doesn't matter whether the feeling is justified, longstanding, or right. If the answer is "no," or if you are not sure, ask yourself, *Would I rather have this feeling, or would I rather be free?* Even if the answer is still "no," go on to Step 5.

Step 5: Ask yourself a simpler question: *When?* This is an invitation to just let it go now. You may find yourself easily letting go. Remember that letting go is a decision you can make any time you choose.

Step 6: Repeat the preceding five steps as often as needed until you feel free of the particular feeling with which you started the process.

Note: If you are having a hard time deciding to let go or simply feeling a difference, then you can also give yourself permission to hold on for a moment. If you give yourself permission to do what you are already doing, you will find that it becomes much easier to make a new decision. This will usually make getting to a genuine "yes" and the corresponding letting go much easier. You will probably find yourself letting go a little more on each step of the process. The results at first may be quite subtle.

Very quickly, if you are persistent, the results will get more and more noticeable. You may find that you have layers of feelings about a particular topic. However, what you let go of is gone for good.

Spiritual Growth

Lester Levenson

This session is composed of aphorisms compiled from various talks by Lester. Allow yourself to ponder them one at a time. Give yourself enough time to gain the maximum benefit that each has to offer before moving on to the next.

The whole object on the path is to let go of the ego. What remains is your Self.

The only growth there is is the eliminating of the ego.

Ego is the sense that "I am an individual, separate from the All." In the extreme, it is egotism.

Growth is transcending yourself, your habitual self, which is none other than ego.

Growth is the ego getting out of its misery.

Recognize that all joy is nothing but your Self, more or less.

There is no happiness except that of experiencing your Self. When you see that, it makes the path very direct. You stop chasing the rainbow, and you go for the happiness where you know it is—right within you.

Everything you are seeking you are and very foolishly saying you are not. That's part of the enigma: everything everyone is seeking with such intensity, one has—and much more.

It is you. When you say, "I," that is the Infinite. Great big joke! Here you are, infinite and looking for your Self which you are!

When anyone says he is not a master, he is lying.

Your effort should be for proper identity—identify with your Self!

Spiritual advancement is determined by how much you identify with your real Self.

The ego is very tricky. It often talks us out of this path for a short period of time, sometimes for a longer period of time. But once we've gotten into it, we usually almost always come back to it. So, you have to be careful of the trickery of the ego part of us. It can really take us away. No matter how far we have advanced on the path, the ego is always a treacherous companion that can take us off the path, sometimes for an entire lifetime.

This is something we should be on guard against. The ego-sense latches on and says, "I am God." It latches onto the progress, and it feels good, and it says, "I am It." By doing so, it sabotages further growth.

When you recognize the opposition of the ego, you can let go of it. After practice, it is easy; and after you let go of enough ego, you just naturally feel the peace and joy of your Self.

It's actually a path of taking on more and more of your natural state of being infinite. You give up limitation. You give up misery, but you never give up anything worthwhile. You never give up anything good.

On this path, you constantly give up trouble.

The first teacher is misery. It is usually the first thing that causes us to seek the way out.

First, we start on the path to escape misery, then we taste the Self and want It because It tastes so good.

On the path, you never give up anything—you just take on more and more of what you really want until you have the All.

Take it for the sweetness that's in it, not to get out of the bitterness that's out of it.

We discover that we never give up anything on the spiritual path but our self-imposed bondages and miseries.

If you are weakly for the path, you are strongly for the sense-world.

You think you can't, that's why you can't. It's only the thought *I can't do it* that stops you from doing it. Those who can't don't really want to.

Your growth depends only on you.

It will happen as fast as you can do it.

The only one who is going to change you is you!

Wishing won't do it, nor will trying. You have got to do it!

Good intentions are no substitute for right action.

To change more rapidly, expect it!

You must have a very strong desire to change, because you are such a victim of habit that you want the world as much as a drowning man wants air. To offset that, you must want to know your Self as much as a drowning man wants air.

Your success is determined by your desire for it. If you get discouraged, you are not really interested.

Your only real friend is you. Your only real enemy is you. You are an enemy to yourself to the degree you limit your Self. You are a friend to yourself to the degree you remove limits from yourself.

What you do to yourself, it being of your own doing, only you can undo. You did it, you must undo it.

This entire path is a do-it-yourself path.

Do what is available to you to do. Do your best.

Every experience is to bless you, not to hurt you. If you stay in accord with principle, you will come out higher!

Every place and every situation in life presents an opportunity for growth.

The best place to grow is right where you are. The best time is now.

Be thankful for the opportunities to grow.

The greatest of all tests are those at home, with your immediate family. Therefore, home is an excellent place to grow.

A lot of spiritual growth can be had by practicing the real, selfless love on your mate and family.

It is a good opportunity to grow when people are saying things about you, opposing you. It gives you a chance to practice the real Love. It gives you a chance to practice the real peace, Just because they are making sounds with their mouths is no reason why you should feel bad about it. Opposition is a very healthy thing. It provokes and firms growth.

It is necessary to remember that everyone can be our teacher. If we react to praise or pleasantries, that is developing ego. If we're depressed over criticism, that is ego. When we are our Self, there is no reacting.

There isn't anything that happens that can't be used. There's no incident that cannot be used as a teacher.

Every minute of every day should be used to grow by.

If we assume that we are there and we are not, circumstances soon awaken us to the fact that we are not.

If you tell others of your high experiences, of your gains, because of their jealousy, they might say, "Ah, who does she think she is?" And that works against you and tends to pull you down.

Any time you brag about anything, you're inviting a test of it. So, I warn you, if you are growing into these things, when they start coming—unless you're so sure you know by experience you can't lose it—it's better not to tell anyone.

Be proud of your spiritual accomplishments. Be happy with them. Be proud of them to yourself.

When you have false spiritual pride, you invite a challenge of the thing that you are proud of, and it is necessary to do away with doubts.

It takes more than faith. It takes knowledge. You start with faith, but you must convert it to knowledge. You must test it out, and then you know it.

In order to really understand, we must experience the knowledge.

When you experience, it is no longer intellectual.

You can get understanding without being able to put it into words.

The only maturity there is spiritual understanding.

Stand ye out and be different, and don't let the others trick you back into where you were. It's not easy. It takes fortitude.

We should try to go all the way. To us, it is given to do that. We have the possibility of going all the way back home, right to the Absolute.

Expect infinity, no more. You cannot expect too much.

Toe the line to the very end. The more you toe the line, the sooner the end.

Every gain is an eternal gain; every step forward you make now is forever.

We climb a ladder, and each time we get up to another rung, we forget about the rungs below. Then, when we get to the top, we kick the ladder away.

The proof of this subject is the result you get.

The more you grow, the less you feel the need to grow.

The higher you go, the less the incentive to go further.

You never learn anything by disproving; you learn only by proving.

Studying the illusion helps make it real. If you want to know the Truth, don't study the opposite.

The whole process of growth is letting go of thoughts. When our thoughts are totally eliminated, there is nothing left but the Self.

Don't try to complicate it—it's too simple.

We can only expand out of the ego. The Self is.

Growth is letting go of being what you are not.

Let go of your ego and be your Self!

As you grow, the whole world opens wide for you—you experience so much more. However, even if you have this whole world, you've only got a dot. Take the whole cosmos!

Longing for liberation is the key. Once you get that, you'll be carried all the way.

In our desire to attain liberation or realization, we are helped to the degree that we help all others.

Grow to the point where your whole attention is off you and on others.

Why shouldn't we all be masters, all of us, here and now?

The moment we decide to be the Self—really decide—it is so!

The higher you go, the more nondifference comes. You accept the leaders of all religions alike.

Having peace under ideal conditions isn't indicative of spiritual growth, it is escape.

When people are not growing, they are going in the opposite direction.

You should thank those who oppose you, because they give you an unusual opportunity for growth.

When we start concerning ourselves with what they are doing, we're turning away from what we are doing.

You need constant confirmation until you don't need it anymore.

Perseverance is necessary.

Adversity is a prod to growth.

The more intense the crises in this world, the more we have an opportunity to grow.

It would be so fast if people would, with constant, intense effort ask, "What am I?"

When you get that answer, then you have control over your body and mind.

If there is anything you don't like out there, there is a need to change yourself.

You may see fully who you are and not be able to maintain it. What happens is that, being the infinite Self, we can get a glimpse of the infinite, hold it for a while, and then suddenly feel as though we've lost it. The reason for that is that the mind has not been eliminated. The subconscious thoughts of limitation are submerged for the moment. You may go completely into your Self and let go of the mind temporarily. You haven't eliminated the mind, you just momentarily let go of it.

So there you are, for the moment, totally the infinite Self. However, the mind that has been submerged reemerges, and then the ego takes over, and you just can't understand what happened to you, what brought you back into the heaviness of the world again. What is required is that we reestablish that state of the Self again and again until it becomes permanent. Each time we do it, we scorch more of the mind, until finally we have scorched the entire mind. Then we are permanently established in the Self. Then you sit back, and the mind is out there and the body is out there, and you are not the mind, you are not the body. As long as you know you are not the mind and the body, both of them can go on to their heart's content, and you know that they cannot touch you.

Releasing Explorations by Hale Dwoskin

What do you long for? Are you longing for a new car, financial security, the perfect relationship, more radiant health and well-being, or simply to get out of your pain? Take an inventory of your desires and you will see what your deepest desires are. If there are external desires, allow yourself to honor and fulfill them and/or just let them go. If you deny what you truly desire, it has you. It generates resistance in your consciousness that you will keep coming back to, yet, if you acknowledge it, you have the ability to either bring it into your consciousness or let it go. Either way you are taking charge of your growth and your life.

As you start to see progress on the path, know that freedom is not for you, it is from you. The "you" that I am referring to here is the apparently limited you. Not the true limitless you that you have always been. If you get attached to or take ego credit for any of your growth, you will find that it can become a sticking point. Allow the free you—the impersonal power that knows the way to be your guide—to have the credit, not you. The less you take personal credit, the more you are freed inside. Plus, anything that you think that you have accomplished on the path is only in the past, and if you try and return to the past, you are missing the only place that true growth can take place, which is here and now.

Make a list of your desires and be as ruthlessly honest as you can. Go through each item on the list and ask yourself, "Can I allow myself to turn this desire into a desire for freedom?" If you can do that, allow the switch to occur naturally inside you and notice the freedom you will naturally feel from just making this inner change.

Another question you can use to help you let go of the desire is, "Would I rather have (the desire) or would I rather be free?" If you cannot change the desire or let it go, then set it up as a goal and allow yourself to accomplish it as best you can.

A third way of letting go of desire is to allow yourself to let go of wanting to change what is and allow yourself to accept it, as it is, as best you can. You can even ask yourself the question, "Can I let go of wanting to change this and allow it to be as it is?" The more you accept things as they are, the more you will discover the freedom that is always here and always available to you just waiting for you to acknowledge it. Plus, you will find that as you let go of wanting to change what is, you will find yourself changing what needs to be changed with greater ease, joy, and clarity.

You may resonate with all three ways of letting go of desire or you may only resonate with one or two. Allow yourself to experiment with all three and then concentrate on the one that you most resonate with.

Even when you do achieve any desire, notice whether the happiness is permanent or fleeting. How long are you truly happy with your new toy? This will also help you to start converting all your desires into the desire for freedom, your true source of lasting, unshakable happiness.

Happiness

Lester Levenson

I'll start with that which we're all interested in, all right? The word that I like best for our subject is happiness. When we analyze that which everyone is seeking or looking for, it is happiness, right? And when you find God, your Self, that turns out to be the ultimate happiness.

When we seek and find the full Truth, the absolute Truth, that again turns out to be the ultimate happiness. We're all seeking the greatest good for ourselves. The ultimate good turns out to be the ultimate happiness. Every being is seeking freedom, and complete freedom or liberation is nothing but the ultimate happiness. So, in the end, the words *God, good, Truth, liberation, freedom,* and *Self* turn out to be the ultimate happiness. And everyone is seeking these: good, happiness, liberation, Truth, God, Self. There isn't anyone who's not seeking it. The only difference between us and others is that we're consciously seeking it in the direction where it is. The others are seeking it blindly through seeking happiness in the world and never really getting the full happiness that they're striving for. We go after it directly. We seek for it where it is. We seek it within.

Everyone wants a continuous, constant, eternal happiness with no sorrow whatsoever, and no one is ever satisfied until he or she finds that. Everyone is seeking what we're all seeking. The major difference is that they are seeking it in the world and are frustrated, while we are seeking it within and are successfully becoming happier. When we go within, we discover that all happiness is there. The only place where we can feel happiness is right within ourselves. That is exactly where it is. Every time we attribute this happiness to something external—to a person or a thing external—we get more pain with it than we do pleasure.

Anyone disagree with that? If you have experienced enough, if you've lived long enough, and if you've examined it, you've discovered this. The happiness that we're seeking and thinking is out there external to us isn't there. The "happiness with no sorrow" can only be found by going within. Point number one.

Now, point number two is that this great happiness that we're seeking is nothing but our very own Self, our very own Beingness. Our most basic, inherent nature is this thing that we are seeking, and it is ours, here and now. We are that happiness that we are seeking, looking for it externally and not finding it there. Looking within, we discover it to be our very own Self unencumbered with our self-imposed limitations. There is not one of us who is not in direct touch with, in possession of, an infinite Beingness that's all perfect, all present, all joyous and eternal. There is not one of us who is not in direct contact with that right now! But due to wrong learning, by assuming, over the ages concepts of limitation and by looking outwardly, we have beclouded the view. We have covered over this infinite Being that we are with concepts of "I am this physical body," or "I am this mind," or, "With this physical body and mind, I have heaps and heaps of problems and troubles."

So, in order to discover this truth, this unlimited Being that we are, we must quiet the mind and finally let go of the mind. And only in this way may we achieve it. The mind is nothing but the sum total of all thoughts. All thoughts are concepts of limitation. If anyone of us could stop thinking right now and remain that way, he would be an unlimited Being from this moment on. It really is that simple, though not necessarily an easy accomplishment. The job is first to undo negative thinking in order to get positive enough so that we may go in the right direction, then to drop all thinking—drop all negative and all positive thinking. When that happens, we discover that we are in the realm of knowingness, of omniscience. We have no need to think, since everything is known, and we are all joyous and totally free. Knowing everything, there's nothing to think about!

Thinking is just relating things to other things, connecting things together. Knowing everything, we know the unity, the oneness, and there's no necessity for relating things by thought. Thereby we are free, free of all concepts of separation and limitation. This leaves us free to use a mind should we want to communicate with the apparency of the world. The process of going within is a process of looking within and discovering what the mind is, of discovering that the mind is nothing but thoughts, and the thoughts are nothing but numerous concepts of limitation. We quiet the mind by letting go of these thoughts until the mind gets quiet enough so that we see the infinite Being that we are. This takes away the mist—the clouds covering this infinite Being—and leaves us totally free.

When we first see this infinite Being that we are, the job isn't finished yet; we still have the remaining habits of thought to do away with. Then, when there's no more remaining thought, subconscious and conscious (and the subconscious thoughts are the difficult ones to let go of), when there are no more thoughts, that's the end of the road of playing limited. Then we are totally free—forever! Actually, we have no choice. We are infinite Beings. If there is a choice, it can only be to choose to be limited! We have chosen to be limited to such a degree that now we are blindly behaving as though we are extremely limited Beings. Consequently, all the apparent troubles, troubles that are only an apparency, because they are assumed as real through our mind. Everything we see in the world, we see only in our mind. There's nothing but our consciousness; nothing can be seen except through our consciousness.

Whatever we see is in our consciousness is in our mind. When one begins to realize this, then one works to change one's consciousness, and, by so doing, one changes his environment. Changing one's environment is a step on the way. In doing so you have the proof ; do you understand what I'm saying? Nothing should ever be accepted on hearsay.

Never believe anything you hear. If you accept what I say to you just by listening to it, it's only hearsay. You must prove everything for yourself. When you do, it's your knowledge, and it's useable. To progress in the direction of wisdom and happiness, it's absolutely necessary that everyone prove it out for himself.

As it's said above, Truth can never be found in the world. The world as we see it now is multiple, dual. When we go just behind the world, we discover the absolute Truth: that there's a singular Oneness throughout the world and universe, and it turns out to be our very own Self, our very own Beingness, which some call God. The world is, but not as people see it. The world is truly only our very own Self. The "I" that we use when we say, "I am" is the exact same "I," falsely appearing separate and divided. When we see the Truth, we see that you are me, that there is only one Beingness, there is only one consciousness and that we are the sum total of all the Beingness or consciousness that formerly appeared separate.

So, again, to find Truth or happiness, you have to go within. You have to see the Oneness, you have to see the universe as it really is, as nothing but your consciousness, which is nothing but your Self. Now, this is difficult to describe; it's something that must be experienced. Only when someone experiences it does one know. It cannot be picked up from listening to anyone. Books and teachers can only point the direction; we must take it. That's one of the nice things about the path. There's nothing to be believed—everything must be experienced and proved by each one to his own satisfaction before it's accepted.

To sum it up, I can take two quotes from the Bible: "I am that I am," and "Be still and know that I am God." In other words, "Thou art that which thou art seeking." Quiet the mind until you see it. Okay? Now we may go into questions.

Q: I come upon a difference: these people, all of us in this room, each of us has a form, and I see it.

Lester: You're seeing wrongly. You're seeing in error. When you look at me, you should see the Truth, you should see your Self. Strive until that day in which you will see this Truth.

Q: After one has a certain amount of inner experience and begins to believe, there still comes an important decision as to what to do with yourself as you find yourself at that point. And then you have to decide what to do with the rest of your life.

Lester: Yes. You must decide whether to pursue your welfare by seeking it in the world or by seeking it within you.

Q: You've had a certain amount of experience, but you will always be called back to a certain contact with the outer world unless—

Lester: Unless you make the outer world you. However, be not attached to the world and it cannot disturb you. Then you may carry on with equanimity.

Q: In order to make the outer world me, I would think I have to self-purify myself.

Lester: Yes. Practicing serving the world will purify you.

Q: I would have to almost go out and sacrifice what remains of myself in some kind of service.

Lester: The only thing you will ever sacrifice in this direction is your misery. Rendering service would give only happiness, to the degree your heart is in it. The more you willingly serve the world, the more you discover that you are related to everything and everyone. There is no isolation. It is serving and becoming the All that should be our direction. You don't cut out and let others be separate from you. You become them through the practice of serving them.

Q: The only reason I would make an effort in this direction is so I could better help other people.

Lester: Good, but you can't help other people any more than you can help yourself. So, the best way to help others is to help yourself. It's automatically so that you'll help others to the degree that you'll help yourself. Do both.

Q: So help yourself by helping others? Isn't it a two-way action?

Lester: Yes. However, it's the motive that counts. If I'm helping you with selfish motives, it doesn't help you or me. If I help only to help you, I grow. But there are many people in the world who help for their own ego-glorification, and it doesn't help them any; nor does it help you, because they then help you ego-wise, i.e., they help validate your ego.

Q: That's a very subtle thing, a very difficult thing to get rid of, that ego.

Lester: Right. When there's no more ego, the only thing left is the infinite Being that you are. Ego is the sense of separation from the All. I am an individual, Lester, and I am separate from the All, and all you people are other than I. That is the sense of ego, separateness. The moment I'm not the All, I lack something, and then I try to get it back. I think I need the missing parts of the All, and I start trying to get them. Thus, I assume I don't have the All, I am limited, and this starts a downward spiral, and we continue until we get where we are.

However, we're all on the way up now. And the big problem is to get rid of our ego, the sense that I am an individual separate from everything. We can do this by looking at our motivations. When our motivation is selfish, we change it, make it altruistic. When we act for others rather than for ourselves, in this way we grow.

Q: Is growth a constant becoming aware?

Lester: Yes. You must first want to. When you want to, then you do become aware of your thinking. Then you become aware of your non-thinking, which shows up as periods of peace and well-being.

Q: Like trying to find out, for instance, why one feels things, or why one is sick, like these past two years of illness for me. It's tremendous, Lester. Even this morning when I was talking to my sister on the telephone, after speaking to her, I kept thinking, *Why? Why? Why?* and I tried to be still—as still as I could possibly be. All of a sudden, a realization of the why I had been so negative came to me with such tremendous clarity. And I thought of you so intensely and I thought, *Well, this is what Lester possibly means.* It's finding out the why, and when one sees it, one immediately turns it into something positive, and one is released.

Lester: Right, very good. Keep that up until there is no more.

Q: That's what you always meant about making the subconscious thought conscious and then letting go of it.

Lester: Yes. Pulling the subconscious thought up into consciousness, and, when it's there, you'll see it and naturally let go of it because of its negativity. But as long as it remains unconscious, you don't see it and can't do anything about it, can you?

Q: No. And tremendous things come up when one begins. Wow! Alligators! It's not easy.

Lester: Ego-wise, you don't like what comes up, and you tend to fight it.

Q: Many times I go along on an even keel, and then something comes up in personal relationships or from other directions; all of a sudden you feel a severe pain, and then you realize that any time you feel pain, you're showing your own limitation, and you step back, look at it and release yourself from the whole situation.

Lester: Yes, every situation can be used for growth by observing what's going on, the way you do. *Do this all the time*, until there is no more needed to be let go of, until there is no more ego.

Q: Creative work, for instance, has the ego involved in that too. It's very subtle. And the more one sees spiritually, the more one is able to paint a picture, or make music or whatever one does. This is a point that has always bothered me, the ego-involvement in this. It has worried me. How can one channel it, commercialize it, sell something?

Lester: The answer is simple: Commercialize it, but be not attached to this creativeness.

Q: Difficult. It's the ego saying, "I am the creator."

Lester: It doesn't matter what you do, be not attached to it. Let go of the sense of, "I am the creator." Let the creativeness flow through you.

Q: I would think that in almost any creative act, there has to be a spiritual part, the stem of it is basically some pure motivation, but it's almost always mixed with ego.

Lester: Let me clear up one thing: everything you do is creative. It's impossible to do anything that's not creative. That's because the mind is only creative; but when we create things we don't like, we call it noncreative and destructive. When we create things we like, we call that creative and constructive. But the mind only creates. Everyone is a creator. What we hold in mind, we create.

Q: So all this ego of ours is our own creation?

Lester: Right. It's better to create constructive things like beauty, health, and affluence as they do not demand as much attention from us as a sick body or a sick pocketbook. Consequently, we have more time and ease to look in the direction of Truth and to discover our Self.

Q: Sometimes I think that one thinks too much of the ego and then the ego grows, and you want to fight it more and you give it more importance.

Lester: Yes. But it's too well-grown right now, far more than you can see, in the unconscious part of your mind. Mind is nothing but the sum total collection of all thoughts. The unconscious part of the mind is holding all the thoughts that we are not looking at this moment. But those hundreds of thousands of thoughts are there, and they're active. Unconsciously, you're operating that body; you're operating every cell. You're working a chemical plant, a circulatory, a cooling and a heating system—all these thoughts are active and are actively operating your body.

Also, there are thousands of thoughts of wanting things and not wanting things, likes and dislikes. But even if they're unconscious, they're active; whether we look at them or not, they are still active, and they are sustained and motivated by our ego. This is the difficult part for us, to make these ego-motivated thoughts conscious so that we may let go of them. However, someday we reach a place where we will not be that ego-mind. When we see that, "I am not that mind, I am not that body, I am not that ego," then we'll really see. And when we really see we are not that, it's possible to drop that ego-mind-body, once and for all.

Q: Because one has re-become what one is?

Lester: Not re-become, one has re-remembered, re-discovered, re-recognized what he always was.

Q: So the ego thing falls off like a crust.

Lester: Right, gone forever. Now that's what we do eventually. At first, we work at dropping the ego until we get enough attention free so that we can seek who and what we are. Then, when we see who and what we are, we say, "This is ridiculous," and we don't identify with the ego-mind-body anymore. Then we watch the body go through life like we now watch every other body. You watch it, and you know that the body is not you. You're really above that body; you're not limited or bound by it. You know you are eternal, whole, perfect and free, and you let the body go its way, like a puppet.

Q: And then you use the body for whatever you like if you want to, or, if not, the show just goes on.

Lester: Yes. You let the show go on. It's a show that you wrote called "Bodies Playing Limited." However, you are free to choose to use the body to communicate with others, to help them grow.

Q: Isn't everything we see, a piece of wood, a potato chip, part of that eternal Truth?

Lester: Yes, but you have to see it as nothing but you, then you see the truth of it. The world doesn't disappear, our perception of it changes—completely. Instead of the world being other than us, it becomes us, or we become it. When you see the world as you, it will look entirely different from what it looked like when it appeared separate. You will love and identify with it and everyone in it. When you fully love someone, you identify with and you become one with that one. When you become the universe, you love the universe, or, if you fully love the universe, you become the universe. Love is absolutely necessary. When we love totally, we totally identify with the grand and glorious infinite Being that we are!

Releasing Explorations by Hale Dwoskin

What if we already are what we are seeking—the ultimate happiness—and even an apparently external object like a new car is not separate from us? Everything is already always being satisfied from within because we are the totality. There is no thing and no one that is separate from or outside of who we are. As you live with this idea and make this understanding your own, your life will change forever.

Allow yourself to explore the oneness that is already evident all around you and within you. You can do this in any of the following ways.

Look at your direct experience and see if you can actually find anything that is separate from Awareness. You can ask, "Is this separate from Awareness or is this appearing in or on Awareness?" As you allow yourself to relax and open to this exploration you will start to see all as the Awareness that you are.

Also, practice seeing you—Awareness—everywhere you look. Start by seeing other people as you—Awareness. Then other things as you—Awareness—and finally it will lead you to seeing every atom as you. Also make sure to focus on that which surrounds and interpenetrates all that appears. It is often easier to see this underlying unity when you focus on the emptiness or the vastness that allows all the apparent diversity to be.

Another way to open up to happiness that is right within you is to welcome or allow what is to be as it is. As you welcome the feelings that are blocking your happiness they dissolve naturally all by themselves.

Welcoming

When you allow or welcome a feeling, you are opening your consciousness, and this enables the feeling to drop away all by itself like clouds passing in the sky or smoke passing up an open chimney flue. The Beingness or Awareness that we are is all welcoming. It has no agenda and is like the sky in the analogy above. It is so natural to welcome that as you practice even a little you will notice that it becomes second nature and goes on in the background even when you are not trying to make it happen through a process.

Because we spend so much time resisting and suppressing our emotions, rather than letting them flow freely through us, welcoming or allowing an emotion to be is often all that is necessary to allow it to release.

Here is an example of a student who learned to use welcome to release effortlessly by acknowledging her feelings in the moment. As a daily commuter, she often used to have trouble passing trucks on the highway because she was anxious. Noisy thoughts and gruesome images of accidents would rush into her mind and she'd panic. Then, she began listening to a guided releasing recording from one of our audio programs while traveling to and from work on the interstate. She would dialogue with herself.

"So, you're feeling anxious?"

"Yes, I'm feeling anxious."

"Could you allow yourself to feel as anxious as you do?"

"Yes."

She discovered that, in a short time, she'd be free of the fear and anxiety. Instead these contracted feeling were naturally replaced by a calmness, ease, and flowing feeling. Just by allowing her panic rather than resisting it, her physical sensations of rapid breathing and shakiness would evaporate, and her mind would become quiet and clear.

You can explore this way of letting go by asking yourself questions like these.

Could I welcome that?
Could I allow that?
Could I be present with that?
Could I embrace that?

Do your best to practice welcoming as you read this book. It will help you to allow Lester's message to open you up more deeply and profoundly. It will also help you to live life wide open and at peace.

Love

Lester Levenson

This session is composed of aphorisms compiled from various talks by Lester. Allow yourself to ponder them one at a time. Give yourself enough time to gain the maximum benefit that each has to offer before moving on to the next.

Human love is that which most people think love is. Real, divine love, however, is a constant, persistent acceptance of all beings in the universe—fully, wholly, totally—as the other beings are, and loving them because they are the way they are.

Divine love is wanting and allowing the other one to be the way the other one wants to be. Divine love is seeing and accepting everyone equally, and I think that this is the test of how divine our love is. Is it the same for every person we meet? Is our love for those who are opposing us as strong as for those who are supporting us?

Real, divine love is unconditional and is for everyone alike. The greatest example of it is Christ with his teachings of turn the other cheek, love your enemy, and so forth. If we as a nation were to practice this, we could make every enemy of ours completely impotent, just by loving them. They would be powerless to do any harm to us. However, we would have to do it as a nation, at least the majority of the people would have to love their enemy.

Real love itself is something we can't turn on and off. Either we have it or we don't have it, and with it, it's impossible to love one person and hate another. To the degree that we hate anyone, to that degree we do not love the others. Our love is no greater than our hatred is for any one person.

What most people call love is simply a need. If we say that I love this person but not the other, we feel that we need this person, and therefore we'll be nice to this person so that we can get what we want. But that's not real love.

Human love is selfish, divine love is completely selfless. It is the selfless love that gives unlimited joy beyond our greatest imagination. Try it and discover this for yourself.

The real love is the love we feel for others. It is determined by how much we give ourselves to others.

Full love is identifying with every other being.

When we identify with everyone, we treat everyone as we would treat ourselves.

Love is the balm, the salve, that soothes and heals everything and all.

When you love, you lift others to love.

The most you can give is your love. It is greater than giving materially.

When you understand people, you see that they are doing right in their own eyes. When you understand, you allow, you accept. If you understand, you love.

When we love, not only are we happy, but our whole life is in harmony.

Happiness is equal to one's capacity to love.

If we love completely, we are perfectly happy.

There is always either love or the lack of it.

When one is not loving, one is doing the opposite.

The highest love is when you become the other one. Identity is love in its highest form.

If you love your enemy, you have no more enemies!

The powerful effect of love is self-obvious. Just try it!

If you will look at it from your very own center, the words *love, acceptance, identification, understanding, communication, Truth, God,* and *Self* are all the same.

The original state of man was all love. His troubles are due only to his covering over of his natural state of love.

Love and discover that selflessness turns out to be the greatest good for yourself.

Love is effortless, whereas hate requires much effort.

Apply love and every problem resolves.

Human love is needing the other one. Divine love is giving to the other one.

Love equals happiness. When we are not happy, we are not loving.

The concept of possessiveness is just the opposite of the meaning of love. Love frees, possessiveness enslaves.

Love is a feeling of oneness with, of identity with, the other one. When there's a full love, you feel yourself as the other person; then, treating the other person is just like treating your very own Self. You delight in the other's joy.

Love is a tremendous power. One discovers that the power behind love, without question, is far more powerful than the hydrogen bomb.

One individual with nothing but love can stand up against the entire world, because this love is so powerful. This love is nothing but the Self. This love is God.

Love will not only give all the power in the universe, it will give all the joy and all the knowledge too.

The best way to increase our capacity to love is through understanding ourselves.

I think everyone knows the wonderful experience of loving one person, so you can imagine what it's like when you love three billion people. It would be three billion times more enjoyable.

Love is a constant attitude that evolves in us when we develop it. We should try practicing the love first on our family. Grant everyone in the family their own Beingness, then apply it to friends, then strangers, then to everyone.

The more we practice love, the more we love; the more we love, the more we can practice love. Love begets love.

The more we develop love, the more we come in touch with the harmony of the universe; the more delightful our life becomes, the more beautiful, the more everything it becomes. It starts a cycle going in which you spin upward.

The only method of receiving love is to give love, because what we give out must come back.

The easiest thing to do in the universe is to love everyone. That is, once we learn what love is, it's the easiest thing to do. It takes tremendous effort not to love everyone, and you see the effort being expended in everyday life. But when we love, we're at one with all. We're at peace and everything falls into line perfectly.

In the higher spiritual love, there's no self-deprivation. We don't have to hurt ourselves when we love everyone, and we don't.

With love, there's a feeling of mutuality. That which is mutual is correct. If you love, you hold to that law.

Love is smothered by wrong attitudes. Love is our basic nature and a natural thing, that's why it's so easy. The opposite takes effort. We move away from our natural self, cover it, smother it with concepts of the opposite of love and then, because we're not loving, unloving comes back at us.

We feel the greatest when we love.

The real love wins the universe—not just one person, but everyone in the universe.

Behind the concepts of nonlove, there is always the infinite love that we are. You can't increase it. All you can do is peel away the concepts of nonlove and hatred so that this tremendous loving Being that we are is not hidden anymore.

Love is an absolutely necessary ingredient on the path. If we ever expect to get full realization, we must increase our love until it is complete.

When you really love, you can never feel parting. There is no distance, because they're right in your heart.

Only through growth do we really understand what love is. When you really love, you understand the other one fully.

Love is an attitude that is constant. Love doesn't vary. Love cannot be chopped up.

All love, including human love, has its source in divine love.

Every human being is basically an extremely loving individual.

When you love, you think only the best for those you love.

The more you love, the more you understand.

There's one word that will distinguish the right love from the wrong love, and that is giving.

You could hug a tree the same way as a person when you are very high. Your love permeates everything.

Total self-abnegation is the most selfish thing we can do. When self-abnegation is total, we think only of others and are automatically in the Self.

Love is the state of the Self. It is something you are.

Consideration is a necessary part of love.

Anything but full love is, to a degree, hate.

Can you see why you can't be against anything? The ant is God, the enemy is God. If you're limiting any part, you're holding God away. Love cannot be parceled. Love has to be for all.

The greatest of all progress is love.

Your capacity to love is determined by your understanding.

If you don't trust someone, you don't love him fully.

If we love this world, we accept the world the way it is. We don't try to change it, we let it be. We grant the world its beingness. Trying to change others is injecting our own ego.

The more we love, the less we have to think.

Being love is higher than loving. The real devotee of God has no choice to love—he is love.

Love is your Self, that is the highest love.

Love is an attitude that is constant. Love doesn't vary. We love our family as much as we love strangers. To the degree we're capable of loving strangers, to that same degree we're capable of loving our family.

Love is togetherness.

Love is the Self. The Self doesn't love, the Self *is* love. (Only in duality can you love.)

It's not loving, it's being love that will get you to God.

Each one glorifies himself by service rendered to others and must, therefore, necessarily receive from others. Thus, God flows back and forth, and we delight in his exoticism. There is nothing so delectable as the spirit of givingness. It is intoxicating beyond any other experience capable to man. Discover this.

Service is the secret to bathing in the ever-new joy of God. Service opens the doors to the greatest fields of beauty and charm wherein is enjoyed the nectars of the infinite variety of tastes all blended into one drink—that of superlative love.

Come into the garden of the most delicious and everlasting joy by an everlasting desire to love and serve. Let go of the emptiness of selfishness. Fill yourself to the fullest with selfless love.

Releasing Explorations by Hale Dwoskin

Lester used to say, "Every feeling except love is a nonlove feeling and is therefore varying degrees of hatefulness." How loving are you? Do you have other feelings besides love? If you do, do not despair. Love is your basic nature even when you are lost in the strongest feeling or most limiting story to the opposite. All you need to do to uncover this Truth within yourself is to release or let go of your nonlove feelings, and what is left over is the real you, which is only love. Because love is what you are, you can experience this natural love right within you at any moment without needing to change any internal or external circumstances.

Lester used to suggest a technique that he called "Square All with Love." To experience this technique in your life, do the following: Allow yourself to begin the process of changing all your nonlove feelings to love. Remember, these feelings only appear to cover over your true loving nature, and as you release, the natural love that you are will come shining through more and more. Simply ask yourself, whenever you have a nonlove feeling that you want to release, "Could I change this feeling to love?" You can also ask yourself, "Could I let go of wanting love and simply be the love that I am?"

Letting go is always merely a choice, and if you allow yourself to make this choice, the nonlove feeling that is appearing on the surface will dissolve, revealing the love that is always right in the background waiting to be uncovered. It is an invitation for love to dissolve whatever other feeling is on the surface.

Since love has infinite power there is no feeling that love cannot dissolve. Keep working with the same feeling until you feel only love in that situation, not the feeling with which you started out. This may seem like it will take a while to accomplish, and sometimes it will take a few releases before it is all gone, but if you are persistent in practicing this technique you will find it goes much faster and gets much easier to do.

Start by experimenting in this exercise with feelings that are less intense and ingrained. As you practice this on the easier feelings, you will find that even your deepest hurts and disappointments can be easily released in this way.

Another powerful releasing exploration is to ask yourself these questions and allow it to lead you into the heart of love. "What is love?" Whatever the response is inside take it deeper by asking, "And if it is even deeper or more than that, what is love?" Keep going deeper with this until there is only silence, pure love, and peace.

Realization

Lester Levenson

We try not to be intellectual. That knowledge may be gotten from reading books. Most of us already have the intellectual knowledge and yet are not realized. What we want is knowledge through experiencing it, through feeling it, through realizing and integrating it into our very Being.

The only knowledge that is useful for growth is the knowledge that we realize with our inner sight and feeling. As we contemplate, knowledge should fit in with our feelings, i.e., feel right and should integrate with our whole Beingness. Then, it is a realization, a revelation; then we know, and we know that we know. A realization is seeing something really for the first time, although you've heard it again and again. When it's realized, it's as though you've heard it for the first time. It's like an electric light bulb turning on in the mind, and you say, "Oh, now I see." It is something that you might have heard a hundred times before, but this time, on seeing and experiencing it, it's a realization. It has become real to you.

This perceived and experienced knowledge is the only knowledge that does us any good. We can read everything on the subject, but it doesn't help. Our life doesn't change much, and it doesn't because we don't integrate the knowledge into our beingness through realization. Realized knowledge is nonintellectual, although the means we use are intellectual. We use our mind, we direct our mind toward the answer, but you will discover that the answer does not come from the mind. It comes from a place just behind the mind. It comes from the realm of knowingness, the realm of omniscience. By quieting the mind through stilling our thoughts, each and every one of us has access to this realm of knowingness. Then and there you realize, you make real. You know and you know that you know. Is there any question about what I've just said?

Q: Are knowingness and feelingness the same thing?

Lester: No. The feeling comes just before the knowing.

Q: Is knowingness beyond feeling? Is knowledge that which feels true?

Lester: The answer to both your questions is "yes." It's something you'll have to experience. There's a feel to things, and also there are times when you just know and you know you know, and there's no feeling to it. Knowing is really a higher level. We start with reasoning, thinking, in the realm of thinkingness. Then we move into the realm of feelingness. The top realm is the realm of knowingness.

Q: Is ego implied in feeling?

Lester: Yes. The ego does the feeling. It is a higher ego state. Therefore, there's duality: "I" feel "emotion." Knowingness is Awareness. When I said, "You know and you know that you know," you're aware, and you're aware of the fact that you are aware. There's nothing conditioning it. The very top state is the state of all Awareness, of all Beingness. Beingness and Awareness turn out to be the same thing when we get there. Before, it seemed as though they were two different things. But when we move to the top, Beingness, Awareness, and consciousness are all the same thing, because the Awareness you are aware of is of Beingness being all Beingness. We see that we are not only this body, but that we are every other body, every other thing, every atom in this universe. So, if we are every being and atom, we are all Beingness.

Q: You mean I am that?

Lester: Yes, definitely! It's "I!" The top state is "I." That's all, not even "am." Just below the top, it's "I am." A step below that is "I am that I am." A step below that is "I am unlimited." A step below that is "I am great."

Q: Or one with God?

Lester: Well, where is "one with God"? One with God is not a top state because it's in duality. If I am one with God, there is "I" and "God." In the ultimate, we discover that "I" is God, there's only a singular Oneness in the universe, and we are, we must necessarily be, that Oneness. That's what we discover at the end of the line, or the beginning of the line, whichever way you look at it.

We are unlimited Beings covering over this limitlessness with concepts of limitation, the first of which is "I am an individual separate from the All." That's the very first and a very big error that we make. "I am separate, I am a personality, my name is Lester, I have a body," and I spiral right down. After we assume a mind and a body, then we assume all these troubles and all these problems, and they're nothing but assumptions. They are only a fiction that we see after we go within, quiet the mind, and discover all this Truth right there.

This whole world, as now seen, is nothing but a dream-illusion that never was. The Truth is just behind the outward world. So why make trouble? The growth is simply the elimination of all the concepts of limitation. That infinite, perfect Being that we are must always be infinite and perfect and therefore is perfect right now. That's one thing we can never change—our unlimited Self. That is all the time. But I, the unlimited Self, can assume that I am limited and that I have a mind, I have a body, I have problems. However, it is only an assumption.

Q: What's the technique for cutting through all that, for getting right to that state where you have that total Awareness?

Lester: Pose the question, "Who and what am I?" and await the answer to present itself. The thinking mind can never give the answer, because all thought is of limitation. So, in quietness and meditation, pose the questions, "Who am I?" and "What am I?" When other thoughts come up, strike them down. If you can't, ask, "To whom are these thoughts? Well, these thoughts are to me. Well, then, who am I?" and you're right back on the track of "Who am I?" Continue this until you get the answer to the question "Who and what am I?" regardless of how long it takes.

The answer is the unlimited Self. The only way It becomes obvious is when the mind stills almost completely. The only obstacles to immediate full realization here and now are the thoughts, every one of which is limited. Eliminate those thoughts and you'll see this infinite Being that you always were and are and always will be.

The difficulty is the past habit patterns of thought, the unconscious constant turning and churning of thought in a mechanism we have set up that we call the unconscious mind. The unconscious thoughts are simply our thoughts now that we do not look at, so we call them unconscious. This is the enemy we set up. To lessen these unconscious thoughts, we first make them conscious. When we make them conscious, then we may let go of them, and they are done forever. This quiets the unconscious mind. Now, the more we eliminate the thoughts, the more obvious our real Self becomes. The more obvious our real Self becomes, the more we are able to scorch the remaining thoughts until the mind is totally quieted.

Q: You have to still the conscious thoughts before you can get to the unconscious thoughts?

Lester: The conscious thought is only the unconscious thought made conscious.

Q: They come through dreams too at that state don't they, the unconscious thoughts?

Lester: Yes, but it's only in the waking state that we can eliminate them and thereby grow.

Q: You still your conscious thoughts through meditation, other techniques, etc. Now the "Who am I?" will go right through both, is that correct?

Lester: Yes. Also, you can use "Who am I?" to still or eliminate thoughts. Pose the question, "Who am I?" and when a thought comes up you say, "To whom is this thought?" The answer is, "To me." Ask, "Well, who am I?" and you're back on the track. Thus, you eliminate the thoughts as they come up.

Q: But what keeps the unconscious thoughts from popping up at that time?

Lester: They will and should pop up. If they pop up, they're conscious. Then you can drop them. Eventually you eliminate all of them.

Q: How many minds do we have?

Lester: There's only one mind. What we are looking at this moment is what the world calls the conscious mind. The part of the mind we're not looking at this moment the world calls the unconscious mind. It's the mode of mind that we give a different name to. That which we are talking about now, that which we are aware of now, is what we call the conscious mind, the conscious thought.

The unconscious mind is all the thoughts we are not interested in at this moment. What some call superconscious thought, there's really no such thing as superconscious thought. The superconscious, that which is above consciousness, is already out of the thinking realm—that's the omniscience, that's the realm of knowingness. The superconscious realm is all Awareness, all knowingness. There is no thinking when you know.

Q: Is unconscious different from subconscious?

Lester: Subconscious and unconscious are the same.

Q: Do you agree with Jung's collective unconscious theory?

Lester: I only agree with Truth. And this is one thing I emphasize: *Truth is the only authority for truth.* Accept nothing until you can prove it out. Don't even accept what I say, no matter how much I speak as though I know. If it doesn't fit into your knowingness at present, you can accept it for checking. But only that which you can prove out for yourself, only that should you accept.

This is basically important. *It is absolutely necessary to prove all this knowledge for yourself.* Otherwise, it's hearsay to you. You must make this knowledge your knowledge. Now, there's only one Truth, one absolute Truth. So putting names to it doesn't mean anything.

Whether so-and-so said it, or I said it doesn't mean anything. Is it true? Does it integrate into your understanding? That's the only thing that matters. That's the point wherein we are different. We try to make this very practical so that you can use this knowledge and move toward the total understanding as quickly as possible.

Q: Is it necessary to go through stages?

Lester: No. How long should it take Infinite Power, Infinite Knowledge, to know that It is infinite?

Q: Wouldn't take any time.

Lester: Right. When man so wills with full intensity of will, it happens quickly. If you would want this more than anything else, you would have it in a matter of weeks or months.

Q: Is there any way of making yourself want it more and more?

Lester: Yes, make yourself want it by experiencing the wonderfulness of it, or make yourself more and more miserable. Well, there are two incentives: misery is one, but not the best. The sweetness of it, the wonderfulness of it, the glory of it should make us want it more than the misery should.

Q: The glory in what sense?

Lester: The glory of it, of knowing what you are. It's a tremendous experience, it's an ecstasy, a euphoria. There are no real words to describe it, because, well, we're in an age where these things are not experienced and therefore not understood, so how can there be words for things that are not understood? There are no words to describe these feelings, they're so beyond present understanding. So you pick the words you know best to describe it and that's it.

Paramahansa Yogananda uses the words *ever-new joy welling up every second,* and that's a practical way of describing it. At first, it's a joy that spills over every second, just keeps pouring out, pouring out—you feel as though you can't contain it. Later on, it resolves itself into a very profound peace, the most peaceful peace you could ever imagine. It's a delicious peace that is far more comfortable than ever-new joy. But please, get the ever-new joy!

Q: But don't stay there.

Lester: That's it. It's very easy to get stuck in the ever-new joy state. That's what they call the *Ananda sheath*. It's the last veil we have to remove. It is the last wall we must break through. When you start this ever-new joy, it's so good you just want to continue it. Also, you have no feeling of need to change, everything is so wonderful. But it isn't the final state. The final state is the peace that passeth all understanding. It's a deep, deep peace. You move in the world, the body moves, but you have absolute peace all the time. Bombs could be dropping all around you, and you have that perfect peace regardless of what's going on.

Q: How do you maintain that state?

Lester: If you get it, you don't have to maintain it, because you have it—you *are* it.

Q: Well, in that particular state, then, you are really omniscient and all the other things, and there's no necessity for thinking.

Lester: Right. That's the top state. Now, it is possible to dip into this state to a certain depth that's very deep and not maintain it because of the habits from the past. The habits of thoughts that have not been eliminated re-emerge and take over. We can feel this infinite Being that we are, and it's a wonderful experience, then, the next minute, "Oh, so-and-so wants me to do this, and I don't want to do it." A thought comes in, and there you are, identifying with unhappy limitedness. You, the Self, are trying to be this unlimited Being through a very narrow ego, a very limited ego, and it hurts. That's all it is.

Q: How do you bombard that ego and get rid of it?

Lester: First and foremost, with an intense desire to let go of the ego. Second, listening to someone who knows the way and following through on the direction, especially if that one is a fully realized Being.

Q: That's hard to find.

Lester: No, they are available right where you are. Wherever you are, they're right there. I can name some of them: Jesus, Buddha, Yogananda. I don't know of any in the United States in physical body. India has, I believe, several. But there is no need for a physical body when you can get the others wherever you are, because they're omnipresent. All you need to do is open your mind's eye and see them. They're omnipresent, so they must be right where you are.

Also, they, wanting to help you, must necessarily come to you if you open yourself to them. They have no choice. They have made a commitment. So all you need to do is to ask for their help and guidance and open yourself to it, and it is there. However, since we think we're physical bodies, sometimes we more readily accept a fully realized Being when he is in a physical body. Therefore, we will take more help because, in our physical sensing he seems to be more real. Because of that, it's good to have a fully realized Being in the flesh. However, if we don't have one, it doesn't mean we can't take the guidance of those who are omnipresent.

Q: Some aspect of the Hindu thought says you can't do it without a live guru, but I think they've evolved beyond that now, and you're confirming it.

Lester: Yes. However, a guru is alive, whether in physical body or not.

Q: Do people need a live guru?

Lester: People need a guru, a teacher. He doesn't necessarily have to be alive in a physical body, but he has to be accepted as being alive. He doesn't have to be in a physical body. The reason why we need a guru is that we are in a very difficult age. It's an age of materialism where everything, everyone, is shouting at us, "This is a material world. This is it!" We have been in this world again and again and again, so we really need the assistance of a fully realized Being to offset that constant weight of the world that says we are physical, limited bodies. We should want the Truth more than we want air. Then we would get full realization very quickly.

Q: Did you coin that? Is that yours, an aphorism?

Lester: Nothing is mine. Anything I say will have always been said before. I might just twist the words around this way or that way in my own style, but there's nothing new. Truth always was and always will be.

There's a story in the Eastern writings of a master and his disciple. They were bathing in the Ganges, and the disciple asked, "Master, how can I know the Truth?" And the teacher took him by the hair and held him under the water until he was about ready to go unconscious. Then he let him up and said, "Now, when you want Truth as much as you wanted air, then you'll have it."

They have some great stories. That snake and the rope story is an excellent analogy of the physical world. I guess everyone knows that, don't they? A person walks along the road at dusk and sees a rope on the ground, mistakes it for a snake, goes into an intense fear and a complete involvement as to what to do about this awful snake. Well, the snake is only an illusion. The real thing is a rope. So he spends a lifetime of maybe sixty-five years struggling and fighting this snake-world and then takes a rest on the astral side and comes back and fights it again and again and again until he wakes up to the fact that the snake was only the rope, and it really never was. And that's exactly what happens to this physical world. It's just like that snake: it's an illusion.

The example I like best is that what goes on in this world is exactly the same as what goes on in a night dream. While we're in the night dream, it's very real—we are there, there are other characters, it's either beautiful or ugly, and, when it's a nightmare, we're being killed. It's a real struggle. All the time we're in the dream, it is real to us. But when we awaken we say, "Oh, my gosh, it was only a dream; it never really was." And that's exactly what happens when we wake up out of this waking state dream of the world.

Releasing Explorations by Hale Dwoskin

Would you rather believe in freedom or be the freedom that you are right now? Most of us substitute belief for direct experience and knowing. As you open to that which already is right now, it will lead you to direct recognition of the Awareness or freedom that you are. I highly recommend that you shed your beliefs and not settle for anything except the real thing.

Self-inquiry is a great way to know and be the Truth, and I highly recommend that you explore this for yourself. In coming chapters, we will explore it in greater depth as we explore the part of the Sedona Method we call the 5th Way, but for now allow yourself to explore it in just the way Lester described in this chapter. You may also want to add another question to your repertoire. After you ask yourself, "Who or what am I?" whatever answer arises, you can follow with, "If I am more than that, what am I? And if I am even more than that what am I?" Keep going until you just rest as That.

Another great way to experience and be the Truth of who you are is by shedding the beliefs about this Truth that you have accumulated since you have been on the path. Most of us have heard a tremendous amount about what is true and what is not and most of us have accepted much on hearsay before we proved it out for ourselves. Anything that we accept on hearsay can act as powerful obstruction to direct experience.

This simple process will allow you to experience, realize, and then be the Truth, rather than just believe it. Make a list of your spiritual beliefs and then use any of the following questions to let them go. The first question is quite direct. Simply ask yourself, "Could I let go of this belief?" "Would I?" "When?" and then do your best to just let it go. The more you let go of the belief, the more you will uncover what is true. Another question you can use is, "Would I rather believe in [the belief] or would I rather be or know the Truth?" You can use either of these sets of questions and they will have the same effect of dissolving the belief and revealing the underlying Truth.

Love, Giving, and
the Christ Consciousness

Lester Levenson

It is now the Christmas season; so let us direct our attention toward Christmas. Maybe I ought to allow you to lead me into what you would like to hear about Christmas—or should I just talk? All right.

Christ-mass, the day when the masses look toward Christ, when mass is held in reverence to Jesus. When I interpret the Bible, it's the way I see it, not the way I've read it or someone else has said it's so. Christmas is related to Christ. Christ is not the man Jesus. Christ is the title of Jesus who has attained the Christ Consciousness. And I think if you separate the two, Jesus and Christ, you will far better understand the meaning of his words and the meaning of the Bible. When he says, "I am the way," he doesn't mean Jesus, he means Christ. So, first I'd better explain what I mean by Christ and Jesus.

Jesus was a man who was born on this earth approximately 2,000 years ago, who, through righteousness, or right-useness, rightly used the world to attain the Christ Consciousness. In so doing, he showed the way to immortality that each and every one of us must take. We must die to death, i.e., eliminate from our consciousness all thoughts of death and hold in its place only eternality and immortality. In order to show us, he allowed himself to be crucified so that he could prove immortality by resurrecting himself. He was a way-shower and dedicated and gave his life only to show us the way.

Christ Consciousness is the consciousness that saves us from all this mess that we find ourselves in when we try to be worldly man. It is the attaining of the Christ Consciousness that saves us from all the horrors and miseries of the world. It is the Christ Consciousness that

89

gives us liberation from all difficulty and leads us into our immortality. If we were to try to be Jesus, we would have all the trials and tribulations that he went through. However, when we become the Christ, by being Christ-like and thereby attaining the Christ Consciousness, we eliminate all and every misery and have nothing but infinite joy.

So, Christhood is a state that was attained by the man Jesus. He attained his Christhood before he was born, and he came back to show us the way by actual example. And if you will keep these two in their meaning as you read the Bible, I believe it will make much more sense. Christmas is known mostly by the spirit of givingness, of goodwill toward all men. Locked up in that word "givingness" is the key to all happiness. It's in the spirit of givingness that we have and experience the greatest joy. If you'll think back, you'll see that when you were giving, you were most joyous.

"Love" and "giving" are two words that are synonymous. It's in the spirit of givingness that the secret to joy lies. When we fully have that, we want to give everything that we have to everyone we meet, and we have infinite joy. It's so important. It's in the spirit of givingness, it's not in the givingness of things, unfortunately, because Christmas is a great time of gift-giving. People are giving, giving, giving. But it's not in the givingness—it's in the spirit of givingness that the joy lies. The feeling of the spirit of givingness is felt more around Christmastime by more people than any other time of the year. It's a wonderful thing. We should make every day Christmas. When we get full realization, we do just that. There isn't a moment in which we're not wanting to give everything we know to everyone.

Q: You mean giving things, or giving of yourself?

Lester: Well, first givingness. If we give with strings attached, with reservations, with recriminations, there is little joy in it. But when we give freely, we have the greatest of feelings, and it's this constant spirit of givingness that is the secret of eternal joy.

Now, the greatest thing we can give, as the Bible says, is wisdom, because when you give one wisdom, you give one the method of attaining everything, not just one single thing. So, the greatest of all givingness is giving wisdom, is giving understanding, is giving knowledge of this subject that we are interested in.

I might explain it this way. If you give a man a meal when he's hungry, he's made happy for the moment, and he's satisfied. But three hours later he needs another meal, and probably thousands of meals after that. So what is one meal that you give to him? Relatively little. However, if you give the man the understanding of how to produce a meal, he will never go hungry! You will give him the knowledge of how to always have all the food he wants. You will have given him sixty thousand meals! So, that's the greatest givingness, giving understanding and wisdom.

Practicing this would be an excellent method of growth, and I think as a group you're ready for it. Give this understanding to everyone whom you meet who asks for it. It's excellent in that it takes you out of your little self onto others. It's an act of love. I'm suggesting that this givingness be taken on as almost a way of life from here on to help others to get this understanding. It will help you to rapidly attain mastership, and it will give you the greatest of all joys. It's good to give gifts. They should be given from the heart. However, I think we are all at the point where we can give much more than just things. We should try to give wisdom and understanding. Did I answer your question?

Q: Yes.

Q: This is only if we are asked?

Lester: Yes. If we try to help people who are not asking for it, we are just expressing our own ego. "I know something you should know," see? "I" talking down to "you," trying to teach you something when you're not asking for it, is just ego-expression on my part, so it should only be given when asked for.

Q: Is there a time when you become sensitive enough so that you do say things to people that they need, even without them asking?

Lester: Yes, there is. As you let go of your ego, you automatically tune in more with others. The less your ego, the more you are attuned to others. You reach a state in which they don't even have to ask. You'll discover that some people who ask don't really want help. Likewise, some people who say, "I don't want any help" are really wanting it.

It takes a little experience to handle situations like that. But it's true that as we grow, as we let go of our ego, we become more attuned to others, and we automatically help them. And we help at all times, no matter what or where a situation is. It could be the cashier in a market or someone you meet on the street. There's always a certain givingness that should be going on all the time. And it doesn't have to be only words of wisdom, it could be a kind word, an expression of love. It wouldn't hurt to try helping others. That would be the greatest of all givingness. Any more questions?

Q: What is the second coming of the Christ?

Lester: The second coming of the Christ is not the same as the second coming of Jesus. The second coming of Jesus will be the time when he returns and walks on this earth again in a physical body. I believe it will be the body that he had the last time he walked the earth. The second coming of the Christ is when we attain the Christ Consciousness.

As a group, we are very fortunate in that we are close to Jesus. This was very evident the very first time we had a meditation when Jesus came into this room and walked around to almost everyone here. It was a very definite and a very important sign that, as a group, Jesus is very interested in us, is trying to help us with all the power that he has. That power is never given unless we are receptive to it. There's no forcing it. He can only use his power when we open ourselves to him. If and when we do, he is right there, ready and very capable. Just try him.

We need this direct connection with a master if we want to go all the way this lifetime. As I've said, it's so difficult in these times to achieve mastership that it is necessary to have this connection with a master, so that when we are ready to leave this plane, he will assist us in getting full realization. There isn't anyone in this room who cannot make it this lifetime, if he or she will just stay faithful to the path until the end. Every one of us can make it this lifetime if we really want it.

Q: Will you define "making it"?

Lester: Christhood and full realization. "Making it" is becoming a master. What is a master? A master is one who is master over all matter in the universe and who is master over his mind. A master is one who sees his own infinity right within him. A master is one who has undone all thoughts of limitation, who has ripped off all these sheaths of limitations and is free.

Q: And this we can do in this lifetime?

Lester: Yes, definitely! You must want it more than anything else. You must want it more than you want things of the world. And if you do, when you're ready to leave this place, you'll get the assistance from the master that you look to, and he will help you over.

The way he will do it is this way: If you don't make it before you die, you will make it at the time of your so-called death. When a person dies, all thoughts of this lifetime and all thoughts of prior lifetimes come up for review. The master identifies with us. He sees us as himself, and as these thoughts come up in our mind, it's like coming up in his mind, and he, identified with and as us, helps us undo them. When they are totally undone, we are totally free!

Q: This is what we are doing every day when we say, "We're not limited. I won't accept this. I'm not this limited being." Isn't this what we should be doing all day long?

Lester: Yes. We should continue it until the end of all thoughts. We should not be limited by any thing or any thought.

Q: But this is jumping so far. I'm interested in being able to walk down the street without getting mad at the fellow in front of me.

Lester: I'm trying to show you the entire way. What I'm trying to do is to give you a map that takes you all the way. I'm not saying, "Bob, be this today." But I think if you have a map that shows the entire route, you can take it all by yourself. You don't need to have people like me say this to you. Once you've got the map, all you need to do is to follow it. I'm trying to give you a complete picture, a complete understanding of what full realization is and the way to accomplish it. And it's a very difficult thing to do, because you'll never really know what it is until you attain it.

Q: And the ego is simply the feeling that I am not this.

Lester: Right. The ego is a feeling that I am a separate individual, separate from the All, and I need a body and a mind to be separate.

Q: That's limited?

Lester: Well, if I have a body, and I have a mind, I have thousands of limitations. I have to feed the body, take care of it. I have thoughts. My feelings are hurt. This goes on and on and on. Realize what you are. You'll see that you are not the body, you are not the ego. Discover what you are and be infinite.

Q: Can Jesus save us?

Lester: Jesus doesn't save, the Christ Consciousness saves. We should believe not in Jesus but believe as Jesus believed. When we make an effort to attain the Christ Consciousness, Jesus helps us to realize it. Jesus is always available to anyone who asks and is receptive to his help. You may and can contact Jesus to the degree you actually accept the fact that you can. Were you to accept that you could talk to Jesus in a physical body, then you would meet with him in a physical body. If you can accept meeting with him in a vision or in a dream, then you would meet with him in that manner. If you can accept him as a presence, then you will feel his presence and receive his support. It is all up to you.

Releasing Explorations by Hale Dwoskin

Do you live every day with the same feeling of giving as you do, at times, during the Christmas season? What is standing in your way? You will discover as you allow yourself to explore giving with your heart that your heart overflows with the love that you are. The more giving you feel, the more you will feel that you already have everything that you need or want for yourself, and the more your world will reflect that. The expression, "The giver is blessed," refers to one who gives without wanting something in return. Just the feeling alone that comes from giving freely is exquisite, let alone whatever else comes back to you. But this can happen only if you give from your heart without wanting anything in return.

Practice giving without wanting anything in return. This is something that you can do all day every day with everyone you meet. Start by giving everyone you meet your love, compassion, and understanding. This is more than enough. You can also share with them what you are learning from this book. And if you are able, also give what is needed on a physical level.

When you give, make sure that you give to those who want to receive. Refrain from forcing those who are not interested. Also allow yourself to feel that the person to whom you are giving is your equal and is already whole, complete, and perfect, as opposed to being in need. The highest gift you can give anyone is to grant him or her their Beingness—to see them as they truly are. The more you give without wanting anything in return, the more your heart will overflow with love and your life will be filled with the abundance of the universe.

If the giving does not bring with it a feeling of joy, it is because there are strings attached to your gift. To keep yourself honest, you can make a list of what you have given that day and then check to see if you wanted anything in return. If you did, simply ask yourself, "Could I let go of wanting anything in return for this gift?" "Would I?" "When?" This will help free you of the strings that you have attached to your giving and will open up the universal flow.

Ego

Lester Levenson

This session is composed of aphorisms collected from various talks by Lester. Please allow yourself to ponder each one individually before going on to the next in order to get the maximum benefit.

The ego concept is the root cause of all delusion and therefore all trouble. It is the false identifying of "I" with a body rather than with the Self.

Ego is the concept of individuality, of separation from the "I," the All. Therefore, ego is a false assumption. We are really the "I," we are not separate from It.

The ego is all the evil there is, and your Self is all the good there is.

The ego is the source of birth and death, and when the ego is let go of, you die to death.

Everything that isn't good has its source in the ego sense and is therefore unreal. Our real nature is an ultimate goodness.

Everything of the ego is the opposite of everything of the Self. Everything an ego sees is a lie in the light of Truth. Everything an ego sees is in duality. An ego can't see Oneness. The ego has an eye of duality only. There's nothing true that an ego sees. On the opposite side, the Self sees only the Truth, the Self.

The coloring agent of Truth is ego. The less the ego, the less the coloring of Truth.

The entire trouble is wrong identity. We say we are the limited ego—ego can't do anything but be limited.

There's only one single growth, and that is letting go of the ego.

Whenever you are not growing spiritually, you are growing in the other direction.

Every time you express ego, you are growing downward.

The more you grow, the more you can face your ego.

When things bother us and we look for the source, we find our ego.

The whole object of the path is to let go of the ego—what remains is the Self.

The whole thing is simple: Any complexity in life is the ego trying to undo the simplicity of reality.

It is the ego that makes life difficult.

Think you are a limited ego, and the more you think so, the more effort you need to get along. It is the ego that requires effort.

There is only one basic trouble in this world. It is the common denominator of all problems. It is trying to be an ego.

Identify with the ego and you identify with trouble.

We should shift from a desire to get out of misery to a desire to let go of the ego.

The ego dies hard, but once you know the ego is the source of all misery, and the Self is the source of all happiness, then it shouldn't be so hard to work at letting go of the ego.

When we start moving into the Self, the ego starts putting blocks in the way: we get sick, we go to sleep, we have other things to do, etc., because we feel we will be destroyed if the ego is destroyed. We have convinced ourselves over the millennia that we are these limited bodies, and we think it takes time to let go of these concepts of limitation.

Time is an ego-thought.

The ego will always trying to keep us from letting go of the ego.

Getting involved in intellectual questions and discussions validates the ego and avails you nothing.

To pose a question, an ego is necessitated. There are no questions when one is realized.

All inquiries about the non-Self are directing one's attention away from, and are delaying, one's realization of Truth. Any question about the ego directs the attention to the ego. The ego is the unreal, the untruth. No matter how much you talk about illusion, it will not give you the perception of the real, the Truth.

In the beginning, the ego is the only thing you know.

There is only one thing to do: let go of the ego! There is no other way to grow. You are fully realized now. Just let go of the ego! That's how simple it is.

The weaker the ego, the more you can put attention on the Self. However, if you spent all your time on the ego, you would never see the Self, not until you looked at the Self. It amounts to weakening the grip of the ego enough so that you can turn toward the Self.

The more you do away with the ego, the more unselfish you are.

When a person is ego-centered, almost all of his attention is centered on himself. Everything he sees or hears is colored because it has to filter through his self-attention.

When you have completely let go of your ego, you are not interested in yourself, you are interested only in others.

If you do things to win approval, then you are doing it for yourself. If you are doing anything for yourself, it isn't selfless.

A problem is created whenever you want to assert your ego.

Whenever we react, it is always because there is something we selfishly want.

Whenever we want to make the world different than it is, that is ego-motivated.

When there is no ego involved, we see things exactly as they are.

We are blinded to the degree of our ego.

Wanting our ego to be accepted, we see things the way we think they will help us to be accepted.

If you have any emotion, it is ego-motivated.

Any human need or desire is ego-motivated. My ego thinks it needs things; my Self feels and knows that everything is mine.

We should have no wants. Then we are never in trouble.

Talking is asking for ego attention. It's wanting ego approval. If you will remain quiet, you may feel that happiness that you are seeking through making the noise.

Almost every time we talk, we are asking for ego acceptance.

Ego is only destructive to one.

Everyone who has ego is destructive to the degree he has ego.

Ego is the opposite of love. Love is the Self.

Egos want to direct the universe.

If you want to be most creative, do away with the ego.

Ego is the most expensive thing in the universe, dollar-and-sense wise.

Any sense of doership is of the little self.

Ego equals blindness, blindness equals ignorance.

Seeking any ego fulfillment is seeking the letting go of the agony of the concept of lack.

Any lack is necessarily an ego concept, for the ego is necessarily a sense of limitation or lack.

Ego is a mere notion that feels like the deluge of an ocean.

When you are unhappy, you are looking for ego approval and not getting it.

Another definition for trouble is trying to be an ego.

Any defending of oneself is asking for ego approval.

If you want to be good at anything, the less the ego, the better you are. The ego is a limiting adjunct on the Self. Since the ego is a limiting adjunct of the Self, the less the ego, the more capable you are in everything, except one thing—misery.

It took you millions of years to develop this ego. Keep letting go of the ego until you begin to see the Self. When you see your Self, you quickly drop your ego in short time.

After having eliminated much of the ego, when one is acting ego-wise, at that moment the ego seems like all. However, what has been eliminated has been eliminated.

It's the ego's sense of being an individual separate from the All that is the source of all trouble.

Soul is a glorified ego concept of the ego.

It doesn't matter what you do, but it does matter with what you identify. If you identify with the limited ego, then you are unhappy.

After dropping enough ego, it gets weak, and the Self takes us the rest of the way.

All growth is letting go of ego.

The ego is a false imposition of the "I." When you say "I," that is the eternal you.

The ego cannot be subjugated by one who takes it to be real.

Seek the source of the ego, and it turns out to be your Self.

Humility is letting go of ego.

If you are hurt, look for the ego motivation and let go of it. You'll then feel happier.

Unless you are eliminating ego, you're not growing. You see, you can't grow into the Self, because that's what you are. You just lift off the cover, which is ego.

The ego creates and maintains the subconscious.

All subconscious thought is originated by the ego and hidden away in the subconscious by the ego.

The ego-principle is the cause of the seeming separation of you from the All.

The high states should be used to scorch the ego. The higher we go, the more we are capable of scorching the ego. When you are high, you can say, "All this silly reaction and ego, I'm through with it!" and be through with it!

The real you, your Self, is infinitely grand and glorious—whole, perfect, and in total peace—and you are blinding yourself to this by assuming that you are a limited ego. Drop the blinder, the ego, and be forever in perfect peace and joy!

Be yourself!

Releasing Explorations by Hale Dwoskin

How real do you see yourself—your ego? What if all your troubles, all your problems are not your own? They belong to a figment of imagination called ego—the personal thought called "I." Were you born with your name or did others give it to you? As babies, it takes about two years of repetition to finally believe that we are the name that we are called. Allow yourself to discover that glorious being that you have always been, never having been limited by any name or form. In fact, if you look for the ego—"I"—in this moment, you will find that it is not really there.

Many times on retreats, when someone is looking to discover who he or she is, or he or she is lost in "their" story—the false reference point of me—I have asked, "In this moment, if you do not go into memory, can you actually find this 'me' that you are talking about?" I have yet to have anyone find a "me" in this moment. For most people, this brings their minds to a complete stop, and they are left resting as the presence that they have always been.

If you struggle with this question at all or you simply prefer this exploration, you can use the question, "Am I that or am I that which is aware?" As I mentioned earlier in the book, any time there is a thought, feeling, or sense of a personal center, simply ask yourself this question and allow it to reveal the unreality of the ego and uncover that which is already shining in plain view.

Many people, rather than allow themselves to remain at rest, reidentify with the false reference point of "me" after some time of enjoying this rest. Most also find that the sense of ease and rest never fully leaves, even when it appears that presence is being obstructed by the reemergence of this false reference point of "me." Either way, when you examine the Truth of who you are in this way, know that what you are never comes or goes, and what does come and go cannot be who you are by its very nature.

If the false reference point does reappear, this does not mean that you have missed something; it only means the habit has not completely dropped away. You can always continue to remind yourself of what is actually here now or use any of the other tools that make up the Sedona Method that are at the end of each session.

Allow yourself to look beyond the ego—I thought. Look, feel, and hear that which is not limited by what you used to call you. Freedom or the Self is always closer than your next thought and is present before, during, and after every experience. Allow yourself to hear the silence that supports all sound and then see and feel the space or emptiness that contains all objects. If you get caught in ego, do not suppress it. Just allow it to be and then switch your focus as best you can back to Beingness. In fact, you can allow yourself to switch back and forth until all apparent separation disappears. As you switch your focus from always focusing on who you are not, who you are will shine through with greater clarity.

Mastering Mind and Matter

Lester Levenson

Our subject is happiness. We say that, when understood, happiness and all the following—God, realization, wisdom, understanding—become the same; that the happiness that we're seeking is only the real infinite Being that each one is. And when we recognize this, we then attempt to discover this inner Being that we are more and more, until we see it completely, totally and only.

When we do, the ultimate happiness is established permanently, forever, and with it goes immortality, unlimitedness, imperturbable peace, total freedom, and everything that everyone is seeking. The way to this inner Being that we are is to direct our attention inward. We first focus the mind back upon the mind until we discover what mind is. We then focus our attention on our Self to discover our real nature. And it turns out that our real nature, the infinite real Self that we are, is simply us minus the mind—that the mind was a limiting adjunct covering our Beingness, that all thoughts have limitation (and we develop millions of thoughts of limitation) that prevent us from seeing this infinite Being that we are and that, by turning our attention inward, we discover all this. When we do, we naturally let go of all these limitations. Then we see that we have always been, are now, and always will be this unlimited Being.

The prime obstacle that we meet is the subconscious mind. It is full of thoughts of limitations that propel us every day, automatically. And we have made these habits of subconscious thoughts so strong that even when we recognize the direction we would like to go in, the subconscious thoughts keep directing us for quite some time (even lifetimes) until we finally succeed in overcoming them. We overcome them with thoughts of what we really want to do in life and, in that way, become master over the mind, controlling the thoughts until only the thoughts we want determine our behavior. Then we're in a position where we can do something about the mind, and we start to transcend the mind. We rise above it, and we drop it. We let it go, and when we do that, we find ourselves this pure, infinite, limitless, totally free Being that we naturally are. And then happiness is complete.

The direction is to go within, seeking and meditating to quiet the mind enough so that we can see the infinite Being that we are. The major steps are first becoming aware of the fact that we are master over matter (and matter includes the body). Then, the second major step is becoming master over mind. And when we become really masterful over mind, we are able to, and we do, let go of mind and operate in the realm of omniscience, in the realm of knowingness. Then we are fully aware of the infinite Being that we are and are in the ultimate happiness.

We should start with the first step, consciously controlling matter. Whether we are aware of it or not, everyone is controlling matter all the time. Whether one wants to be a demonstrator or not, he is. It is impossible not to be a creator all the time. Everyone is creating every day. We are not aware of it, because we just don't look at it. We have demonstrated or created everything we have! Every thought, every single thought, materializes in the physical world. It's impossible to have a thought that will not materialize (except that we reverse it). If we think the opposite right after we have a thought, with equal strength, we neutralize it. But any thought not reversed or neutralized will materialize in the future, if not immediately. So this thing of demonstration that we are all trying so hard to accomplish, we are doing all the time, unconscious of the fact that we're doing it. All we need to do is to direct it consciously, and that we call demonstration.

Everything that everyone has in life is a demonstration. It couldn't come into our experience had we not had a thought of it at some time prior. If you want to know what your sum total thinkingness is, look around you. It has determined exactly what you now have. It is your demonstration! If you like it, you may hold it. If you don't, start changing your thinking. Concentrate it in the direction that you really want, until those thoughts become dominant over the sub-conscious thoughts; and when you begin to consciously demonstrate small things, you may then realize that the only reason why they are small is because you don't dare to think big.

The exact same rule or principle that applies to demonstrating a penny applies to demonstrating a million dollars. The mind sets the size. Anyone who can demonstrate a dollar can demonstrate a million dollars! Become aware of the way you are demonstrating a one-dollar bill and just increase it next time to a much larger amount. Take on the consciousness of the million, rather than the one-dollar bill. The material world is just an out-projecting of our minds into what we call the world and bodies. And when we realize that it is just an out-projecting of our minds—just a picture out there that we have created—we can very easily change it, even instantly, by changing our thought!

So, to repeat: everyone is demonstrating, creating, every moment what he or she is thinking. You have no choice. You are a creator, so long as you have a mind and you think. Now, to get beyond creation, we must go beyond the mind. Just beyond the mind is the realm of perfection where there is no need for creating. There is a higher state than creation—it's the state of Beingness, sometimes called Awareness or consciousness. That state is just behind the mind. That's beyond creation. The mind finds it very difficult to imagine what it's like beyond creation, because the mind is involved constantly in creating. It's the creating instrument of the universe and everything that happens in the world. So, if you take this thing called mind, which instrument is only a creator, and try to imagine what it is like beyond creation, it's impossible. The mind will never know God or your Self, because you have to go just above the mind to know God, your Self.

To know the infinite Being that you are, to know what it's like beyond creation, you must transcend the mind. The final state is beyond creation. It is the changeless state. In creation, everything is constantly changing, and therefore the ultimate Truth cannot be there. So, to demonstrate what one wants, one needs to become aware of the fact that all we need to do is to think only of the things that we do want, and that is all that we would get, if we would do just that. Think only of the things you want, and that's what you'll be getting all the time, because the mind is only creative. Simple, isn't it?

Also, take credit for creating all the things that you don't like. Just say, "Look what I did." Because when you become aware that you've created things that you don't like, you're in the position of creator, and if you don't like it, all you have to do is to reverse it, and then you'll like it.

After you can master matter by consciously creating that which you want, then master your mind and get beyond it. Any questions?

Q: No, but I think you did a good job of laying it out like that. I could almost understand everything you said.

Lester: The most perfect explanation yet!

Q: Am I to assume that everything that I see and meet during the day has been created by subconscious thoughts?

Lester: Yes. The difficult thing is the unconscious thinking. Every unconscious thought is active whether we are aware of it or not.

Q: So, if I have a habit of having someone who doesn't pay rent, this is a subconscious thought that was put there by parents or someone before.

Lester: No, put there before by you, it's your thought.

Q: All right. It's best to look at it and say, "Where did this habitual thought come from?" By looking at it, I can see where it came from and erase it from my consciousness and erase that particular habit of thought, can't I?

Lester: Yes. Putting it a little better, rather than see where it came from, see that it's been in you. Then you see how silly it is to have this thought working against you, and you automatically drop it.

Q: I wish I would. I just don't automatically drop it.

Lester: No, you do. There isn't just one thought on each subject, there are millions. I don't like to say this, but there are millions that you've acquired over many millions of years.

Q: If I have a habit of having something recur in my life—let us say a delay in getting things done, which is quite common in my business—is this purely my consciousness?

Lester: Yes.

Q: And it's nonsense to say this is the way real estate people operate, isn't it? I've got to look at my consciousness, and if I say this is nonsense because it's my thinking, I can eliminate this type of delay.

Lester: Yes. It's possible.

Q: How does one eliminate recurring conditions in one's life?

Lester: By constantly working to undo it—looking for the subconscious thoughts that are causing it and dropping them.

Q: It's my thoughts. I don't look at anything but my own thinking.

Lester: Yes. Now there's another way, a better way. If you can't pull up the subconscious thoughts, you can now put in a conscious thought with strong will, so strongly that it overrides all the prior unconscious thoughts. This is possible. This is called using willpower. You can will it, and if you will it strongly enough, it'll override all the subconscious thoughts. When you're feeling high, that's when you have your greatest will. Just will it to be the way you want it to be. The mechanism is: You put in a thought with so much power behind it that it's more powerful than all the former subconscious thoughts put together.

Q: A man died last night, and he left $25,000,000! And the man next door had nothing. He died and went to Heaven.

Lester: It's easier to get to Heaven when you don't have $25,000,000 holding you here.

Q: It's easier to go if you don't have $25,000,000?

Lester: That's right. He's attached to that twenty-five. He's trying to hold on to it right now, even though he is dead. And when he tries to pick it up, his astral hands go right through it, and he's in trouble. It holds him back, whereas a man who didn't have anything will just go off into higher, freer realms.

Q: You mean now that he has so-called "died," he can still be attached to his money?

Lester: Oh sure! What he was the moment before he died, he is the moment after, except for the fact that he has let go of the dense body. The physical body is an exact copy of the astral body. And when you step out of the physical body, it feels the same to you, and you try to do the things that you were doing just before in the physical body, if you have attachments to the physical world. If you don't have attachments, you adapt much easier to the freer way of life in the astral body.

Q: I like your explanation of creation.

Lester: For the intellectuals, there are schools that argue this way: Is creation gradual or is it instantaneous?

Q: It's gradual because—

Lester: What makes it gradual? The mind, by saying it's gradual.

Q: True.

Lester: And if you keep thinking on it, you'll discover that creation is instantaneous.

Q: Sure it's instantaneous, but it appears differently.

Lester: And the instantaneity—the instant also has the concept of time in it. That's just something I'm throwing out for you to work on, if you want to.

Q: An instant—you're confining it to a certain amount of time. You are limiting it.

Lester: I'll give you a clue to it. You went to sleep, and you had a dream, and you dreamed that you were born into a little infant body, and you went through one year, two years, three years, into youth, middle age and old age, all the way up to ninety years. And it took ninety years to get up to that old body. It was a long, long time, right? Ninety years? Until you woke up and then realized it was a dream and it might have taken a second or two. The dream lasted a few seconds, and in that time you went through a ninety-year period! And it seemed like ninety years while you were in the dream. It wasn't until you woke up that you realized it was only a few seconds. Someday you'll see that creation is instantaneous, with the mental concept of time in it.

Q: How do you equate our effort in trying to create that which we might desire with the statements, "Seek ye first the kingdom of God and all good things will be added unto you," and, "Think not of what you shall eat and where you shall sleep"?

Lester: Well, it fits in. "Seek ye first the kingdom of God:" God is the essence of our very beingness. If we see that and discover it, we find the secret of everything. So, seek ye first the kingdom of God: go within, discover who and what you are, then you have the secret to everything, not only to creating, but to everything.

But, you see, that's been part of several years of what we have been going through as a group: how to go within and discover this infinite Being that we are, which is the God part of us. And when this infinite Being is discovered, everything is known—how to create and, more than that, how to uncreate. And still more important, how to get beyond creating and uncreating, which is the ultimate state. Then you will not think of what you shall eat and where you shall sleep. Did I connect it for you?

Q: Until you reach the higher state, I wonder if it isn't possible to get caught up in still trying to create before you become aware of the higher state?

Lester: Yes, I say that you are caught up in trying to create. You now have no choice whether to be a creator, you are that all the time. You should now consciously create only the things you want and stop creating the things you don't want. One of the grossest errors we make is to try to create in the future: I will have this, I will get that. When we do that, it keeps it in the future all the time, thereby keeping it away. This is the greatest stumbling block for most people. When you create something, it has to be seen in present time, in its isness, now. It is mine now!

Q: Well, even if I can't believe that I may be going to have something, at least I can believe that the thought is mine. So, if I build on, "The thought is mine," this gives me more foundation.

Lester: Yes. Discover who the thinker is.

Q: What happens when you reach the desireless state?

Lester: Well, what is desire? Desire comes from thinking we are not the All. When you reach the desireless state, you see yourself as the All, as the sum total, and there's no more need, there's no more lack. Everything is you. It's not yours, you are it!

Q: So, it's really a state of seek ye first the kingdom of God and all this shall be added unto you.

Lester: Everything, every last atom in the universe. Please note that most of your questions have been on havingness, the havingness of things. This indicates what you think happiness is. However, you will discover that should you obtain all the things you desire, you would still find yourself unhappy. You must go beyond the havingness state and reach the Beingness realm where you only are. There you know that you lack nothing and that you are the infinite All. There lies the ultimate joy, which is a deep and a most profound peace, the ultimate satiation.

114

Releasing Explorations by Hale Dwoskin

Be honest with yourself and check to see if you would like to create more of what you want in your life or if you are ready to move beyond creation. If you want to create more in your life, allow yourself to do it by letting go of the thoughts and feelings of lack and limitation. If you are ready to move beyond creation, then allow yourself to let go of wanting to change what is and allow yourself to feel grateful for and accepting of that which already is right here and now. Then allow your attention to dwell on the changeless background that allows all creation to be.

These two directions are not mutually exclusive. Allow yourself to pursue your worthwhile desires, knowing that you are the creator and at the same time allow yourself to rest more and more as that which is beyond creation. If you let go in order to get what you want, you will automatically be uncovering your true nature.

Anything that you want to change or improve in life, which you cannot let go of wanting to change or improve and allow to be as it is, can be set up as a goal. Write down your list of goals. Then take one at a time and allow yourself to write it at the top of a page. Make sure to phrase it in the now and put in only what you want, not what you are trying to get rid of. Then read the goal silently. Write down the first thought or feeling that comes to mind that is the opposite of accepting this goal as having already been accomplished. Then ask yourself, "Could I welcome that?" "Could I let this go? "Would I?" "When?"

Continue working on each goal until every time you look at the goal only feelings of "I can and do have it" only feelings of courageousness, acceptance, and peace come to mind. In this way you will start to demonstrate more and more of what you want in your life, while at the same time you will be letting go of the attachments and aversions that keep you lost in limitation. We go into a much more in-depth exploration of the goal creation process in the Sedona Method book and in our seminars and programs.

You can also move beyond creation by using the following questions regarding any of your goals: "Could I let go of wanting to create [your goal] and to rest as that which is beyond creation?" "Would I?" "When?" Letting go of wanting to be the creator in this way will not stand in the way of the goal coming into fruition, but it will help you to dissolve the pain that comes from delaying your happiness until it is achieved.

Make a list of that which has already been created in your life, both what you would label as positive and negative, and allow yourself to accept, as best you can, that everything on this list is a creation of mind. You can ask yourself, "Could I allow myself to accept this as a creation of mind?" "Would I?" "When?" The more you can accept that, the more you can direct the creation process, and the more you will be undisturbed by whatever is or is not created.

The Mind

Lester Levenson

This session is composed of aphorisms collected from various talks by Lester. Please allow yourself to ponder each one individually before going on to the next in order to get the maximum benefit.

The mind is an instrument created by you to image the Oneness as chopped up and separated into many parts, interrelated.

The mind is simply the sum total composite of all thoughts.

The mind becomes habitual.

The subconscious mind is merely the thoughts that we are not looking at now.

The subconscious mind is running us, making us the victims of habit.

The thing that keeps us from recognizing and expressing our infinity is simply the mind, conscious and subconscious. If we are to express this infinite nature, we can do it only by getting behind this mind. When we reach the realm behind the mind, we operate without thoughts—intuitively—and are in harmony with the whole universe.

The direction is to still the mind. Quiet the mind and you'll see your infinity right there.

Just let go of the mind completely, and what's left over is your infinite Beingness, all-knowing, all-powerful, and everywhere present.

Were we to direct all our energies to stilling our mind, we would soon be realized.

The mind quiets spontaneously in the company of a great soul.

The more you quiet the mind, the more you feel the Self, and the better you feel. You feel as good as your mind is quiet.

Then the mind vanishes, and there the Self is. Where the Self is, there is no mind.

The mind is reflected consciousness, reflected from its source—the Self—just as the light from the moon is reflected from the sun. While the moonlight may be used to reveal objects, it is no more needed when the sun rises. Although the moon may remain in the sky while the sun shines, it is dim and useless. Likewise, the mind is useless when we let the Self shine.

Your mind is an instrument used to identify your real Self with your body and world.

If you do not identify with your body or mind, neither your body nor your thoughts will affect you. So it is when you sleep. While not identifying with your body or mind, you have no problems, no suffering.

In meditation, one subdues the mind and feels the wonderful peace of the Self. This is the start. The finish is the total dissolution of the mind. This is accomplished by *recognizing* the mind as not being apart from the Self, by seeing it as a phantom product of the Self.

In this dream-illusion, there's a thing called thought. And thought determines, and is the cause of, all matter.

In your imagination, you have written and projected a cinema show of acts, actors, and audiences on a screen who have lost sight of the fact that it is all in your imagination, all in your mind. Discover this and you discover the absolute Truth.

The world and universe are a mental concoction. Mind subsidence is realization. There are two ways to obtain it. On recognizing what the mind really is, it is seen as an illusion and therefore subsides. By concentrating on your Self and discovering it is you, mind also subsides. Complete subsidence is full realization.

The reason why thoughts wander back into the world is because we believe the world is real. But for this belief, realization would be!

Mind distraction is wanting more the things of the world than the Self. In wanting more to hold your Self, the world is not looked at!

A thought is an assumption of lack causing a wish to fulfill it.

All thoughts are of non-truth. It's so simple: you just stop the thoughts, and the infinity that you are is self-obvious.

You've got to use the mind to quiet the mind, and you need to use determination to still it.

When you begin concentrating on the mind, you begin rising above the mind.

Once you see what the mind is, you won't be subject to it anymore. Strength of mind is the ability to concentrate, without distraction, on a single thought.

Without a concentrated mind, progress is relatively small.

A wandering, wagering mind is one that dissipates one's energy in the form of many thoughts. Hold one thought, and the energy is less dissipated and more conserved. Direct this conserved energy toward the Self, and your Self will be revealed. The more you do this, the stronger becomes your direction, and the easier it becomes to abide in your Self.

In the beginning, the mind pursues the Self intermittently between long intervals. As one continues, the intervals shorten. Toward the end, the mind is constant in this pursuit and does not wander from it.

The power of the mind is almost infinite. When there is only one thought, all that power is right there.

Restless thoughts keep the Great Ones away. A quiet mind keeps the door open to them.

The more you eliminate mind, the more peace you feel.

The mind will never discover the Self because the mind is the cover-up of the Self. It's only by letting go of the mind that the Self is seen. You get the mind quiet enough to allow your Self to be obvious to you so that you may use it to let go of the mind.

Eliminating what you are not is growth.

The biggest difficulty is the subconscious mind. We have relegated things to the subconscious, stored them there, and thrown away the key.

If we could make our subconscious fully conscious, we would be fully realized.

Every mind uses the very same unlimited intelligence. Everyone uses it as much as he believes he can use it to fulfill his desires. When he learns that his mental limitations are self-imposed, he lets go of them. Then his intelligence, his IQ, can be raised to the degree that he knows he has no limits.

We are all in the same mind, and the only thing that keeps us from reading the other one is that our attention is too centered on our own little self.

Everyone *unconsciously* reads everyone else *and* thinks that it is his own thoughts.

All minds are influencing each other.

A high-level mind tunes in with other minds of high level. A low-level mind tunes in with other minds of low level.

Mind is catchy. It's immediately infectious, because thought is a mechanism of limitation.

The only intelligence the mind has is what you give to it.

Thoughts smother the capacity to be happy.

Every thought causes a demonstration.

There's no limit to the number of new ideas that man can have.

Anything man can think can be.

You use your mind to still your mind. When you are meditating, holding one thought, other thoughts drop away.

Since mind is always seeking external knowledge, direct it internally.

Introvert the mind and realize to full realization.

The ego-mind struggles for survival and tries to subvert your direction.

The mind cannot give the ultimate answer because it's part of the ego, part of our limitation.

Real knowledge lies just behind thought—which is relative knowledge—and relative knowledge is ignorance.

When the Self, which is just behind the mind, is discovered, you see that the mind is limited and you can let go of it.

There is a mind that runs this planet. There is a mind that runs the solar system and a mind that runs the universe. All these minds are in the illusion.

Where is the world without your mind? Is there such a thing as world when you submerge the mind? The thought of the world creates it. This whole solid universe that you mentally say is a solid universe is just your thought that it is a solid universe.

Anything your mind is absolutely convinced of materializes instantly.

Mind can do anything with the body.

The utmost that the intellect and reasoning can do for us is first recognize its limitations and, secondly, do that which helps the quest for the Self.

Every thought is an affliction. When the thought waves are completely stilled, there are no more afflictions.

Every thought is motivated by a desire for pleasure or an aversion to pain.

Letting go of all attachments and aversions is letting go of all your thoughts.

Thought and desire are the same.

The only thing we are aware of is our own thoughts.

What we're seeing out there is our own mind.

That which you really want you never forget—it's always on your mind. Really want to discover your Self.

The mind is the brain of the astral and causal bodies.

The mind can be made quiet wherever you are. The place to do it is right where you are.

Don't mind the mind, and the mind won't need minding!

The mind is not made noisier, it's just that you get quiet enough to notice how noisy it is.

Everything falls perfectly into line effortlessly and harmoniously without thoughts.

As mind gets quiet, first the sense of havingness decreases until a measure of security is felt. It becomes less necessary to have in order to be. Then the sense of doership decreases until a further security is felt—a security in that one is not the real doer, that the real doer is a higher power, and that one can actually be with much less doing. Then it becomes less necessary to do *in order to be*. Finally, your real Self (that has always been in the background) steps in and takes over, and you feel that there is nothing necessary anymore that you must have or do, that there is no choice but to be!

Use omniscience, don't use the mind! The goal is to eliminate the mind.

If there are no thoughts, then there is no mind. Mind is only thoughts.

If you take away your mind, what's left over is omniscience. You are that omniscient Being that you are seeking, clouded over by mind.

Mind detached from the world and centered only on Self is liberation.

Depth in meditation is the degree of quietude of mind.

Unless we're eliminating mind, unless we're eliminating ego, we're not progressing.

The more we keep looking into the mind, the quieter we become.

Where the mind is all quiet, there is all knowledge.

A quiet mind is full realization.

The first thought of all thoughts is "I am an individual, separate." In order for there to be a he, she, or it, first there has to be an I. So, we create I, and then there are others. Without the first thought of I, there can't be any other thoughts of anyone else. That's the first basic error: I am a separate individual. If I am separate, then there have to be others, and you start dividing up the one by first becoming an individual that is separate from it. Thought first divides and separates you from the one Beingness and then creates a multitude of beings and things and all their relationships. It's all your thought—that's all it is. Let go of thought, and what's left over is you, infinite, eternal, glorious, all joyous, serene!

Methods of Mind Revelation

1. See the source of the mind, and you will find your Self.
2. Turn the mind back upon the mind, and it will reveal its secrets.
   a. Concentrate the mind on one thought and all other thoughts will drop away. Then, drop this one thought.
3. Learn to control the breath, and you will automatically control the mind.
4. Eliminate the ego. The ego thinks and causes all thought. The ego is the identifier of the Self as the body.
5. Surrender the mind to God.
6. Eliminate all objectivity and the mind resolves. Then, there is only subjectivity.
7. The mind must be eliminated permanently by realizing that it is not real but only an apparency, an illusion that has its source in your Self.
8. Where there is only subject and no object, there the Self is.

Releasing Explorations by Hale Dwoskin

Try finding your mind right now. If you look honestly, without going into memory, I propose that you will not be able to find it. We remember a series of recurring thoughts that we identify as our own and we call that our mind. However, if you look right now, there is no mind, and if there is no mind now, what if there has never been a mind that you could call your own? All the previously mentioned exercises in this session will lead you in the direction of discovering the unreality of the mind. You can also explore the following.

Whose thoughts are these anyway? If you allow yourself to observe the thoughts that arise in consciousness, you will find that you claim them as your own. Experiment throughout the day with switching back and forth between seeing, hearing, and feeling that the thoughts that you become aware of are your thoughts and then perceiving them as belonging to no one, or, if you would like, as belonging to God. For instance, you may think, "This is a weird exercise," and, without trying to change the thought itself, allow yourself to perceive it as your thought and then as no one's thought. Allow yourself to switch back and forth inside between these two perspectives until you feel your identification with the thought dissolve.

If you do this throughout the day, without forcing it, it will help you to dissolve the identification with the thoughts that arise in consciousness. This will free your mind to get progressively quieter, and it will help you to gain enough distance from what you call "your mind" to see that which is always just behind the mind—the Self. After all, what if freedom or the Self is always closer than your next thought?

You can also simply allow yourself to pay attention to the silence that is here, before, during, and after every thought. As you do that, the thoughts fade into the background and you are at rest as the silent Awareness without which there can be no thinking.

Meditation with Quest

Lester Levenson

The prime purpose of meditation is to quiet the mind. When we hold one thought with interest, as we hold it, other thoughts keep dropping away. Thoughts of the day, what he did to me, what she did, what I should have done, etc., all these thoughts are active on a subconscious level. As we hold to one thought, these subconscious thoughts quiet; they become still. They drop into the background and that quiets the mind.

Now, the most important thing in quieting the mind is interest. When you are very interested in something, you'll override all other thoughts. Likewise, if, with intense interest, you want to know, "What am I? What is this world? What is my relationship to it?" If there's a real burning desire to get the answer, then all other thoughts drop away, and the mind becomes extremely concentrated. Then the answer shows itself. It comes from within. The answer is there all the time. The quieting of the thoughts allows us to see it, to see the answer that was there all the time, in the realm of knowingness, in the Self.

The starting point should be a strong desire for the answer. When that desire is strong, we get the answer. That's why man's extremity is God's opportunity. Extreme adversity causes in us a desire to get out of it with such intensity that we concentrate our mind and discover the answer.

When I started my quest, I thought "thinking" would give me the answers. I had a mind that was as active as any mind could be. But I was at the end of the line. I had had a second heart attack, and they told me I was finished, that I had only a short time to live, and so I *had* to have the answers. And even though my mind was far more active than the great majority of minds, the intensity of the desire for the answers caused me to hold to one question at a time, obliterating all else.

This concentration did it! I started seeking with no knowledge of metaphysics, no knowledge of the way. In fact, I was anti-religion and anti-metaphysics. I thought they were nonsense, for the weak minded, for people who believed in fairy tales. But it was only because of the intensity of my desire to get the answers—I *had* to have the answers—that they began to come.

And they came relatively quickly. Over a period of three months' time, I went from an extreme materialist to the opposite extreme where the material is nothingness and the spiritual is the All. The wish to get the answer was so strong that, in spite of my mind being one of the noisiest of minds, the answers began to come. I automatically fell into things (I knew no words for them) like *samadhi*. I would concentrate on a question with such intensity that I would lose awareness of the world, lose awareness of this body, and then I would be aware of just a pure thought. The thought itself would be the only thing existing in this universe.

That's absorption, when the thinker and the thought become one. One loses consciousness of everything but that one thought. That's a very concentrated state of mind, and the answer is always discovered right there. I started with, "What is happiness? What is life? What do I want? How do I get happiness?" and I discovered that happiness depended upon my capacity to love.

At first I thought it was in being loved. I reviewed my life and saw that I was very much loved by my family and friends, and yet I was not happy. I saw that that was not it. Continuing, I realized that it was my capacity to love that gave me happiness. The next question was, "What is intelligence?" I held to it and held to it until, "Ah!" I saw it! There's only one intelligence in the universe, and we all have a direct line to it.

Then I worked on responsibility and discovered that I was responsible for everything that happens or has happened to me. Creation was something I created! Finally, I held the question, "What am I?"

until the answer presented itself. And in a matter of three months' time, I believe I saw the entire picture, believe I went all the way, but *only because of the concentrated approach*. I knew nothing about the subject; I knew nothing about the direction, the way, the path. But I wanted to know.

"What am I? What is this world? What's my relationship to it?" You discover that the whole world is nothing but you, that there never was anything but you all along, because there's only One and you are It!

But that isn't the final state. You come out of it, and there's still a certain amount of mind left. So, you go back into the meditative quest until there is no more mind controlling you. When you've eliminated all the habits of thought, all the tendencies of mind, you are free. You can then use your mind, and you are the master and director of it. It no longer determines you, you determine it. At present, we are over ninety percent of the time controlled by the unconscious mind.

Q: That's the conscious and unconscious mind both?

Lester: Well, the conscious mind is easily controlled. The subconscious is not, because it is not easily seen. It's a mechanism we set up of not looking at our thoughts, of making them operate automatically. We did it to our entire body—it's all automatic now—and then we did it to all thoughts except the thought we're interested in at the moment.

Q: Why is it that we did it to all thoughts except the one we're interested in at the moment?

Lester: Because we don't want the thoughts in the first place, so we push them away to the background. We are happiest when there are no thoughts. Sometimes, when you work with your hands, you're very happy, right? Why? The thoughts are quiet.

Q: Then your mind is quieted at that time? Or is it operating on the subconscious level?

Lester: Well, consciously, and even subconsciously, it's quieter. We really don't want thoughts. Thoughts are the things that make us unhappy. Even the happy thoughts make us unhappy, because while we are enjoying something, we're concerned about the possibility of maintaining this pleasure that we know is not going to last. The *thought* of the pleasure at the same time evokes the thought that it's not going to last. Even thoughts of happiness are limited. The really happy state is the no-thought state; it's the state of knowingness and is beyond thought.

We started with the subject of meditation. Meditation does seem to be a question in many peoples' minds who have meditated for years and years. The best type of meditation is with question. When you just drop into a nice quiet state without question, you get a good feeling but no progress of getting the knowledge.

Q: There isn't any progress when you're just quiet?

Lester: There is in that you're moving toward the quiet state, and the quiet state is a better state than the noisy state. In that sense, it's a step forward. But the only problem we have now is called ignorance.

We're ignorant to the fact that we are infinite. To get rid of ignorance, we need the knowledge of our infinity. To get the knowledge, we have to inquire. So, when we go into meditation and just get peacefully quiet, that's good, but don't stop there—get the answers. It's necessary to get quiet to get the answers. Only the answer to "What am I?" gets us to the top. That is easy to see, isn't it? So, if we want to take the quickest way, we start with the question that we finally have to answer: "What am I?"

I want to relate this to meditation. For more rapid growth, meditation should be with question. Here's where the Jnanis get the advantage over the Bhaktas. Surrender and devotion throw us into nice feelings, and they're good, but a Jnani goes further. He says, "All right, don't stop there, get the answer." It's only when we fully know who and what we are that we're at the end of the road. So, the fastest and best way to meditate is to pose a question, get quiet, and stay quiet until the answer shows itself. Then, go to the next one until all the answers are there.

Q: If we find we aren't making much progress, could we pose the question, "What's holding me up?"

Lester: Sure. You should. It's a good one.

Q: You know I think you had it easier, because you didn't have a lot of preconceived ideas.

Lester: You're right. I was very lucky that I knew nothing, because intellectual knowledge about the subject is an obstacle. The ego substitutes the intellectual knowledge for the real experiencing of it. I was very, very fortunate not to have had any knowledge of it.

Q: You also didn't realize that it's as difficult as most people think it is.

Lester: Yes. However, knowing what you're telling me helps one let go of that obstacle of intellectual knowledge. I prod you in this direction, don't I? I say, "Don't believe anything. Start from scratch. Build up your knowledge on the solid foundation of proof, step by step." Everyone must do this.

Q: You can't take someone else's experience?

Lester: Right, you would be working on hearsay, on what they have said, and the only useful thing is that which you experience. I relate it to driving a car. If I say I know how to drive a car after reading a book that directs you to turn the key on, start the motor, shift into drive, and step on the gas, do I know how to drive a car? No, not until I experience it can I drive a car. It's the same thing on the path; we must experience everything.

We must, of course, adopt the attitude that what the Great Ones say is so, that they have experienced it. However, you must check it out and prove it for yourself. And the basic Truth is that there's only one reality, there's only one absolute Truth, and that is that this whole world or universe is nothing but God—but, better than that, is nothing but my very own Self. God could be far away. He could be miles and miles away in cosmic space, but my very own Self is right here, is something I know about, is something I can perceive—it is my very own Self! So, using Self as God is far more practical than putting him out there, putting him apart from us. But each one must start from the bottom and prove this whole thing for himself. As the proofs come, the more they come, the more we accept until we experience the whole thing. You still want to hear more on meditation?

Group: Yes.

Lester: *Every* aid should be a means of quieting the mind. If meditation is difficult, we can prepare the way by chanting. Chanting puts our minds on the meaning of the chant itself, and the thoughts of the day drop away, and that quiets the mind. Exercising the body, doing certain *Asanas*, etc., do the same thing. Anything that helps is good, whatever it is. The basic thing is to quiet the mind.

Being loving and good makes the mind quieter. *The mind is the only thing that keeps us from seeing our Infinity.* The mind is nothing but a collection of thoughts of limitation, and, in meditation, we try to quiet that mind so we can see this infinite Being that we are. Meditation should never be passive. We should never try to force the mind to go blank. Meditation should always be with question for the best results. The more we practice meditation, the easier it is to do.

To get the real deep insights requires momentum. When meditation gets to be more enjoyable than things of the world, then we go at it with enthusiasm and desire for it. And then we just can't wait until we get back to it. When we get that momentum going, the mind gets quieter and quieter until this infinite Self is self-obvious and just glares at us, and we laugh. Now maybe with all this talk on meditation, we ought to try it, okay?

Q: Just one question: does concentrating on your hands help to get your mind quiet? It seems to me.

Lester: If it helps, it's good.

Q: It's not harmful, then?

Lester: Oh no. There are several centers one may concentrate on. A good place is up here, between the eyebrows. Concentrating here takes your mind off other parts of the body. It is the center for the third eye, the astral eye, the spiritual eye. It pulls us away from the lower centers of the body when we come up here. Some prefer the heart center. But anything that helps, helps!

Q: I used to concentrate between the eyes, but now when I do inquiry, I let the "I" sink down to the heart.

Lester: The heart is a good place, because it is the center of feeling, and feeling is closer to the Self than thought. It depends on your background. If you're a Vichara Jnani, it'll be the heart, but not on the left side, on the right side. If you're a Raja yogi, it'll be between the eyes. When I did my concentrating, it wasn't on any location, it was on wanting to have the answer. Concentrate on seeking the answer.

Q: I haven't thought in terms of answers, I just thought in terms of getting there, that's all.

Lester: You see, anything in life that you wanted with intensity you always got. This goes for everyone. It's the same with the path, but it's the unconscious conviction that our joys lie in the world that keeps us away from getting the answer.

Q: It sounds so easy the way you say it.

Lester: The thing that determines the ease is *the intensity of your desire for the answer.* That's the crux of the whole thing.

133

Releasing Explorations by Hale Dwoskin

Most of us are obsessed with trying to find our location and define or confine who we are based on our bodies and minds. We ignore the true source of the answer and instead we look in the wrong place, in the reflection called the world. Are you the reflection that you see in the mirror or is that merely a reverse image of the body? The world is a reverse image of who we appear to be, yet we act as though it is the only reality. We pretend that we are the victims of this external force called the world. To break free from this dilemma all we need to do is to rediscover our true nature. Then the world and all its comings and goings loses its grip on us and we discover our freedom, our natural stateless state.

Lester's explanation of self-inquiry is complete. The following suggestions are designed to help you get the most out of his comments. Remember self-inquiry can be an all-day everyday activity.

As best you can, make self-inquiry a constant part of your moment-by-moment experience, as opposed to a process that you need to take time out to do. Every time you become aware of the personal self—the sense of "I," "me," or "mine" and its stories, feelings, and desires—it is an opportunity to practice self-inquiry and/or releasing.

Use self-inquiry as an aid in your letting go, not a substitute for it. In fact, you may notice that each time you ask yourself the self-inquiry questions, you experience a spontaneous release happening. Be open to this and allow yourself to relax into the opening that is created by this release.

Ask the questions below with your heart not your head. There are no right answers. If your mind answers the question in words or images, use those for further self-inquiry as well as grist for the releasing mill. Be open to whatever comes up in the process and allow yourself to keep going deeper.

Remember, you are freedom right now and there is nothing that you need to do about that. Just be still and know that you are.

Any one of the following questions, if answered fully, can take you all the way Home—that Home that you have never left. Use them to further your exploration of self-inquiry.

What am I?

Who am I?

If I'm not that, what am I?

If nothing I experience is real, what is real?

If I am the Formless Nothing upon which everything appears to exist, what am I?

If I am everything and nothing and all that appears is merely imagined, what am I?

If this is all a dream that never really was, what am I?

If this is merely imagined, what am I?

From what do I arise? In what am I contained? To what do I subside?

If I'm not that, which can be imagined or understood, what am I?

If there is no body, no mind, no doer, and no one to go free, what am I?

If there is no dream and no dreamer, who is there to awaken?

If this is merely imagined, on what does it appear?

If there is nothing to want and no one to want it, what am I?

If there is nothing to release and no one to release it, what am I?

If there is nowhere to go, nothing to do, and no one to do it, what am I?

What is that, that needs no effort to be?

What is that, that needs no eyes to see, no ears to hear, and no body to be?

What is that, that has no name, no form, and no action?

What is that, that is always effortlessly present?

Desire

Lester Levenson

This session is composed of aphorisms collected from various talks by Lester. Please allow yourself to ponder each one individually before going on to the next in order to get the maximum benefit.

A desire is a disturbance of one's natural, inherent peace and joy. Desires keep one involved in trying to satiate the desires, consequently detracting one from his constant, natural, inherent happiness. In short, desire is the enemy of happiness and the source of misery.

The more desire is let go of, the less disturbed the mind becomes, allowing it to become concentrated. The more concentrated the mind, the more capable one becomes of discerning or realizing his Self.

Silence silences the noisy demands of ego desires and allows your Self to be seen.

Solitude is the absence of desire.

The absence of desire is serenity.

Every time one tries to satisfy a desire, he creates a greater intensity of that desire. This comes about because the momentary pleasure, which is inhering more in the Self due to momentary stilling of thoughts, is attributed to the object of the desire. Therefore, one wants the object more and more, vainly attempting to satiate the desire, which is satiable only in being constantly quiet from thoughts, i.e., constantly inhering in the Self.

The simultaneous fulfillment of all desires is in the finding of your real Self.

Desire is a bottomless pit that can never be filled up.

Desire constitutes the world, and desirelessness constitutes the Self, God.

Desire is seeking the joy of being our Self through objects and people. The mind originally creates the thought of need, or lack, which agitates the mind and covers the Self. When the object is attained, the mind stills, the joy of your Self shines forth and this joy is attributed to the object. Then the mind goes on seeking the object as the source of the joy. But the joy being not obtainable from the object, the mind seeks it more and more from the object and is never satisfied.

Desire is the mother of all motion, the disturber of all peace.

The basic mechanism of desire is first, that we create a lack and then desire whatever is necessary to fill that lack. The desire creates thoughts. The thoughts cover the Self, and this makes us unhappy. Then we look to relieve that unhappiness by fulfilling the desire, which momentarily stills the thoughts. The stilling of thoughts removes a bit of the cover of the Self, and it's the feeling of a bit more of the Self that we call pleasure. We wrongly attribute that joy or pleasure to the thing or person that was used to fulfill the desire to relieve the agony of the thoughts of desire that were covering the Self. Because of this wrong attributing of the joy to the person or thing, the desire will never be satiated, because the joy is not in the person or thing. The only possibility of satiety is to remain in your Self.

Fulfilling desire is momentarily letting go of the agony of the feelings of being limited by lack. This understanding should help you let go of the frustrating drive of seeking happiness where it isn't, which is in the world!

Desire is mind disquieted.

Recognizing who and what you are instantly satisfies all desires.

We should desire only God.

Desire leads only to misery and death.

Any desire upsets and disturbs the natural, inherent tranquility and peace.

If one will stop thinking of something, his desire for it will disappear.

After you discover that desires are undesirable, you discover that there's a joy and peace that's ever-constant and more profound than any joy you have experienced before.

Desire is the start of all agitation.

A desire is an artificially created lack.

Ignorance creates the universe, desire sustains it, and enlightenment dissolves it!

If there were no desire, there would be no world or universe of limitation.

Desire is the source of all trouble.

If desire overwhelms us, it is because we want it to. Who turns on the desire? If it's in your power to turn it on, it's in your power to turn it off. The more it is turned off, the weaker it becomes.

Desire only growth. Everyone makes the goal eventually, but the intensity of the desire determines when and how soon. If your desire is strong, you think only of that. The doubts then drop away.

Don't suppress desire, actually let go of it. If you create the desire in you, you can uncreate it.

The worst thing to do is to suppress a desire, any desire. When it is suppressed, from that moment on it will try to express itself. Recognizing it does not mean we must try to satisfy it, but it does prevent suppressing it.

Nervousness is caused by wanting two opposing things at the same time, one consciously and the other subconsciously. The battle is resolved when you make the subconscious desire conscious. On the other hand, if you will know what you are, there will be no conflicts. You can do that through seeking. It's not necessary to understand the negative. It's far better to be the positive. Be your Self.

Seeking any ego fulfillment is seeking the letting go of the agony of the concept of lack. Any lack is necessarily an ego concept.

In order to be infinite Beings, we must have no desires, because any desire is a limiting action upon ourselves. If we think we need something, we think of ourselves as being limited. If you have every-thing, if you are everything, how could you want something? You know you don't need anything, and you go through life knowing all the time that you need nothing. Your attitude is different. With this attitude, should there be a need of the body, it's immediately fulfilled. You don't have to think about it; it's taken care of immediately.

The only thing that creates thought is desire. As long as there is one single desire, there will be disturbance and lack of complete contentedness.

Any desire satisfied disappears forever.

There's an easy way to realization: just get rid of all desires.

One way to overcome desire is to have a very strong desire for God. And, in the end, you have to get rid of your desire for God. Then you are It!

Every little ego wish is a clamp-down on your freedom, which is tantamount to saying every desire is a clamp-down on your freedom.

Desire creates thoughts, the desire to have or not to have. Before desire is ego, so ego is the starting point. I'm an individual separate from the All, so I've got to desire to get the All.

The only thing that disturbs peace is desire.

Internal pressure is caused by desire.

When things are approached with pure love, there's no more desire.

Desire plants seeds for the future.

Decrease desire for the world and increase desire for the Self.

You must get rid of all desire. You can enjoy without desire. In fact, if you really want to enjoy things, you can enjoy far more without desire.

Desire is the cause of everything. Any time you have any problem, there's desire behind it.

Any desire except desire for liberation is causing misery.

The odd thing about desire is that the more you try to satisfy it, the stronger it becomes. The more people try to satisfy their desire by having things, the stronger that desire becomes. People have more things today than they have ever had, and they are unhappier than they have ever been.

Desire just cuts off happiness.

You should have only one desire, a desire for complete liberation, complete realization. Any other desire will keep you in trouble. We should try to let go of all desires. We should not try to fulfill desires. Every time we fulfill a desire, we strengthen that desire rather than weaken it. I believe that is obvious to all of us that we never satiate desires. The more we try to satisfy them, the more we want of them. So, it's better not to satisfy desires; by doing so, the mind gets quieter. When the mind is quieter, we have a better chance to see the Truth. When we see the Truth, we scorch the desire, and this is the better way, actually the only really effectual way of getting rid of desire.

When you see the Truth, desires are scorched, because a desire is really trying to be your own real Self through some indirect means, through some thing, through some person. When you see this, you let go of these silly desires, because why struggle through an indirect means to be that which you are? The indirect means *cannot make* you what you are, so it's fruitless and extremely frustrating. Consequently, we have this frustrated world. We're all trying to satisfy desire; it's absolutely impossible to do it, and we go on and on, lifetime in, lifetime out, until we recognize that desires are our enemy.

Desire is an admission of lack. If I am the infinite One, I desire nothing; I am the All. We must get back to that state by behaving as one would in that state. The greatest behavior, the greatest ritual we can perform is living as a fully realized Being would live. Try to attain the state of dispassion—no attachments, no aversions. Try to attain a state of equanimity, a feeling of equal mindedness toward everything, everyone. Try to attain the desirelessness state. Then you will see that you are the All, that you are That!

Releasing Explorations by Hale Dwoskin

Do you live life as the All, or do you live life craving little pieces of the All? How would you behave if you knew and fully trusted that you already are that which you are seeking—you are the All? Probably not the way you are now. Another way to say this is: Would you rather seek or desire freedom, or just be it? It is our choice what we focus on. The more you let go of the agony of lack or desire, the more you discover that you are now and have always been that which you were seeking.

You may also ask, if you are already this freedom, why even desire it? Or isn't the desire for freedom creating a lack of it? Lester and Ramana Maharshi used to explain it in this way: "If you fell into a thorn bush and your body was covered in thorns, it would be helpful to take one of those thorns and use it to pry out all the other thorns. Then you could throw that away as well." The bush is the world, the thorns in this case are your desires, the desire for freedom is the thorn that you use to pry out all the other thorns, and then it naturally drops away.

If you find yourself unable to let go of any particular desire, you can ask yourself, "Would I rather want this [the desire] or have it?" If you would rather have it, then let go of wanting it. If you would rather want it, then notice how you already have what you want and there is no problem. You can ask yourself too, "Would I rather want that, or would I rather be freedom?" If in this moment you would rather be freedom, you will find yourself spontaneously letting go and being the exquisite freedom that you already are. You can also just ask yourself directly, "Could I let go of wanting that?" "Would I?" "When?" What you will discover as you explore this direction is that, except in the case of freedom, our wanting for things actually gets in the way of having them.

What Am I?

Lester Levenson

I thought that a summary of what we have been through, where we are going and what there is at the end might be a good idea for the last talk of this series. The way I like to look at our direction is that the ultimate goal of every Being is total and complete happiness with no taint of sorrow whatsoever. We are all striving for this in our every act, but somehow missing the goal.

The reason why we miss our goal, our target, is simply that we do not have a clear vision of the target, and we therefore are aiming blindly. So long as we remain blinded, we can never attain that goal of perfect happiness. Someone comes along and says, "Attention! You have spent many lifetimes looking in the wrong direction! Stop looking without and look ye within! Only there will ye find that which ye have spent lifetime after lifetime seeking!"

And then you meet someone like Lester who tells you, "Seek ye your very own Self. Therein lies your complete happiness. Stop looking for happiness in people and things. Here you merely eliminate the pain of the desire for something, and the relief you get you call pleasure. And the pleasure is short-lived, because the desire is not eliminated and is still there, and therefore the pain of it continues to gnaw at you."

Now the starting point is you. You must take the way toward discovering you, and only you can do it. Accept nothing unless you can prove it yourself. Prove it and it is yours. Prove it and then you can use it. The uniqueness of this science, and it is a science—someday you'll see it is the science of all sciences—is that this is a subjective science. We have to seek it within. We can't put it out on a table in front of us and examine it. We can only examine it within our own mind or, better, within our own being.

Also, the intellect does not avail it to us. The intellect can get us in the right direction to find it. The right direction is turning within, stilling the mind and experiencing this Truth, this knowledge. And only by experience can we get to know it. The methods are many, but the very highest is the method that everyone uses in the end, and that method is finding the answer to "What am I?" This quest should be kept up all the time, not only in meditation, but also during the day. While we're working, no matter what we're doing, in the back of our mind we can always keep that question posed, "What am I?" until the answer makes itself obvious to us.

Now, any answer the mind can give us must necessarily not be it, because the mind is an instrument of limitation. All thoughts are qualified; all thoughts are limited. So, any answer the mind gives cannot be right. The way the answer comes is simply by our getting out of the way of the blindness that we have imposed upon ourselves by assuming thoughts that we are thinking. When the thoughts are quiet, the limitless Being is obvious. It's Self-effulgent; it is there all the time. It's just covered over by thought-concepts, every one of which is limited.

So, the way is to pose the question, "What am I?" and quietly await the answer. Other thoughts will come in, and the biggest difficulty is quieting these thoughts. When other thoughts come in, if we pose the question, "To whom are these thoughts?" the answer is naturally, "To me"; then, "What am I?" puts us right back on the track again. That way we can continuously keep our attention on "What am I?"

In addition to posing this question until we get the answer, it is good practice in our daily life not to be the doer, not to be the agent. Just be the witness! Acquire the "It is not I but the Father who worketh through me" attitude, which several in this group already have. This is the main conduct of life that we should strive for. The more we become the witness in life, the more we become nonattached to the body, the more we are our real Self. So, there are two things I'm suggesting: one is the quest, "What am I?" and the second, in life itself, is not to be the doer, but be the witness. Let things happen;

allow life to be. That's the way we are in the top state, and the best behavior in life is that which is characteristic of the top state.

There are many other things, which I'm sure you're aware of: humbleness, goodness, kindness, honesty, etc. All these things help, but the greatest aid is not to be the doer, but to be the witness.

Now, when the Self of us presents itself to us, it's a tremendous experience! It's a very difficult one to contain. We feel as though we're going to burst, because we recognize our omnipotence, omniscience, and omnipresence! But just seeing it once doesn't establish us in that state. However, once experienced, you'll never let go until you re-establish it. You'll continue to try, and you should continue to try, to get back into that state.

The next time, it'll last a bit longer, the third time, longer still, until finally we are in it twenty-four hours a day. When we attain this top state, we are not zombies, we are all-knowing and everywhere present. Everything falls perfectly into line. We move in the world just like anyone else moves; the difference is that we see the world entirely differently from the way everyone else sees it. We see our body and every other body equally as our Self. Likewise, every animal and everything is our Self. Seeing everything as "I" gives us that singular Oneness throughout the universe, which is called God, or the Self. We watch our body moving through life like an automaton. We let it go its way, and since we are not really that body, nothing that happens to that body can affect us. Even if it were crushed, it wouldn't mean much to us, because we fully know that we are not *that body*. We know our eternal Beingness and we remain that!

So, one who has attained the top state is difficult to distinguish from anyone else. He'll go through the same motions of life, and whatever he was doing before, he might continue to do. But his outlook on life is entirely different. He is completely egoless; he has no concern for his own body. He is interested in others and not in himself. He is interested in all humanity. Whatever he does has absolutely no ego motivation. His body will continue to live its normal span and usually goes out, in the eyes of the unknowing, the same way most bodies go out, via so-called death and coffin. But the one who was originally connected with that body never sees any of this death. He sees this entire world and body as an illusion that was created mentally just as we create scenes, cities, and worlds in our night dreams. When we awaken, we realize there never was such a thing. And in the same way, when we awaken from this waking state, we see that the whole thing was a dream and never really was. That the only thing that *ever* was, was my Being, the absolute reality, being all Beingness, infinite, all-perfect, all-knowing, all-powerful, omnipresent.

To reiterate, the main two points that I wanted to bring out today were that, first, the very highest method is the quest, "What am I?" As we pose this question in quietness, when other thoughts come in, ask, "To whom are these thoughts?" The answer is, "To me." Then, ask, "Well, what am I? and we're right back on the track again until we get the total answer. Secondly, the way in life is to be the witness not the doer. I believe that sums up what I've been trying to get across up until now. Any questions on this?

Q: To not be the doer, don't you plan? Don't you do everything normally?

Lester: No, the right way is not to plan. Let it happen. Let go and you'll be guided intuitively. Instead of planning with thought, you'll do the exactly right thing, perfectly, at the right moment, from moment to moment.

Q: There is a situation where someone might take a position of that kind when he hasn't really felt it. For example, he will say, "I'll just stay in bed until I'm moved." Meantime, his rent isn't paid.

Lester: So he'll have to move! If we assume that we are there and are not, we are soon awakened to the fact that we are not there, see?

Bob, I'm talking from a higher level now, the perfect state, where everything is in absolute harmony every moment. There, you never think and at every moment you know from within just the right thing to do. You're guided intuitively each and every moment and everything falls perfectly into line. Now, if you're not there, of course, *you have to think*, you have to plan.

Q: Well, in practice then, in the beginning, it's probably a combination of the two where things go very easily, and then there's a hump in which you have to plan.

Lester: Definitely, yes! In the top state, you do by knowing; you just know from moment to moment. One feels, "I know it!" That's just the way it feels, and there's no thinking to it, only "I know it!"

Q: I know, from my own experience, I slip back and lay out a plan, but sometimes that plan comes very easily and quickly to me, and sometimes I have to struggle like the devil to work it out, step-by-step, and I don't know what's going to happen. Other times I just lay out a plan, and I *know* what's going to happen, and I have no difficulty with it.

Lester: The word *know* as you use it is the key. You know how that word feels when you say, "I know it!" There's no doubt, not one iota of doubt there. And it happens. That's the key. That's the realm of knowingness. Make that all the time. Keep working for it until it comes and stays. The quickness with which we attain this is determined by the intensity of the desire for it. The more we desire this top state, the sooner it comes.

Everyone makes it eventually. I'm convinced the majority of people on earth today will probably take millions of years. But any one of us who is consciously seeking the way out can do it this lifetime. The so-called grace of God is always there also. All those who have made the top grade before us are radiating the consciousness of perfection to us. We have tremendous grace being actually pushed our way all the time. However, they have no right to impose themselves, and don't. We have to open ourselves to it in order to receive it. We need this grace.

Because of the state of affairs today, man is relatively low. We are very strongly convinced that we are a limited body, and by long habit we are trying to hold on to it. So, it's not easy to let go of this body, and because of that we need the grace of the Great Ones who, in our eyes, have passed on, but in their eyes they're still here. When we recognize that they are still here, we can see them and talk to them the way we talk to each other. If we accept them partially, we can talk to them in a dream or a vision. The way we meet with them is determined by our acceptance of them.

If any one of us believed that he could go down to a restaurant and have a snack with Jesus—the way you believe you could do it with me—if you had that much acceptance, then you could do it. Now, some of us know that he came into this room. He gave a sign proportionate to our degree of acceptance. If he were suddenly to appear in a physical body in the room, it would be too much for most of us to accept, and therefore he doesn't. But the way he comes to us is determined by our acceptance of him. He gave signs to some here, and some did not recognize that he did. However, most of us did!

The point I'm trying to make now is that we should open ourselves to the help of the great masters. Jesus and the Great Ones want each and every one of us to know our perfection. They can't force it upon us, but their hands are always extended. It's good to keep this in mind—then we open ourselves more to the help.

Q: How do you request and receive this help?

Lester: You have to be accepting of Jesus as being alive, just as much as we are, and capable of meeting with you, the way we meet with you. Then it can happen. You have to be open to it. The help is always being sent to you.

Q: Are there words to say? Thoughts to carry?

Lester: Yes, but I can't give them to you. That's up to you. See, I give you the general principle: acceptance of him the way he is. Don't expect him not to be Christ-like, because he won't be that. However, he can appear as a very humble human being in form. Being omnipresent, at any moment, he can appear to anyone and speak with him.

Q: Lester, he will be as Christ—he won't be in disguise, will he? The beggar at the door?

Lester: No. The only disguise is the one we put on him. He would never disguise himself. He wants to be recognized as Christ. That's not his name. The man named Jesus had the Christ Consciousness—and we have to accept him and his consciousness, which is extreme humility, simplicity. No Hollywood glamour.

Q: Would you define humility?

Lester: Yes. The greatest humility is through surrender: not I but thou. It is not I, but the Father who worketh through me. Everything I do is God's work; I am not the doer. It is surrender of the ego, the ego being a sense of separate individuality.

Q: If you surrender yourself as an individual, how about the other person? I think we mentioned before that we recognize the other person as ourselves, and we treat them as though we are the same. Who is this other person?

Lester: From where you stand now, the other person should not concern you. The only thing that should concern us is what we do. For me, it matters not what your attitude is toward me. You could hate me with every cell in your body. But it's of extreme importance what my attitude is toward you. While you're hating me, I should love you fully and completely. Then you'll understand the answer to your question, and you will see only the One. When you separate and then ask what's up here in the One, it just doesn't fit. When we love, and only love, we are using the most formidable power in the universe. No one and nothing can harm us. We can never ever be hurt or unhappy, if we would only just love without any hate.

You can never be hurt when you love, in the sense that the love is full, complete, divine love. It's just love with no hate, not one bit of hate, in it. It requires turning the other cheek, loving your enemy. That's the kind of love it takes.

Q: Love is understanding?

Lester: When you love fully, you understand the other one fully. Love is understanding. It's identifying with the other one, being the other one. Coming down a step, it's wanting the other one to have what the other one wants, loving the other one, the *way* the other one is.

Q: Then who is our enemy?

Lester: In reality, we have only one enemy and that's ourselves. No one can do anything to us; no one can do anything for us. Someday you'll see this, that we in our consciousness determine everything that happens to us.

Q: Then it is our idea of ourselves that is incorrect?

Lester: Right. And that could be made better! When you say understanding, do you mean understanding in a logical sense, or do you mean acceptance of them without question of the reason why they're doing things, good or bad? Just acceptance of whatever they are in their entirety. It's acceptance in an entirety. But the real understanding requires knowledge of what the universe and the world are. When we see someone doing wrong, we have to know that this is a god-being misguided. He's looking for God in the wrong place. Am I making sense? That's the understanding.

Q: Which in his mind would be happiness, right?

Lester: Yes. He's looking for happiness the way he sees it. Even a Hitler, in his mind, is doing right, and therefore should not be hated, but should be loved, wanting him to be what his real basic nature is. Now, this doesn't mean approving of his program—it doesn't. But whether we approve of his program or not, loving and hating are different things than not approving of his program.

So, we love everyone, see them as misguided Beings, forgive them for they know not what they do. They're like children, misguided. Attain the highest state of loving everyone equally as Christ did!

Releasing Explorations by Hale Dwoskin

Are you the doer? Before you answer this question, allow yourself to observe what you call your actions. I think you will discover that while the act is being accomplished, there is no sense of personal doer; there is only the action. We claim the action as our own only in retrospect. We only appear to be the doer based on memory and assumption. We assume that because we have claimed "our" actions repeatedly, they are actually our own, and we don't examine them in the now. In fact, the greatest accomplishments anyone appears to make is when he or she gets himself or herself out of the way.

In sports, this is called the zone. When an athlete is fully in the zone, time appears to slow down and there is a sense of witnessing what the body is doing and appreciating the perfection of what is being done through it. It is only when the athlete stops to analyze what has happened that his or her ego claims the accomplishment.

Practice being the witness, not the doer. Allow yourself to notice as best you can that the sense of being the doer only arises after the accomplishment. As you review what "you" do throughout the day, you can say to yourself, "This was my accomplishment," and then say to yourself, "This is merely happening." Allow yourself to switch back and forth a few times until you feel your sense of being the personal doer dissolve. You can also occasionally allow yourself to check while you are in action to see if there really is a doer you can find in this moment. If you really look into the moment, not into memory, you will probably discover there is no doer. And if there is no doer in this moment, has there ever been a doer or has it always just been an assumption?

The Key to
Constant Happiness

Lester Levenson

I made the statement that I would give you the key to maintaining constant happiness. I was aware that several individuals were dropping in the level of their happiness and not coming up, which is one of the reasons why I didn't get here sooner.

You see, when you were down and you were frantic, and you thought things were terrible, I couldn't have communicated with you very easily. Also, if I had come and you had received this lift and gotten out of it, you would have said that I did it. This develops a dependency relationship, which isn't good. You can do anything and everything that you want. You can have, be or do whatever you will or desire. And when the disturbance lasts long enough, you get fed up with it and you let go of it anyway. Then *you* do it. It's much, much better when you do it and don't need someone to lean upon.

What the group would like to know is how to maintain this new-found happiness. Why don't we have it all the time? We should! And so I thought I would give you the understanding, or the key to the understanding, that will help you develop happiness that remains.

All right, now this is the key: When you understand, when you really know what happiness is, then you're able to establish it. Then you do it more and more until it's all the time. But the key is knowing what happiness is. When you do know what it is, you look for it where it is rather than where it isn't. Looking for it where it isn't is what causes you to drop.

Is there any question on what I've said so far? The key is knowing what happiness is, so that you can go directly for it. Not recognizing what happiness is makes it difficult to establish it permanently. When you get to see what this happiness really is, then when you become miserable, you'll move in the right direction and establish that happiness.

All right, what is happiness? Most people call it pleasure, but what it actually is is escape from pain! What most people call happiness is their getting away from their pain through socializing and entertainment. It is really an escape. They cannot stand being by themselves with their own thoughts. They have to run to a movie, a nightclub, or visit someone just to get some action going so they are not facing their own thoughts.

When their mind is taken away from their own thoughts, they feel better and then call that pleasure and happiness. All entertainment is actually that! A happy man needs no entertainment and no socializing. He is content. However, when you become free, if you choose, you can enjoy entertainment far more than before, because you are free from the hunger-need for it. The happiness that I'm going to talk about now is not the escape-from-misery kind. It is really the only happiness. It's the joy that results from being your own real Self.

The more we are our real Self, the more we feel joyous. Sense-joy of the world is accomplished not because of the thing or the person out there with whom we associate it. It's accomplished by satisfying and stilling the thoughts of wanting to acquire that person or thing. When we quiet those thoughts, we feel our Self more so and are happier. The quieter the mind is, the more we just are, the more we abide as our real Self and the more joyous we feel!

But this is something you've got to see for yourself, that the quieter you get your mind, the happier you are. It's good to play with this. Experiment with it until you see it. Whatever that joy was, it *always* resulted in quieting of the mind, and then you felt happy. Seeing this, you will begin to let go of attaching happiness to people and things. You will begin to see that the joy is only in you abiding as your very own Self. Then, when you discover this, you're not going to look for joy where it isn't. You will immediately let go and just be.

And finally, you reach the place where you need no one and nothing to be happy—you just are happy, all the time!

Is there any question on that? I guess intellectually it's seen by everyone? Whether you see it through your own mind's eye or not, you should have it intellectually first. Then experiment with it—test it out—and you'll discover that this is so, that every time you feel happy, your mind is quiet and at ease, and that what you attributed to the person or thing outside of you is something going on within you. It is a quieting of your mind so that you abide more as your Self. Then, when you see this, you won't bog down anymore, because the moment you become unhappy, you'll know just where to look to reestablish the happiness!

Q: That would be within yourself, wouldn't it?

Lester: Yes, but it's first recognizing that the happiness is not the external person or the thing, but the quieting of the thoughts of desire for the person or thing which allows you to go within and just be your Self, i.e., just be. When your mind is on things out there, you're not just being, you're being involved with externals.

But, I say the key is seeing just that point, that your happiness is the quieting of your mind through the satisfying of the desire, which stills the hunger thoughts for the thing and allows you to just be. When you actually see that in your own mind, you can do it directly. You can let go of those thoughts without achieving the person or the thing, and immediately you're happy!

The prime overall thing is that you move toward happiness in the direction of where it really is, in you and not in the externals. In that way you establish a state of happiness that is continuous. Did I tell you anything new? I've told you this before many times, but it seems new to you!

Q: You told it to us, but before it was not received.

Lester: All right, before it was just an intellectual thing or it did not connect, and so it's as though it were new now. But, as far as that goes, I always feel as though I'm saying the same thing over and over again, from this side, from that side, from another side, but it's always the same thing. However, until you see it in your own mind's eye, until you recognize it, until you realize it, it isn't meaningful to you.

Q: It sounds as though you're saying we should not desire automobiles, we should not desire homes, we should not desire wives or sweethearts, we should not desire anything but become nothing.

Lester: Everything was right but the last part of your sentence. You become everything instead of nothing. Become everything and you need nothing. Desire is lack and the consciousness of separation, the source of all trouble. If you are everything, the All, you need nothing. See, everything was right down to that last part of your sentence—just reverse that and you've got it. Okay?

Q: If we become everything, then we become the wife, then we become the world, we become everything. Instead of separating ourselves, we become the other one.

Lester: And that is the greatest of all feelings! That's the highest love, when you become the other one. That identity is love in its highest form. In other words, you think that she didn't break the dish, but we broke the dish; she didn't spend money on a dress, we spent the money. This is the highest love.

Q: I become the automobile, therefore I don't desire the automobile. Or, you become everything, you become—

Lester: Now, you're going to have to work this out for yourself. You are going to have to realize that when you become everything and feel that you need nothing, then the slightest thought for something will bring it to you immediately.

Q: The desire is, "I haven't got."

Lester: Yes! You create an artificial lack, you create a lie when you say, "I haven't got." Desire, causing you to feel "I have not," *will cause you to have not!* Let go of desire and you feel, "I have." This causes things to come to you.

Q: If I look at the world as though I'm writing a novel and say I am the characters, I'm all these creatures that I create in my story. And yet this is what I'm living today. I create my difficulties; I'm writing this story. Instead of doing that, I should say I am the power, and why bother creating limitations? I don't need to. So, I stop it. But what do I have when I don't create?

Lester: What do you have when you don't create? Everything that you really want—your pure Beingness.

Q: I have peace.

Lester: Yes. You are the All. Everything is in you. Feeling that way puts you completely at peace.

Q: Until the phone rings; then I'm right back in my habits.

Lester: Don't allow a little bell to push you around that way. Again, I say each one has to realize this for himself or herself, but when he or she does, then happiness can be made permanent, because then you look for happiness where it is, and you stop looking for it where it isn't. There's no happiness in people or things. Happiness is our basic nature. Happiness is our very own Beingness. And when we are *only* Being, we are infinitely happy. Yes, when we are only Being and nothing else, we are infinitely happy!

Q: In other words, when you have these various things—like you have an automobile—you utilize that automobile, but you have no attachment to it in order to attain the feeling of joy. Because if you become attached to that automobile, then that attachment has some sort of hold on you wherein you have a responsibility to it.

Lester: Yes. The greater the attachment, the greater the unhappiness. Likewise, the greater the aversion, the greater the unhappiness. It's a lack of freedom to be attached to anything. You can have things and not be attached to them. Be attached to them, and you are necessarily putting yourself through unhappiness.

Q: Now, when you're in a state of Beingness, that does not mean that you're an ethereal being who floats from spot to spot. That means that you are in that state where you know the Truth and thereby don't have to go through all the habits that have been piled upon you by your ego.

Lester: Yes. it's knowing your infinite Beingness that is eternal and never changes. Then this world cannot touch you. You see it as a fiction, a dream. You witness it. You move through life with no attachments and no aversions. Then no one and nothing can disturb you, and you have the infinite peace and joy that is constant.

Q: When I try to explain this to people, they think that I become a shadow or substance that vanishes from the sight of everybody, or something like that.

Lester: The only difference between a fully realized individual living in the world and one who is not is his point of view of everything. An unrealized person identifies with a single, limited body-mind. A realized person identifies with everything, every being, every atom and sees them as his Self. He sees the Beingness in everything as his Beingness.

Q: Therefore getting joy out of everything that happens.

Lester: No, your very nature is joy. You don't get it out of everything that happens—your basic nature is unlimited joy. That is your natural state! No need to get it!

Q: Therefore being in a state of joy perpetually.

Lester: Yes. As long as you don't lock it onto a person or thing, it's there all the time. But if you say you can't have joy unless you do or have something, you limit your joy. The natural state is unlimited joy. This is the *real* natural state. The natural state is being infinite, but we superimpose over that all these ideas of limitation, of needs, attachments, and aversions that block out this infinite joy that is natural. If a Being would do absolutely nothing, he would be this infinite Being. He would then be only a witness.

Q: But you can still put in a hard day's work.

Lester: Oh, yes. You go through life like everyone else.

Q: But it's your attitude.

Lester: Right. You see things differently. You see yourself as a witness rather than a doer.

Q: It's there, but you're detached somewhat from it. It's an eerie feeling sometimes.

Lester: It's a nice feeling, isn't it? It's eerie because you're not used to it. When you get used to it, it's dearie rather than eerie!

Q: Lester, is this thing really easy, and we're making it hard?

Lester: Yes. You are so right! *All* your difficulty is keeping yourself limited. You have compounded limitations on top of limitations and are holding on to them in your thoughts. Therein lies your difficulty. You must let go of all your thoughts. Every thought has limitation in it. Drop all your thoughts, and what is left over is you in your infinite happiness, your Beingness. Then you will realize that it is as easy for you to discover that you are an infinite Being with infinite happiness as it is for you to discover that you are a male or a female!

Releasing Explorations by Hale Dwoskin

The bottom line of this session is that you are the happiness that you have always been seeking in all the wrong places. Lester often said, "If you want to find happiness, all you need to do is do a U-turn back to you." This is a lot easier to accomplish than you may imagine. All you need to do to discover this for yourself is to look at what happiness is— what you are? Once you see this clearly you will never be fooled again.

You can also explore the questions "What is happiness?" and whatever response arises within can be followed up with "And if it is even more or beyond that, what is happiness?" Keep going in this exploration until you are feeling more at rest as the living source of all happiness.

Another way to deepen this exploration is to explore the part of the Sedona Method we call Holistic Releasing.

Holistic Releasing

Holistic Releasing is based on the premise that everything the mind experiences, whether real or imagined, arises in pairs. With this perception of duality, if we have *in*, we also have *out*. If we have *right*, we also have *wrong*. If we have *good*, we also have *bad*. If we have *pain*, we also have *pleasure*. Most of us live life as though we can hold on to the good and get rid of the bad, but, in so doing, we miss the obvious. Think about it. When you try to hold on to something good, it always slips away. Whenever you try to clutch on to what you judge as good, or that which you prefer, it is elusive and tends to move through your awareness. And then think about the inverse of this.

What happens when you resist or try to hold away what you don't like? That's right. It persists or appears to gets even bigger. So, in effect, what most of us have been doing is pulling what we don't like toward us and pushing what we do like away! We also spend a lot of time and energy keeping these polarities of opposites alive by trying to keep what we like *as far away as possible* from what we don't like. This takes an enormous amount of energy and creates that which we call "problems." The perception of duality also ignores the underlying unity. which is here before the mind and is unaffected by all the pairs of opposites.

Holistic Releasing is very simple. You simply focus on or welcome both sides of the polarity by going back and forth between them. For instance, a very simple polarity has to do with happiness. Most of us are either feeling relatively happy or unhappy from moment to moment, but we tend to see only one and not the other. So let's just do a little experiment. Ask yourself these questions.

Could I allow myself to feel as unhappy as I do in this moment?

And then, could I allow myself to feel as happy as I do in this moment?

And as unhappy as I do in this moment?

And as happy as I do in this moment?

As you continually move back and forth on the different sides of any particular polarity several times in a row, notice what is happening inside. You may have even noticed it just in doing this exercise: the polarities will actually dissolve each other. And you are left with greater and greater awareness of the freedom and presence that you are. You may also see the underlying unity beneath the duality and separation of the polarities. You may experience it as an energetic shift. You may feel it as a dissolving or a clearing or a lightness. You may have greater clarity and understanding within your own self.

When you bring the two sides of a polarity together, it is like bringing matter and antimatter together or positive and negative energy. They neutralize each other, and you're left with a much greater awareness of freedom, presence, and greater access to your intuitive knowingness. You see solutions, not problems. You feel more open, more alive and more at peace. As you work with Holistic Releasing, you'll discover that this effect expands over time. You will start to see more possibilities and see things more clearly. Each time you practice releasing in this way, you will get more out of it—more access to your own truth.

The Body

Lester Levenson

This session is composed of aphorisms collected from various talks by Lester. Please allow yourself to ponder each one individually before going on to the next in order to get the maximum benefit.

Why should we have need for this body? If we are infinite Beings, why need we a body? The fact that we were born into a body shows that we are ignorant of our infinite Being. It's an indictment right in its own *de facto* situation.

The body is the greatest shackle, imprisonment, that we have, the greatest obstacle we have placed in our way.

The only way out of all difficulties is to know that you are not the body.

We came into this world to be a body in order to learn that we are not a body.

The worst habit we have gotten into over millennia is that we are this body.

The body is a slow-action machine. That's all it is.

The desire to survive as a body is the basis for all our present aberrated behavior. Everyone wants approval (love), struggles hard for it, and spends almost all his effort in life to attain it. As an infant, as a child, in our formative years, we believed our parents would not take care of us if they did not approve of us, and we would therefore die! So, we developed perverted, aberrative behavior patterns through suppressing our own wishes and desires in order to get that approval from our parents, which meant survival. The patterns are so deeply subconscious because of being formed in the very first days and years of our life; with so much suppression, it is extremely difficult to reopen and consciously examine them now. However, once we know that we are not the body, all this behavior is gone.

You fear that if the body isn't, you are not.

All fear is either directly or indirectly the fear of the body dying.

You're infinite, and there's nothing complicated about that, but the habit of being a body is so strong that it complicates and overwhelms your abiding as your Self.

The entire body of misery relates to the physical body. The entire body of happiness is being what you are, the Self. Happiness is exactly what you are. Misery is exactly what you are not. The natural state is happiness. The artificially self-imposed state is misery. That is the choice: to say that the body is real or the Self is real.

How attached are you to the body? That's how attached you are to misery.

The body is life conditioned. You are life unconditioned. This body is nothing but a dying mechanism, from birth till death.

If you have a car, you do not say that you are the car. Why then, if you have a body, do you say you are the body?

Sleep is the pleasure of nonbodily existence.

You actually drop your body when you are in deep sleep and

recreate it in the morning when you wake up. There's no difference between sleep and death, except that after death, you pick up a different body, while after sleep, you pick up the same body. The time between sleep-bodies is short, and the time between death-bodies is long.

Wrong belief that one is a body is the basic cause of desire and aversion.

We shouldn't pay too much attention to the body. Give it what it needs and no more. Do it without attachment.

Because of the extreme limitation of the human body, the incentive to get free is great. It affords the greatest prod for growth.

To make your body perfect and to live in a consciousness of the body is not as high as to live with an imperfect body in a consciousness of your Self.

It's a higher state to have a sick body and not identify with it, and that's why certain masters do that. They will go through life with a weak or sick body, all the time maintaining their peace and equanimity. And they welcome it because it is an opportunity to be constantly reminded that they are not the body.

The body is the disease, not the sickness of it.

A perfect body can keep one in bondage as well as an imperfect one can.

If you know that you are not the body, you are not the mind, so what if they hurt?

The body is just a thought. Everything about the body is a thought.

All functions of the body at one time had to be done consciously before they became unconscious.

People are not aware that they run their bodies entirely. Subconsciously, we know more chemistry than all chemists today know consciously.

The mind is the switchboard for the nervous system of the body.

The body is nothing but a robot, controlled by us.

It makes just as much sense to identify with this body as it does to identify with a body on a movie screen.

"Me" and "mine" are binders to this body and to possessions.

Some people who take no care of the body are very attached to the body. It is our attitude toward the body that counts.

When you think of the body as God, that is conceit.

If you think you are the body, then make it perfect. If you think you are the Self, then it doesn't matter.

Body equals pain, and Self equals infinite joy.

If you think you are the body, you are distracted by it. If you know you are not the body, the body doesn't distract you no matter how sick it is.

The basic motivational force in physical life is the desire to survive as a body. (And it is impossible!) One of the basic troubles today is that people are much too interested in the body. Most people live ninety-nine percent of the time for the body. The body is a real jail. There's nothing about this body that needs glorification. If you want to know how attached you are to your body, consider throwing it off a cliff. There's no mind in the physical body. It's the mind of the astral body that operates the physical body.

"I am the body," is ignorance. "The body is not apart from the Self," is knowledge.

The body is one of the least things that we can have.

All trouble starts with wanting to be a body.

The body operates on the law of cause and effect and is an effect of the mind.

There is always a decision to leave the body when we do.

Only identifying with the body causes misery.

Give the body its due: keep the body healthy, etc., and then forget it.

The healthiest foods are fruits and vegetables from the flower of the plant. The unhealthiest foods are flesh.

Cooking kills the vitality. We should eat fruits and vegetables uncooked.

Exercise is good if one believes it is good. Best method of exercise is seeing cosmic energy flowing in and out of the muscles and body as they are tensed and relaxed.

We should see every body as our body.

It's all right to be that body if you'll be every other body. Then you see every body as your Self.

You are so convinced you are the body that you don't want to look away from it, and, therefore, you look away from your Self.

You feel yourself as you, no matter what body you have on.

You're only free when you know that you're not the body.

If you want immortality, stop holding on to the body.

Once you know you are not the body, it doesn't matter what happens to the body.

Be a body and be forever submerged in misery. Be your Self and be forever at peace.

The body is like a straitjacket when you see the Truth.

You have the concept that you are only that body and only through that body can you be somewhere. That's not true. If you would see the Truth, you would see everything going on anywhere right now.

When you see you are not a separate individual, you transcend the physical, astral, and causal bodies. Separate individuality is the cause of body form. You should see your individuality as the one Being.

In the process of realizing what you are, you will see all bodies as your bodies.

An unusual thing happens: you become all Beings. You give up being one body and become all bodies, but the bodies appear different from the way they look to you now. They become a flimsy, dreamlike substance.

Nothing that the body does should shake you from abiding as your Self.

We should live our way of life so that we are not identifying with this extremely limited, garbage-producing vehicle called the body. It only cuts off joy, because we attach joy to it when really the joy is nothing but the experiencing of our real Self. Our way of life should be to be not the body, but to be the witness of it.

It's impossible to find God if we're accepting the body and the world as real. When you are the Infinite Self, you don't see bodies, you see only the Beingness in them.

Not to be the body is a beginning step. As long as you are trying to be the body, you haven't got a chance of seeing the Truth, because the Truth is you're infinite, and the body is at the opposite end of infinity. It's the most limited thing you can be unless you want to be a stone.

Saying, "I am a body" is tantamount to saying, "I, the limitless Self, am a limited body."

Identify with your body and the extreme limitations of a body are yours. Identify with your Self and you are all bodies, all things, all knowledge and power, with no limits and totally free!

Be not the body and the world is a dream, a beautiful and perfect dream.

There is a physical, astral, and causal body. When you know what you are, you let go of all bodies. When you let go of the concept of being a body, you go all the way to the top. This physical plane is the greatest, because in it we can transcend all planes and be Free!

We have freewill to identify with the body or to identify with our unlimited Self.

If you think the body is so great, after realizing your Self, you can make a thousand of them, all alike, all perfect!

Die to the body and you die to death!

Releasing Explorations by Hale Dwoskin

How would you behave and how would you respond to life if you knew that the body is imagined and only the Self is real? Probably very differently than you do now. If you look at your life you will probably see that it is totally centered around your attempts to make the body real, content, safe, and last forever. Imagine what life will be when you know that the body was the least of you, as opposed to how you often feel now, that it is the all of you.

As the body moves through life, you have the opportunity every moment either to reinforce your attachments and aversions to it and your identification with it or to identify with that which gives the body life yet is totally unbound by any name or form. You can explore this polarity for yourself by experimenting with the following.

Allow yourself first to identify consciously with the body and its stories and problems and then consciously to disidentify with it. You can say to yourself, "I am the body?" Experience what this sounds like, looks like, and feels like. Now explore the opposite. Say to yourself, "I am that which is aware of the body." As best you can allow yourself to experience what it sounds like, looks like, and feels like to be the Self unaffected by the comings and goings of the body. As you do, you will begin to free yourself from the imagined shackles of the physical.

You can also experiment with the following Holistic Releases.

I am the body—I am not the body.

I am the body—I am Awareness.

You can also simply explore this self-inquiry question: "If I am not the body, what am I?" However the mind responds, ask, "If I am not even that, what am I?" Keep going with this until the mind drops away and you know you are not the body or you are simply being Awareness.

Attitude and Action

Lester Levenson

This session is composed of aphorisms collected from various talks by Lester. Please allow yourself to ponder each one individually before going on to the next in order to get the maximum benefit.

Attitude and action in our daily life should be consciously used for growth all the time. When so used, there is no time when you are not growing. It is an excellent way of constant and continual growth. Remember, when you are not growing, you are regressing.

All attitude and action should be in the direction of helping yourself and others toward realization.

Have an attitude of harmlessness toward all Beings and do not want them to behave as you would like. The same thing said positively would be: Have an attitude of love toward all Beings and allow them to be the way they are.

To every action, there is an opposite and equal reaction. This is the law of compensation, also called karma.

Daily toil is a waste of time unless you continuously use it to learn what you need to know from the resistances of it. Square it with love, take full responsibility and the resistance melts. The less toil and more quest and realization of Self, the righter the direction and the easier living becomes.

Every act and every attitude is either a step forward or a step backward.

Everything that we do that is not in the direction of the Self forestalls the continuous bliss and sustains the misery.

Determine the goal of your life, and then find the shortest road to it.

Everyone is doing exactly what he or she wants to.

It isn't right for us to tell anyone anything unless they want us to.

Don't waste your time socializing; use it realizing.

If you can't do it yourself, how can you tell someone else how to do it?

Nothing happens to us that isn't caused by us.

"I can't" means "I won't."

Hurriers are worriers and worriers are hurriers.

Everyone is right as far as he goes.

The more you act out the law of mutuality, the more capable you are of carrying it out naturally.

Praise is destructive, for it encourages and develops ego.

Every act and thought that is not for the good of others creates a bondage, a limitation that must necessarily materialize.

Attitudes are far more important than actions.

No matter what happens to a human being, no matter what it is, the heaviness is caused by his attitude toward it.

When anything bad happens to you, know that only you are causing it. Then you can change it.

Trying is an excuse for not doing.

If two people want to fight, should we stop them? If it is mutual, it's right for them.

Economize your time. Minister only to your needs. Don't waste time creating things beyond your needs.

Spend your time in search of ever-new joy or bliss, then rest in the eternal serenity of bliss, night and day.

Dependency is deadly for growth.

A dependent relationship does not allow you to think for yourself. It admits you are dependent on another human being and prevents you from seeing your infinity. Conformity is dependency, is having to do what others do, wanting their approval. An independent person is always an oddball, misunderstood by society.

Everything you do is with your inner motivation and is motivated from your inner state of Beingness that you have attained.

All action is ritual.

You've got to read behind peoples' words.

Life in the world should consist of only two things: that which helps us grow, or that which will help others grow.

Crying is motivated by a feeling that we cannot do. If we feel that we can do something about it, we have no grief. Our thought goes to doing it rather than thinking, "Oh, I can't, I'm helpless." If you thought you could do, you wouldn't cry. If you have the determination that you can do, you won't cry. It's good not to give into grief. Cancel grief when it comes by affirming that you can do.

There's no such thing as a mistake—we do it! There is no such thing as an accident—we do it!

To be interested in things outside of yourself, you must get your interest off your little self.

You shouldn't support people in their weaknesses—it boomerangs.

Any advice comes back to you karmically.

If you explain something, do it through the other one's point of view.

That which you embrace becomes a part of you.

It's so much faster for your growth to know that only you can do it for you.

There's nothing bad; there's just making errors on the way back home.

Advice is ego-playing God.

Outlook differs according to the sight of the person. In gross eyes, all is gross. In mental eyes, all is mental. If the eye (I) becomes the Self, the eye is infinite, and all is seen as your infinite Self.

Attitude toward a child and an adult should be the same.

Behavior is general. We don't behave one way with one person and another way with another.

Everything one does is motivated from one's basic motivation; therefore one behaves similarly in all situations. Only a free person doesn't. That is why a freed person is an enigma to others.

Your behavior with the world will be the same as it is with your parents.

One is a fool who doesn't use the experience of others. It is a wise man who learns from others' experiences.

Your attitude toward anything will be your blessing or your curse.

We look for confirmation of our feelings, positive or negative. Better to look for the reality of things.

Fully trust a crooked person, and he will be honest with you.

He who excuses, accuses himself.

Don't defend yourself—reform!

Sympathy is something we should never feel, as sympathy is supporting the other one in his misery. Compassion is understanding him and wanting the best for him.

If they think that sympathy is love, you have to grant them their right to think that. When they want sympathy, there is nothing you should do. You can't join them, so you just let them be.

Complexity is the lack of understanding. Tension is caused by wanting to go in two opposite ways at the same time.

Being a skeptic is good if it causes you to prove things.

Nonattachment is the way to happiness. Disown all things from your heart while taking care of them. Consider them borrowed for use only. Use them with gratitude.

Perform material duties with service. Otherwise, you are limiting yourself, your consciousness, your growth.

When you act in the world, you shouldn't care for the fruits thereof. If they are good, okay. If they are bad, okay. It shouldn't matter how it comes out. Whatever you do, don't have attachments or aversions to it, and you will transcend this world. Action does not cause bondage, but the sense of doership does. It is the wrong identifying of yourself as the doer of the action that causes bondage. It doesn't matter what we do in the world, so long as we remember what we are.

If your interest is in God, you should talk only God. If one is on the path, one should never talk about anything but God or the things necessary in living. Other than that, the lips should be sealed. Not talking about God sends you in a downward direction. Any time you are not talking about God, you are actually talking about the opposite.

Nothing said should ever bother you.

Anything that bothers you is not outside you; the bother is within you.

Rebellion is better than the inability to rebel. Best is acceptance with no wish to rebel.

Gratefulness is a very joyous state. Want to be always happy? Maintain a state of gratitude.

Have no doubt and you can do anything. There is no doubt when you have radical reliance on God.

See no obstacles, and there will be no obstacles.

He who gets elated necessarily gets deflated.

Everyone should be your friend.

We've got to attain equal-mindedness toward all Beings to reach the top.

Our attitude should be the same toward all life.

Almost everything that we do lessens God.

When all are included, one is not deluded.

There's one thing we cannot do, and that is to give up our mastership. We only blindly believe we can. We blindly give our power to others to hurt us.

Discussing good actions and bad actions is discussing whether you should be good in the illusion or bad in the illusion. Realize that there is no illusion!

When your understanding is high enough, you see only confirmations of Truth in everything you hear, see or read.

Isolation does not give quietude. Elimination of thought does.

Escape by moving away from problems is not quietude. It's momentarily escaping the disturbance only to meet it again.

The only quietude is within. Get to the place where no one and nothing can bother you.

The highest compassion is to know that no compassion is necessary.

Right action is completely selfless.

The two greatest things you can do are to keep up the quest of, "What am I?" and to be not the doer but the witness.

The greatest act is only to be.

Beingness is higher than doingness, and doingness is higher than havingness.

The more you just be, the more you realize that you are the world, everyone and everything. The more active you are, the more you are being limited by the particular act you are involved in. You are that personality involved in that act doing that particular thing that is quite infinitesimal in the realm of infinity! The greatest action is in the realm of inaction, of being the All. A master is aiding every being on this planet. By his seeing every person as a master, he is supporting them as being a master. So, seeing and supporting nearly four billion people as masters is quite an activity, isn't it?

A contented person needs no action. One who is not content must do.

In reality, there's nothing to be done, nothing to be achieved. If you can realize that, you've got it made!

The best behavior is that which is in accordance with the way a master would act—dispassionate, seeing all as equals, being a witness and not the doer. Maintain the state that is natural in the realized state!

Be what you really are! Be your Self!

You can be, when there is no striving!

All behavior should be that which is characteristic of the egoless state or the state of the Self: changelessness, equal-mindedness; seeing only the Self, seeing only perfection; having the same attitude toward good and bad fortune, i.e., identifying with all with an indifference to praise or censure; having joy only in your Self, having complete passivity, complete humbleness; being not the doer; and having desirelessness, dispassion, nonattachment or forbearance.

It matters not what you believe or do not believe; it does matter what you do. Anything that you do that is not directly related to growth is a waste of time. You can only be interested in negativity if negativity is interesting to you. Never evaluate for the other one; let the other one do the evaluating for himself. "I'll try" means "I think I can't." That's why trying doesn't accomplish anything but trying. Rather than try, do it!

Releasing Explorations by Hale Dwoskin

Every time you are honest about your state of mind and are willing to let go, even a little, you are naturally drawn in the direction of Truth. There is no need to force this. Allow yourself to be open to the exploration of Truth more and more each day until it becomes your full-time endeavor. Then you will discover that you have always been that which you which you were seeking.

For most of us, our possessions possess us. Allow yourself to take stock of "your" possessions. You can do this by making a list or just by becoming aware of what you think you own. Allow yourself to examine these assumptions of ownership. You can do this with one or both of the following questions. You can ask, "Do I own this or is that merely an appearance?" Just by asking this you may see the object as merely an appearance. You may even see that "you" are just an appearance in your consciousness as well. You can also ask, "Do I own this or is this on loan from God?" If you can see your possessions as God's possessions, then inwardly thank God for lending them to you.

If you are having difficulty accepting that you do not own what you think you do, or if you would like to take this exploration even deeper, you can allow yourself to loosen your grip on any particular possession by using these Holistic Releases.

I own that [the possession]—There is no possession and no one to possess it.

I own that [the possession]—That [the possession] has always only been on loan from God.

You can also ask yourself one or both of these questions: "Would I rather have this one possession or would I rather be the All?" and "Could I let go of wanting to be possessed by this possession?" "Would I?" "When?"

As you can allow yourself to feel that "your" possessions are not your own, you will feel lighter and more alive. You will have less need to be on guard against losing "your" possessions because they have never really belonged to the personal you. You will relax more into the knowing that you are the All and therefore need nothing.

You can also explore the following Holistic Releases.

I have to strive in order to be—I am that which needs not striving to be.

This belongs to me—This belongs to no one.

This is my action—This is merely the perfect functioning of the One.

This world is real—The world is only and appearance.

Gurus and Masters

Lester Levenson

Amaster is a fully realized Being. A guru (or sat guru) is a master who has chosen to help others find their freedom. God, guru, and Self are all one and the same. This becomes obvious when the illusion is gone and the reality is known.

There is no greater aid than to have the guidance of a master or guru. To quote the greatest accepted authority on Monism of the East, Swami Shankara, "No known comparison exists in the three worlds (physical, astral, and causal) for a true guru. If the philosopher's stone were assumed as truly such, it can only turn iron into gold but not another philosopher's stone. The venerated teacher, on the other hand, creates equality with himself in the disciple who takes refuge at his feet. The guru, therefore, is peerless, nay, transcendental!"

A guru may be in a physical body, or an astral or causal body. The finer the body-form, the more readily he gets around. Can everyone have a guru in a physical body? No, because rare is the guru who chooses the most extreme of limited form—the physical body. There just aren't enough of them to go around.

Can everyone have a guru? Yes, if he will accept a guru who has transcended the physical body. Having transcended the physical, the guru can use his omnipresence and actually help everyone calling on him. Can we sense a guru who is not in a physical form? Yes, everyone can, to the degree of his acceptance. If we are up to it, he can appear and talk with us in a physical body. If our acceptance is less, he can appear in an astral body and talk with us. If we have less acceptance than this, he may appear in a vision. Least of all, we may feel him as a presence. However, he may come to us and to our aid in any one of the foregoing manners. All we need to do is to demand it and then accept it when it comes.

Is it necessary to have a guru? Theoretically, no. Practically, yes! Our present era is one in which we are so sunk in the apparency and delusion that superhuman means are needed. Should we have a guru? Definitely, yes. Can we find one? Definitely, yes. When the pupil is ready, the teacher appeareth! If you have not found your guru, just expect and know that you have contacted him, and you cannot but experience him!

How can we know a real guru or master? How can we tell the degree of one's realization? A fully realized Being has an inner peace that cannot be disturbed. He is completely selfless, and his every act is for others only. He is equal-minded toward all. He is desireless. He is fearless. He is Love that is all-givingness. He expects nothing from anyone. His every moment is oneness with God. To the degree that one has all the above qualities is the degree of one's realization.

The rest of this session contains aphorisms collected from various other talks by Lester. Allow yourself to reflect on each one before moving on to the next.

Getting a guru, we garner the greatest good and get our Godly goal.

Although we don't see it, the Great Ones work more and more with us as things get worse in the world. Don't lose your head. Keep yourself open to them, and you will be safely led through.

On the stage of earth, a realized one playacts a character as a human and knows himself as divine. He sees no contradiction between human and divine. He merely sees the world as *in* him rather than external *to* him. The unrealized one sees the world as external.

It is hard to judge a master by his behavior, because he is free to be any way he wants to be. He can even choose to be human. The top state doesn't exclude the limited states. It takes them in too without being touched by them.

To the degree we have reservations about the master or teacher, to that degree we cut off his help.

If one's ego feels it can dominate the teacher, the teacher has no chance of helping.

When the pupil is ready, the teacher must necessarily appear.

When a master in this world looks around, he sees his body, and he sees all bodies around him, but he knows that everybody is his Self—that's the difference. He sees everybody as much his body as his own.

Point of view is the only difference between a master and a non-master.

For a fully realized Being, his outer activity does not disturb or effect his consciousness. Likewise, thoughts do not disturb his consciousness.

I think the hard thing for disciples of a master (in physical body) to see is that the master is in the world and not of it, that his body is the least part of him.

You are always pointed in the direction when you are with the wise.

You think a master in a physical body is more effective, because you are unable to see him in his finer body and therefore think he is not with you.

The greatest of all aids is a living teacher who has realized. Why? Because, although we all potentially have infinite power, the more we realize, the more we can exert this power. When a living teacher, who has realized something, is trying to convey that to another one, he puts all his power behind what he is saying to help the other one realize it. He sees the other one as a limitless Being, gives him an inward lift, points and sets him up to receive that which is being said and uses the power emanated to effect the realization.

So, the greatest of all aids is a teacher who has realized what he is saying. The next greatest aid would be reading his words. There's a definite import to his written words. That's why I say that we should read only fully realized masters. Everything that They have in writing is intended and calculated to give the reader a realization. The written word carries the original import of the one who said it.

As to behavior in life, the very best behavior is imitating that of a realized Being, because that is conducive to giving you his realization. When you're acting it out, it points you in the direction of seeing that which you're acting out.

Stay with your master and be with your master all the time by constant thought of him and by constant reading of his words, as though he is talking directly to you.

The masters are living to give us realization, but if you don't accept this, their love does not allow them to impose themselves on you.

All the masters are at every moment helping us to see who and what we are.

A savior is a servant who serves.

A master's behavior is completely selfless. There is a total self-abnegation in a master.

A master feels like a servant. A master does not interfere with the lives and ways and wishes of others.

Masters seldom give advice. They give principle.

It's not that masters mind the world; it's that the world minds them that causes them to withdraw.

There's no realized teacher who wouldn't want you to listen to all other masters. They want you to listen to any realized Being, because they all see themselves as the same. But they don't want you to listen to anyone less than a realized Being.

All masters are exactly the same Self with different names.

When you can accept every master as your master, that's good. Then, when you can accept every person on the street as a master, you're almost there.

Every fully realized Being that comes into the world, in order to come in, must assume some desire and karma. If you don't have some desire, you cannot stay.

Masters will go through life with a weak or sick body, all the time maintaining their peace and equanimity. They welcome it because they use it as a constant reminder that they are not the body.

For one who's in a body, it's near onto impossible to look on a master as not a body.

Christ is against nothing. Love is all-accepting.

Masters never reject, they only accept.

A realized one doesn't *enjoy* bliss, he *is* bliss.

The guru helps set the background for realizations, for peace.

A master is a help in that he points us in the right direction and reminds us of the direction when we want to be reminded.

Reading their words is association with the sages.

A fully realized Being is inactive in his own consciousness. To others, he appears active. He looks at his Self and others look at his body.

It takes a master to understand the behavior of a master. If you could understand his behavior, you would be like him.

Any time you get totally absorbed in any saying of a master, you make contact with that master.

There are no limitations to a master. He can be one body; he can be a thousand bodies. A master can actually have a thousand bodies and talk through the thousand bodies at one time, to a thousand people—a thousand different people. There are no limitations on a master.

There is another thing you ought to be convinced of now: masters are one hundred percent correct!

Masters, isolated, are doing far more good for the world than presidents and kings are.

A realized one, being unlimited, may or may not use the mind.

When we start on the path, we start with much confusion. We don't recognize that what is out there is only that which we have set up. The teacher we look up to is in our consciousness and only there. However, when we look up to a teacher, we humble our ego, the only thing that prevents us from seeing the Truth. Looking up to a master puts our ego into the background, and we take our direction from someone who knows.

Now, the outside master or teacher will always point us inwardly to the teacher of all teachers, our very own Self. This doesn't become apparent at first. When we allow the teacher out there to become successful enough, he shows us that the teacher has always been right within us, that the teacher has always been our real Self. So that, in the end, there's only one teacher, the teacher within, your Self.

When you're moving in the direction, every guru and master is supporting you—yes, every one of them.

If your mind is on a fully realized master, he works to pull you over.

The place where saints are is right where "I am." So, when you find out what you are, you'll see the "saints come marching in."

Read the words of a master. Better still, imagine him saying them to you. Best of all, hear him saying them to you as you read them!

Truth is truth, and all masters speak identically. It appears different because they tailor it to suit the hearer.

The teacher is only as effective as is his conviction that the other one is a master.

When you know your Self, you know everything. A master knows far more about every field than the top world authority in that field.

When an individual becomes a master, he operates by intuition. He doesn't need to think.

Just one master could help every single one of the nearly four billion people on this earth at one and the same time, because masters are unlimited and omnipresent.

What is night to all humans is day to the realized. What is day to all humans is night to the realized. What the human sees, the realized doesn't see.

To the realized one, the world may be likened to a moving picture on a screen. He sees the changeless screen as the substratum of the action. The unrealized man takes the moving pictures to be real, and if he would investigate by grabbing hold of the moving pictures, he would discover the Truth, that it is just a changeless screen. Grab hold of your Self and discover the changeless substratum of the world!

A master sees nothing but the one Self, which others chop up into millions of parts.

Since masters are Beingness, they can never not be. But their Beingness is other than what you attribute to them. Beingness has no body or form. Beingness is unlimited. Form is limited to the form.

A master has equal-mindedness toward all Beings (even animals and insects).

When one is around a guru, if one gets quiet and digs for Truth, whatever one is aiming for, he will get through the assistance of the guru. He gets it through the silent teachings, which are the very highest of all teachings. This can also be done from afar!

In the end, the teaching has to be in silence, because it's an experiential thing; it's not a verbal thing.

A master sees us as himself, as his very own Self. There are no others to a master; there's just one infinite Being. This helps us to see what he sees.

You can meet the masters in a body when you can accept meeting them just as much as you can accept meeting me. You cannot invoke a master without his coming in.

Releasing Explorations by Hale Dwoskin

You are the master you are looking for, however, if you have any doubt about this fact it is helpful to have it reinforced by a master who *appears* to be separate from yourself. If you choose a master, make sure you choose one who has the following characteristics. One of the keys to knowing whether you are with a true master is that he or she will see you and treat you as his or her equal and will neither talk up or down to you. You will find that your mind will get quieter in the presence of a true master and you will become more self-obvious to yourself. A master will also not claim to be a master, because there is no one left to make such claims. They see everyone as themselves, as fully realized.

Lester always suggested that you choose a master with whom you not only resonate, but who is in a body now or has been in one. Lester felt that whether or not a master was in a body you should always contact him directly rather than going through a medium or mediator.

During the last twenty years of his life, Lester changed his opinion on masters. He still thought that they were an incredible aid, but he also felt that anyone who faithfully used the Sedona Method could go all the way on the path without the need of an external master.

Allow yourself to open to the one true master that is already right within you as your true Being. This Beingness will sometimes manifest as an external teacher and sometimes it will not. Either way that which you truly are is always here to support you in your freedom.

Also, allow all the power and powerful ones of the universe to support you in your quest for freedom. Allow the power that knows the way to lead you to the right teacher when you are supposed to have one. If you are drawn to a particular master, allow yourself to honor that attraction and follow his or her guidance as best you can. At the same time, until you have absolute certainty that he or she is right for you, allow yourself to approach everything that the master says both with an open mind and also with inquisitiveness. Once you are absolutely certain, then surrender to the master without reservation. Even if you are mistaken, you can benefit from the surrender.

Here are some Holistic Releases to explore.

I need a master—I am always in the presence of the one master.

I need something or someone to help me be free—I need no one or no thing to help me be freedom.

I and the master are separate—There is only One.

Take Full Responsibility

Lester Levenson

Would you want one practical key for quickly reaching the Goal, I would recommend that you take full responsibility for everything that happens to you. We have lost sight of our mastership and have deluded ourselves into thinking we are victims in a world that controls us, that pushes us around. It isn't so! We are causing what is happening to us by giving power, our power, to the external world. If you want to regain your control, you must take full responsibility.

How do you regain your control? By examining your thinking and correcting it. Develop the habit of honest introspection by asking yourself, "Wherein did I cause this to happen to me?" and holding it until the thought that caused the happening comes out of the subconscious into the conscious plane. Then you recognize your mastership, that you caused that pleasant or unpleasant experience to happen to you. The more you will do this, the easier it becomes, and the more able you become until finally you recognize that you were always the master.

Q: Then I, myself, am my own block, and other people do not influence me?

Lester: Yes. It's not what other people say. If you follow their thinking, it's because you want to.

Q: Yes, because I think they know more than I do.

Lester: I say you know everything. You've got to accept this as a premise at least, if you want to grow.

Q: Well, I can accept that a part of me knows everything, but that part of me does not appear to be operating, because my world out there is not in good shape.

Lester: It does not appear to be operating? You don't operate that part of you? That is the way you're talking! No, you operate it. You choose not to use your omniscience, your basic nature. You choose to be ignorant of your omniscience by saying, "I am a limited mind-body." That's your choice. When you choose to identify with your real Self, then you'll see that you always were omniscient, are right now, and always will be; and you'll stop foolishly saying you're not.

Q: You mean I can actually make that choice?

Lester: Yes, not only you can, some day you will. When you get tired enough of all this limitation, you have set up for yourself, then you'll make that choice. Who thinks all your thoughts? You do! It's all your doing. What we accept is what we choose to accept. It's always our choice. It is now our choice to be extremely limited bodies. And when you don't accept your responsibility for that, you have no possibility of getting out of that extreme limitation.

Q: I say I want to get out of that limitation and think I want to get out of that limitation, and then when certain things happen, I just don't get out. I'm right there in that limitation.

Lester: What you need to do is not to say it but want it so strongly that you override the contrary unconscious habits and do it.

Q: Overriding the unconscious habits is hard to do because they keep sneaking up on you and you don't realize sometimes you've got them.

Lester: It depends on how strong your desire is for the thing that you want as to whether the unconscious habits override it. We have infinite power, infinite will, and when man so wills, he's immediately set free.

Q: Gee, that sounds so easy.

Lester: That's the easiest way to do it. Just will it! And it's possible for every one of us, because we are infinite and therefore have infinite willpower. And the reason why we don't do it is that we don't have that much desire for it. We still have more desire to be limited bodies.

Q: I believe that anyone would take the other choice, if he really had a choice.

Lester: Oh, if you had a choice—pardon me! [laughter] You see what's happened? You're convinced we don't have the choice.

Q: No. Speaking from experience, sometimes when you really want something, it seems like the opposite happens.

Lester: Everything you really wanted strongly in your life, you got, because the mind is only creative. These are things you have got to dig out and recognize for yourself. You're getting exactly what you want, as is everyone. Because you don't look at your thoughts, and you call them unconscious does not mean you don't have them.

Q: I'm afraid of my unconscious. Did you know that?

Lester: How does that help you see your unconscious thoughts?

Q: Consciously, I tell them to go away.

Lester: So they stay operative all the time. Thoughts have no will of their own. You have the will. Unless you pull them up into consciousness and look at them, you can't let go of them. When you see them consciously, you'll automatically let go of them, the ones you don't like, because you don't like them.

Q: How can you become conscious of your unconscious thoughts?

Lester: By practice. Just the way you're doing it now. Anything you want to think of comes to your mind. What you are going to say to me five minutes from now is not conscious right now, it's unconscious. Five minutes from now you'll pull up what you want. Now if we make it a habit of pulling up thoughts, we can do it easily. The more we practice it, the easier it is to do. It's a good habit; it saves a lot of unnecessarily living out of karma.

Honest introspection works quickly and beautifully like a surgeon with a knife. We control the unconscious. We keep back there all that we want to keep back there, and then when we want it up in the conscious, we pull it up.

Q: You really believe that we control it?

Lester: Do I control your unconscious?

Q: No, I don't think you do it.

Lester: Then who does?

Q: Well, I don't know. I think it's unconscious control.

Lester: It's your unconscious. Can you remember right now things that happened yesterday that you're not conscious of? What did you have for breakfast yesterday?

Q: Oh—ham and eggs!

Lester: All right, a minute ago that was unconscious, and now it is up in your consciousness, right? Do you have control of your unconscious? Can you pull things up from it? You did just then!

Q: But you see that does not have any emotional impact—what I had for breakfast.

Lester: It had a good emotional impact. You showed you liked it. However, it does not matter whether there is emotional impact. What matters is the desire to pull up something from your unconscious.

Q: But you triggered her bringing it up. She wouldn't have brought that up otherwise.

Lester: Yes, but so can she. She wanted to. If she had not wanted to, she just wouldn't have remembered. Pleasant things are easy to bring up and unpleasant things are difficult, because we have little desire to bring up the unpleasant.

Q: Do you have to go through this phase of clearing up the unconscious before you can accept the theory that you are unlimited?

Lester: It is necessary in the beginning, and it also makes for rapid progress. Later, after much progress, you can will it out. There are basically two ways of growing: one is eliminating the mind, the subconscious; the other is putting in the positive, seeing who and what you are.

Q: When you put in the positive, doesn't the opposite seem to take effect?

Lester: Sometimes. However, when you see your real Beingness, you'll scorch the opposite. You'll say, "That's ridiculous to remain miserable, sick, unhappy, etc.," and you'll begin to scorch it. There is a tendency in the direction you're asking. If I say "hot," you think of "cold," right? If I say "up," it implies "down." That is in the nature of thought itself. But I wouldn't use that to imply that we can't wipe out the negative by seeing the positive that we are, because we can.

Q: Well, I don't know. You see, at the hospital I went around trying to use light, love, and peace, because I thought that these were the things that were essential. And it seemed like the more I tried to dwell on light, love, and peace, the worse things got.

Lester: Love is something that can't be turned on and off. Either you've got it or you haven't. If you have love, you may say horrible things to people, and they don't mind it. So this thing called love isn't something we can turn on and off like a faucet. We can only express it to the degree that we have it. Now, if you have love for these people, you would want them to have what they want.

Q: So what I'm doing is playing an ego game?

Lester: Yes. Can you see it? When you see it, that's good. Then you will, I hope, let go of it.

Q: By the way, you mentioned before that by bringing up the subconscious, you could eliminate karma. How?

Lester: Karma is in the thought, not in the act. When you do something, it's the thought that's carried over in the subconscious that instigates the act next time. Eliminate subconscious thought, and you eliminate future karma. It's the thought that carries over from lifetime to lifetime. So, if you bring the thought up and you reverse it, karmically it's gone.

Q: I want to know how to control what I think. I do not feel I can control how I think.

Lester: You do it by first accepting the idea that you can. Then you try it, and you succeed once. When you succeed once, then you know you can try it again. When you succeed twice, the second time is easier. The third time is yet easier than the first two, etc. The more you do it, the easier it gets. This leads to complete control and freedom.

Q: By control you mean changing your thinking?

Lester: Yes. We control all our thinking. If I do something wrong, it's because I decide to carry out something wrong, that's all. And if I make it unconscious, I do it. Did I hear you say, "Take full responsibility?" That's it! If you want to grow, you must take full responsibility for everything you do, for everything that happens to you. Trace all happenings to their originating thought in your mind.

Q: I still feel I can hurt people.

Lester: You can't. People hurt themselves; you don't hurt them.

Q: I wish I could finally see that.

Lester: I call you "stupid." You've got a certain reaction there, right? It wasn't good, was it? Who made you feel sad? You thought, *Well, he called me stupid. Well, I'm going to feel sad.* All right, now I say, "You're brilliant." You thought, *He called me brilliant. I'm going to feel happy.* But you do the up and down in your feeling; I don't do it. I come out with a sound: "stupid," "brilliant," and you choose the way you feel about it. It's just a little tiny bit of sound energy that went from me to you, to your ears, and you felt first sad, then happy. You did all the doing there. Can you see that?

Q: Well, if I can't hurt anyone, I can't help anyone, either!

Lester: Yes, that's true.

Q: This business of when you try to put in the positive thought, and oftentimes the negative seems to be strengthened, is it because while you're putting in the positive, you're holding on to what you're fighting? So that all you need to do is just do it?

Lester: Yes. When you want to do it enough, you'll just do it.

Q: When you do that, you just let go of it. You don't hold it in mind, and it isn't.

Lester: Right! When the conscious wish to let go is stronger than the unconscious wish to hold on, then you let go. These habits are very strong; the unconscious wish for them is very strong. The conscious wish has to be stronger to override it.

Q: Then if you have a conscious wish, and you're trying to accomplish something, and you can't do it, it's because you have a subconscious habit that is blocking you. Well, how do you get rid of that subconscious wish that's blocking you?

Lester: By making the conscious wish stronger. Or by pulling up the unconscious wish to the contrary and looking at it. When you see it, you automatically let go of it; you won't hold it down there anymore.

Q: I want to meditate well, and I can't seem to.

Lester: How many hours a day do you practice meditation?

Q: Three-quarters of an hour in the morning, because when I'm working, I can't do any more.

Lester: How many hours a day do you do the opposite?

Q: An awful lot of hours.

Lester: That's why it's difficult. Now, out of a sixteen-hour day, if you spent eight hours trying to meditate and eight hours in the world, you'd have an even push for and against it in your daily doing. Meditating is quieting the mind. Activity in the world is doing the opposite.

Q: But even when, during the day, you try to think of God, you can't.

Lester: Because your mental habit is so strongly on things of the world, and every day you develop that habit further. So, when you take some short time off and try to do the opposite, you don't find it easy. You've got to take more and more time off for meditating until you succeed.

Q: You mean by increasing the desire for meditation, the opportunity will present itself?

Lester: Yes, and therefore you will succeed. If your desire for meditation were intense, you'd be meditating rather than doing other things. Then you would become able to keep your mind on God while in the world.

Q: When you once reach Oneness in meditation, do you regress back into your separateness?

Lester: Yes, when you first see it, it's a tremendous experience that you'll never forget. But the mind has not been undone and therefore re-emerges. But seeing it scorches a good part of the mind each time you see it.

Q: The more you see it then—

Lester: The more you scorch the mind, until the mind is totally undone. Then you're in the steady state. You regress no more. It's possible to see all the way, see the Oneness, by momentarily submerging the mind. But as long as that mind is not undone, it will re-emerge.

But you'll never let go once you drop into that state of Oneness. You'll go into it again and again until it becomes permanent.

Q: You can't will that?

Lester: Oh, yes! Oh, yes, by wanting it that much. The reason why it's so difficult to want it that much is that we have been wanting the illusory world for so long that we don't let go of the illusion very easily. Even though intellectually we know the illusion causes the misery, through long-time habit of thinking that the joy is in the external world, we just don't let go of it easily.

Q: That's why I say traveling is a fool's paradise.

Lester: Yes, it is chasing rainbows. The ultimate joy is closer than flesh. How far do you have to go to get It, that which is closer than flesh?

Q: Right here; wherever you are, that's where It is.

Lester: Yes, that's where It is. It's the "I" of you. Find that "I" and you've got It. So the place to go is within.

Q: Is isolating running away?

Lester: It could be. If one is isolating just to get away from the world, that's escape. If one is isolating to dive into one's Self, that is not escape.

Q: How do you know which one you are doing?

Lester: By being honest with yourself.

Q: There's something about being next to nature.

Lester: The nice thing about nature is it gets one away from worldly restimulation.

Q: That's escaping though, isn't it?

Lester: Right. You go out into nature to enjoy nature. What you're really enjoying is the freedom obtained by the dropping away of all the unhappy thoughts and pulls of society. And that's escape.

Q: You mean you can't enjoy nature and at the same time be going within and trying to go home?

Lester: No, I don't mean that. All joys should be being what you are. We should never enjoy anything. In order to enjoy something, we have to go into the illusion of separateness. The joy should be independent of things, independent of people. However, when one sees the Truth, one can choose to enjoy; and the closer one gets to Truth, the more one is capable of enjoying. One becomes sensitized, and everything becomes far more intense. But there's no need to go out and enjoy nature, because your basic nature is joy. You are the ultimate joy.

Looking for joy would be like me going around looking for Lester. I am Lester. I don't have to go out there and look for him. If I am joy, I don't have to look for it out there. There's no need to go out for joy when it's inside you.

Q: It's simpler to get it in an isolated spot.

Lester: Yes. Even if you're escaping, you'll reach a point where your thoughts will get unbearable. Then you'll be forced to go within.

Q: You're helping us today through throwing back some of the things we're saying and giving other things to us. One needs that, doesn't one, in one's search?

Lester: Yes, it is an aid. The only thing anyone else can do for us is to point and support us in the direction. And when we are pointed in the wrong direction, it's very good to have someone repoint us in the right direction. Mirroring your thoughts back to you helps you see your wrong direction, so that you may change it.

Q: How do you know if you're pointed in the right direction?

Lester: Intuitively, or by the results achieved. Unconsciously, everyone is seeking his infinite Self. We call it happiness. When we beat ourselves long enough and hard enough, we begin to open ourselves to the right direction. Then a Christ, a Yogananda, a Ramakrishna, a

Buddha comes into our experience. Becoming acquainted with these Great Ones is no accident. They point the right direction.

Let me conclude with the following: You are responsible for everything that you feel. It's your feelings; it's your thoughts. You turn them on, you think them, and no one else but you does it. And you act as though you have no control! You turn a faucet on in your head and you say, "Oh, someone is getting me all wet." It's you who's turning on the faucet and getting yourself wet.

So, your direction has been, remains, and will be to take full responsibility for what's happening to you. Then you'll see by looking in the direction of "I am doing this" that you are! Then, when you see that you're torturing yourself, you'll say, "My gosh, how stupid can I be?" And you'll stop, and, instead of torturing yourself, you'll make yourself happy.

Now, no one is an effect of the unconscious mind, the unconscious habits and tendencies, unless he chooses to be. You are cause over the unconscious mind: you set it up, you're choosing to follow it. The day you decide not to, that day you're through with it! It's simple. When you don't look at what you are doing, it's a forever process of being miserable. You think miserable thoughts, and you feel miserable, and you don't take responsibility for thinking these thoughts. So what chance have you got for getting out of it?

Once you take responsibility for your thoughts, you've got control. You can turn them off, change them, or put in good thoughts until you overcome the bad thoughts. Then you'll drop thoughts. You'll see how stupid it is to think. All thoughts are things of limitation, and you're happiest when there are absolutely no thoughts. And when there are absolutely no thoughts, you are in the top state. So, what's difficult about that?

Q: The unconscious mind.

Lester: No. It is you! It's not the unconscious mind. This is the point I've been trying to get across. It's not the unconscious mind. You would like to make it the unconscious mind. You would like to make it other than you. That's why you want the masters, or you want

Lester, to pass a wand over you and do it for you, but you don't want to do that which makes you happy. You're choosing to do that which makes you unhappy. Can you see this? It's so simple. Whose thoughts do you think? Why all these unhappy thoughts? The moment you choose not to have them, you won't have them.

Q: We'll look to you and us.

Lester: Look to you, look to you. Look to find out who and what you are. Only when you know who you are will you know who I am. Only by discovering what you are will you understand what this universe is.

Until you understand what you are, you cannot see this universe clearly. It's a hazy mist. When you discover who you are, you'll see that this whole universe is right within you. Like the universe in a night dream is within you. You must take full responsibility. Otherwise, you have no chance of ever getting out of the mess. If you attribute the cause to it as something other than you, that's not being true—you can never get out of the mess. So, the day you decide to do it, that's it! Be cause! Take full responsibility and have your mastership!

Releasing Explorations by Hale Dwoskin

Do you feel responsible for your life? Or do blame others, even God, for your troubles. What if everything you experience is created in the mind? Everything! As you begin to explore what Lester spoke about—taking responsibility—you will begin freeing yourself from your self-imposed limitations. Plus, you will have the bonus of con-sciously creating more of what you want in your life and letting go of what you don't want. You will also have the added joy of watching God in action.

Allow yourself to explore your life and discover where you believe you are responsible and where you are not. If you can see your respon-sibility for something that you feel was an error from the past, then you can ask yourself, "Could I let go of wanting to create that again?" "Would I?" "When?" If you say to yourself, "I am responsible," and your feeling is not joyous, then you have not taken responsibility. You are blaming yourself, which hurts and only perpetuates your victimhood.

If you are blaming yourself for something that happened instead of taking responsibility, ask yourself, "Could I let go of wanting to blame myself for what happed and love myself no matter what?" This will help move you in the direction of taking responsibility and away from blame.

If you find that you are blaming someone or something else for your problems, you can ask yourself, "Could I let go of wanting to give [the person, situation, or thing that you think is to blame] power over me and reclaim my mastery?" "Would I?" "When?"

As you see that it is your responsibility for creating something that you like, then allow yourself to thank yourself and/or the Self or God for that creation.

Also, be open at least to the possibility that responsibility rests with the All and not with a personal "you." The more you surrender to the power that is the way, the more you discover that all is well and everything is unfolding as it should.

You may also choose to explore the following Holistic Releases.

I am not responsible—I am responsible.

It is my fault—It is no one's fault.

It is their fault—It is no one's fault.

I am responsible—The One is responsible.

Helping Others

Lester Levenson

As we are approaching Christmastime again, I would like to say a word on love. As you know, the real love, the divine love, is a feeling of givingness with no expectation of receiving something for it in return. When we attain this, we see and feel nothing but the most enthralling love everywhere and in everyone. We taste the sweetness of God and are effortlessly locked in harmony with him. We are intoxicated with a joy that defies description.

Loving God, loving All, loving everyone, is the easiest and most natural way to attain full realization. It requires no giving up, as it is an expanding of our inner feeling of love to encompass and embrace All—everyone and everything living. Expand your love, for your family, for your friends, for those of your country, for those of the entire world. Expand it until there is no more room for expansion and then remain eternally intoxicated and one with God! Love is basically an attitude. To express this attitude, we do so at Christmastime with greetings and gifts. As you give, do so from the bottom of your heart, and discover that it is the giver that is most blessed.

Having been away from you for some time, and knowing that you have been meeting and communing weekly, has anything come up that you might want me to clarify?

Q: We just said what we individually thought, and, in that way, we reached for a better understanding, and I think it helped.

Lester: All right. "Reached for a better understanding." See if I can tie in there. We're moving toward a goal that is unlimited. We must become totally free. We have been moving in ups and downs, and our lives have become much better and happier. Yet, as we feel, there is a distance to go, right?

To date, as a group, I would say that you have mastered much of the principles as applied to life. You've learned how to let go of a certain amount of limitation. You've learned to accept the positive, you've learned to accept the power of thought and you've learned that you are the creator in your life. And, of course, the thing that goes along with that is that you have increased your capacity to love.

As we expand our consciousness, our love automatically increases. Likewise, as our love increases, so does our understanding and wisdom. And yet, we have noticed, these things that we have so far gained are not all-satisfying. Even though life has become happier, it still isn't full, complete. Anyone take any issue with me so far?

Q: Not a bit.

Lester: All right. The path we're on is from here on until we make the goal—total freedom. That's the first point I'd like to make. Second, we can do this *this lifetime!* Generally, it takes many, many lifetimes for the great majority of those seeking to make it. However, we can do it this lifetime for two reasons: First, we are an unusual group, i.e., rare are the ones wanting this quickest, most direct way.

Second, we have the right direction to make it this lifetime. Then, if we ever come back in the future, it will be by choice, not by necessity. Those of us who very much want to help others might come back just to help others. But that's a matter of individual choice. The main thing is to achieve the ultimate state.

Now, becoming master over life is really a basic and necessary step through which we learn that, rather than victims in life, we are the masters. Then, after we master the ways of making our environment the way we want it, we look beyond. No matter how happy we make our life, so long as it's involved only in everyday living itself, it will never fully satisfy us, because our real nature is that of being infinite. Are there any questions on that?

Now I'll go into what I think should be our direction in the future. We must become more universal. We should let go of our own livingness to the point where we can live outwardly more for others. If we are universal Beings, we must behave like universal Beings. "Every human being is me" is the way we should feel. "You are me" is the attitude we should have toward all people.

I used the word *attitude*. We can't help people much by giving them things; there's just too much needed, and we do not have it. But we can give them that which is much more than things. We can begin to give them the wisdom that we are getting. Our attitude should be one of wanting to help everyone who wants help. Never help those who don't want it; that would be imposing on them. We should try to help only those who cross our path and ask us.

We don't have to extend ourselves looking for people, as they will just fall into our experience. They'll ask us questions, and, as we give them the answers, we'll find that certain people will feel that we are giving them the right answers, that we are helping them, and they will ask for more. And it's really an obligation to help those who come to you sincerely seeking the right direction. Remember, "You are me."

As we begin to live more expansively and think less of our little self and more of the other one, we really help ourselves. The worldly see it differently. They would probably interpret it as us helping the other one. But there is no other one to help but our Self, and we actually get the greatest benefit. By helping others, we help ourselves toward the goal. We will never make it unless we have an attitude of love and a feeling of compassion, of oneness with everyone, with a wish that they too know what we know.

So, to repeat, we have gotten to the point where we have learned how to better control life and make it happier. Now we should try to make it happier for others who want it. This does not mean stopping our own growth—that we never do. We keep working for our own further growth by helping others. Any questions on that?

Q: I feel that I have to work for a living, and I've got to pile up so much money or so many goods, and that if I give somebody else something, well, then I won't have. Isn't that basically wrong?

Lester: Yes.

Q: Because, in reality, I don't have to work for a living. Isn't that the first thing I have to know to get rid of—that idea that I have to work for a living?

Lester: Yes. However, we should feel that we would like to give away what we have, and this is the way you'll feel later on. You'll just want to give away everything; you'll have to control yourself. The world is in such a state that people think all they need is things, and if we try to provide things, we're not really helping them. We're confirming that they cannot provide for themselves. It's not things that they need, it's understanding. Just look at the wealth and the accompanying unhappiness in our country today.

Q: That is a little different slant, which is very important. Giving them things without giving them the power to be the thing they really want is not giving them anything.

Lester: Yes. Comparatively, things are small when wisdom is gained.

Q: But you see, I don't demonstrate this. We have come to the point where we have an easier life, a happier life—I feel I can talk for all of us—but certainly, at times, we sure fall on our faces.

Lester: Some of us do, but why?

Q: Because we think limited thoughts?

Lester: We're trying to be happy in the business of everyday livingness itself only, aren't we?

Q: I, speaking for myself, would say "yes." When a deal goes through, I'm happier than when it doesn't.

Lester: Right. Try to not be the doer. Let go and let God. Be happy at making others happy.

Q: Because, in truth, all there is is God, perfection. But I put my fingers in and mess it up, don't I?

Lester: Yes, you do. But you don't have to.

Q: Just let go and let God?

Lester: Yes, why don't you do it? Why don't you let go and let God?

Q: I would say habit is in my way.

Lester: It's habit, all right, but why allow the habit to run you? You're living in a world of separation: there are you and people and deals. If you see the Oneness, you begin to live for others. You see them as you.

Q: But the others that I see come to me because they want things. I never had anybody come to me and say, "I want peace."

Lester: That's your consciousness. Expect to meet people who want peace. Then peace seekers will come into your experience.

Q: You spoke of love and compassion. Define what they mean.

Lester: Love is only understood when you love. Basically, it is the attitude of givingness, with an understanding of and an identifying with others. Compassion is understanding what the others are experiencing without sharing their misery and with a wish to promote its alleviation.

Q: Love, as far as I feel, then, should be wanting for others the same as I would want for myself with no feeling of "I am limited."

Lester: Yes.

Q: This group is trying to rise high.

Lester: All right, what should we do now since life has become happier? The next step is to live more outwardly, more expansively; live for others, or live *more* for others. This, in another way, is seeing God everywhere and in everyone. Feel that everyone is you, because there is only one Beingness—you. There is only God, and God is All. Therefore, that which I am, my Beingness, is God!

One who is not in some way helping others is injuring them. This "some way" is basically and generally in thought. Any thought other than one of goodwill or good wishes toward anyone is injuring others and is therefore injuring oneself. The above is effected through the interconnection of all minds, and by the fact that the law of compensation, i.e., karma, is effected in the thought whether the thought is carried through into action or not.

Your helping others is more by your attitude of how much you love them than by your behavior. When you love, you are very constructive whether you are in action or not. Just feel love and your thoughts will be those of love.

Thought is far more powerful than action. Thought is the basis of action. It is the initiator. It comes before it. It determines action. The degree of the lack of recognition of the woes of others is the degree of one's ego. The more one knows his Self, the more compassion and desire one has to help others. The more you are capable of loving, the more you are helping the world. All minds are interconnected; all minds interact and inter-react. The more an individual increases his love, the more everyone is helped.

Your thought force either helps or hurts the world's spiritual progress and is consequently hurting or helping yourself. He who is not helping the world's "upliftment" is helping its degradation. The greatest good is done by the person who best understands himself. Everyone can be helped in every situation that involves more than one person, and no one has to be hurt when love determines. When you let someone know you are doing something for them, they are obligated to return a "thank you." When they don't know and don't return, then the Infinite returns, *overflowing*.

When I give and you give back, you stop me from receiving a blessing from the Infinite. It's helpful to you to help others, provided there's no ego-motivation behind it and that it's done without attachment. A high Being sitting in a cave somewhere all by himself is doing much good for the world by his sending out powerful thoughts of love and peace.

To the degree that we know the other one is perfect, to that degree we are effective in helping the other one. Charity is aiding and abetting the lie that God will take care of the sparrow but not man. Charity is saying, "You can't help yourselves." Charity is good and necessary for one who is at that level of givingness and havingness.

The greatest thing we can do for others is to help them to help themselves. Blessed is the giver, because he is the happier if he gives from his heart.

To the degree you straighten out yourself, you may help others. Again, I say you're not going to help others any more than you help yourself. But try to help others because that will help you to help yourself. You don't need any special training to help others. You do it naturally, from your own state of Beingness. Everyone is a teacher teaching at his level. He does it unconsciously in his daily relationship with others. The greatest givingness is not in things. The greatest givingness is your attitude of love. Giving out money is like giving out snake protection (the snake and the rope concept). The greatest giving is giving the understanding that there is no snake from which to protect yourself.

Have an attitude of givingness. It's not how much you give, it's your attitude. Some people give to hospitals, etc., to get their nameplates on them, and that is the extent of their reward. Whatever we do, we should do with a desire to serve. Serve with the feeling that it is not you but the God in you who serves. The giver should say, "Thank you" and the receiver should say, "You are welcome." (The giver is the more blessed.)

The less ego we have, the more we know the perfection of others. And it's to the degree that you know they're perfect that you support them in their being perfect. A completely giving person always has whatever he wants. We help mostly by raising our own state of Being. The higher you go, the more you lift everyone. When you're holding good thoughts, you're sending out good thoughts to everyone. When you're helping others, where's your attention? Selflessness is an excellent yardstick by which to measure the state of Beingness of an individual.

Givingness is also a good yardstick. One's state of Beingness is proportional to one's feeling of givingness, one's wanting to give. Does a master ask things from the devotees, the disciples? A master is all-givingness. Our feeling of givingness should be equal toward everyone. Giving to someone who likes you is ego-motivated. A master has equal-mindedness toward all.

Anyone who has spiritual pride is only giving out words, and the other one picks it up as words with no import or authority. To help another, you have to equate him to you, i.e., not think you are spiritually higher. When one understands, one sees everyone equally as a master. If everyone lived only for others, that would right the world. It would make it a utopia! When we live only for others, then we're at the top. Any and every relationship should be for the purpose of helping the other one attain realization or for your being helped in attaining realization. Service to mankind will get you full realization if you do it with no interest in the fruits thereof.

Releasing Explorations by Hale Dwoskin

Are you ready to see everyone you meet as you? If we all saw everyone we met as our very own Self, we would all treat one another with respect, caring, and a feeling of giving. There are so many issues in this world that would be completely resolved in this way. Would you steal from yourself? Would you make war on yourself? Probably not. So why do we do it to others? Because we believe in the basic lie that "I am separate from you and I therefore need to look out for 'my' interests even if that means it will hurt you." Discover the truth of the statement, "You are me—I am you—There is only One," and you will end all your troubles.

You are the most helpful to apparent others to the degree that you are aware of your true nature. The more you recognize the Truth of who are, what you are to that degree you automatically share that with others.

Allow yourself to be open to meeting supposed others who are looking to discover their true nature or just looking to find real lasting happiness. Allow yourself to share with them, to the best of your ability, the Truths that you are discovering through these sessions and from all of your helpful explorations of Truth. As you do, make sure you only share that which you have been able to prove for yourself.

Make sure that you share with an attitude of supporting them in discovering their own truth, not by trying to impose what you believe on them. Also, make sure they are truly interested in Truth. Do your best to refrain from imposing this on anyone.

As you meet people, ask yourself, "How can I support this person in their freedom?" As best you can, allow yourself to give support without looking for anything in return—even recognition for your helping. Remember the highest help you can give anyone is to see him or her as already perfect—already freedom. It is to grant the other one their Beingness—Awareness.

You can also explore the following Holistic Releases.

I am not you—I am you.

They need help—They are perfect as they are.

I can help them—the One is the only helper.

Healing

Lester Levenson

I see there are several doctors in our group. A doctor, who is already trained in the field of healing, becomes a better doctor when he seeks for deeper understanding of life and finds more of the basic causes behind the life in a body. Now, getting into the personal life of a doctor, I'd say, "Gosh, you're in a sick business!" And your seeing this sickness is unhealthy for you unless, in your mind, you reverse all this sickness that you apparently see.

Q: Well, that's the one question I had for you tonight. I don't know how you knew that.

Lester: I wasn't conscious of it. When I let go and let God, the questions in the minds of the listeners usually get answered.

Q: I feel this very strongly, and how do I reverse it?

Lester: You see, the mind is only creative, and it creates the pictures we hold in mind. Having a picture of sickness, we tend to create sickness, unless, as we see it, we mentally reverse what we are seeing.

Q: Would you define what you mean by "reverse"? I had a patient today, for example. I'd like to reverse the whole incident, or I'd like to do what Goldsmith writes, which is you see none of the imperfection, you see only the perfection of God. But when I looked at the patient today, it was very difficult for me to see any perfection.

Lester: You're in a most difficult situation. It's easy for me, because I have been doing it for sixteen years. When people say, "Oh, this is bad, and this hurts, and the doctor said that," I hardly hear it. I become aware that they are telling me there is imperfection. I see that they are trying to convince me of an illusion. I look at them, and I know the perfect Being that they really are. I immediately reverse the apparent imperfection by seeing their perfection.

The Truth of our Beingness is absolute perfection. The more you study the Truth of perfection, the more you will realize and know it, the more you will see what they say is an apparency and the more able you will be to take care of it. But it's going to take a knowingness on your part of the Truth behind this world. That Truth is its Beingness, its existence, which is the source of its apparency.

Q: Well, you say exactly what I read, but I have not had the realization of it.

Lester: Because you are so much with the apparency as being real, it makes it extremely difficult to see the absolute perfection that actually *is*, here and now. If you've read Goldsmith, I guess that what I'm saying is very familiar to you. However, you must discover the real you in order to discover the apparency of the world.

Q: Yes.

Lester: Let's take the snake and the rope idea—have you heard that? We see a rope on the road at dusk, and we think it's a snake. The moment we think it's a snake, we're very involved in fear and want protection from this snake. There's quite an involvement so long as we think it's a snake.

Now, the reality is the rope. The illusion is the snake, and that is compared to the world. The world is the snake. The reality (the rope) is just behind it and is the basis for it. So long as we keep looking at the illusion of the world, we do not see the reality of it. It requires getting quiet enough with oneself to see the reality, the basic reality being, "I Am That I Am."

We are that infinite Beingness of the world, and what is required is quieting the mind enough so that this infinite Beingness that we are is self-obvious. When you discover that you are a perfect Being, then you will know it. When you see your real Self, then you see that the perfection that you are is omnipresent. And this perfection is the rope, wrongly seen as the snake. So, what is necessary is to stick to this path, meditate, dive within, and dig within until you see the reality of you.

When you see the reality of you, you'll see the reality and perfection of the world. And although it now looks like many bodies and much separation, when you see the Truth, you'll see an absolute Oneness wherever you look. You'll see nothing but you wherever you look. You'll see that this whole world is in your mind. You'll see it's your universe. You created it just as you create a world and people in your night dreamworld.

So, to sum it up, you're in a very difficult situation because of your profession, but that doesn't make it impossible. If your wish to discover the Truth is strong enough, you'll see it.

Q: When you see it, and that so-called "ill" patient comes to you, you don't see that at all. You just see perfection.

Lester: Yes. By your knowing he is perfect, you help him drop the image of illness that he holds in his mind. If people come to me and tell me of body ailments, I don't see it, I don't hear it. As they're telling it to me, I'm mentally saying, "You are perfect." You should do this.

Q: And you're speaking of the perfection of the spirit.

Lester: I'm speaking of the perfection of the person I'm talking to. The sick body is an illusion. The person is real.

Q: You mean the twisted—

Lester: The distorted body is an illusion. But, until you see it, it doesn't seem that way. Take a mirage on a desert where we see water in the mirage. If we never check it, it always seems to be water to us. If we go over to the spot and discover it is sand, from that point on we know the water is a mirage. The next time we see the mirage, we still see the water, but with this great difference: we know the water to be an illusion.

Until we discover the reality of the body and the world, we are looking at an illusion as real. Discover the real you, your Beingness, and only then can you know the reality of the body and world.

Q: In dealing with a patient, if I see the perfection, that helps me. By seeing the perfection, am I helping the patient?

Lester: To the degree that we know the perfection of the other person, we support the other person in knowing his perfection. To the degree that he accepts it is the degree of his healing. When these faith healings, or instantaneous healings, happen, it's because the one who had the sickness within him sees the perfection, and there's an instantaneous healing.

I can't have a sick body without having a mental picture of sickness. It's impossible to hold anything in the body that's not in the mind. The body is composed of carbohydrates, minerals, etc.; that is, it is only matter. It has no intelligence. We are the intelligence; we image and hold the life of the body. It's impossible to be sick without holding that sick picture in our minds, unconsciously, of course. If it were conscious, we would correct it immediately. Being unconscious, it's difficult, because we are not looking at it. Have you seen spiritual healings? Have you seen so-called "miracles"?

Q: Yes.

Lester: Well, then you know it is possible. It's done simply by the individual who's running the body—mentally changing things, that's all. The instant we change the mind picture, the body changes. But, again, because the sick picture is unconscious is the reason it's difficult.

Q: How can we become aware first of our unconsciousness and make it conscious, and secondly, how can we help the mind visualize much more perfectly that which we wish if we do not know perfection ourselves?

Lester: To become aware of our subconscious, we must engage ourselves in the practice of honest introspection. The more we turn our attention within, the more we become aware of our subconscious thoughts. When we become aware of any subconscious thought, we are able to do what we want with it as it is now on the conscious plane.

The more we practice this, the more proficient we become. We get to know the perfection by looking in the direction of where the perfection is. The perfection is in here, where we are, where the "I" of us is. So, first, we have to direct our attention inwardly; we have to pose the question, "What am I?" until the answer comes. When the answer comes, you know, and you know you know. And to get the answer to "What am I?" it's necessary to still the thoughts. The thoughts are the noise blanketing the Truth. The thoughts are concepts of limitation, and there are many of them constantly bombarding us.

Q: Yes, yes, when I've sat quietly, I've had this experience. How can you make the mind quiet?

Lester: Intense and persistent desire to discover what you are. When your interest in knowing what you are becomes stronger than your interest in this world and body, then your thoughts of the world and body are quieted, and you discover that you are not the mind, that the mind is an instrument you set up and is other than you. Then you are in control of your mind. Intense and persistent desire is the key.

Q: The reason I asked this is because I've come to a point in my life where I've made it real for me that nothing that happens in my life that is bad or good is outside myself. In other words, I create this. If something is wrong, I originated it. I'm responsible for my life; I'm creating my life from moment to moment. Now I've come to this; I accept it. I take full responsibility, but I'm stuck. I've seen this, now I want to go beyond this. I want to break the barrier. See what I mean?

Lester: Yes, you want to go further. Taking full responsibility is an excellent means of growing, because you will get to see your mastership. You will get to see that whatever is happening to you, you caused.

Q: Oh, yes, yes, definitely, I agree.

Lester: All right. You first become master over matter—and body is part of matter—then you become master over mind. Now this is the part you want.

Q: Right.

Lester: When we are master over mind, then we are a full master. So, you keep on until you gain that mastership. In the Eastern teachings, they call this *tapas*, discipline. Mastering the mind is: consciously changing your likes and your dislikes; walking out into the cold and not minding it; walking into a high temperature and humidity and feeling comfortable; having pain in the body and not being bothered by it.

Q: That's conscious suffering?

Lester: No, you don't have to suffer when you can do this. When you know you're not the body and the body pains, you know the body is in pain, but it just doesn't bother you. Just as when someone else's body hurts, you do not feel it because you do not identify with it. If you would identify with that other body, you would feel the pain of it.

Q: Yes, I understand that. I've come to a point where my body might be hurting me and I say, "My body is hurting," but in my mind, I feel good. This is what I mean, I feel good. I had tremendous disorder this past week: I misplaced a few things, and I went through such a mess, and I was observing myself constantly, but behind the whole thing, there was something that was always, you know—

Lester: Always okay, all right. There's a well Beingness behind the whole thing.

Q: Right. Now, how do I get to it and *hold* it?

Lester: By continuing to do it, you develop it more and more until someday it remains permanently. You'll have complete mastery over the mind, and then you're a master. Are you your mind?

Q: Am I my mind? My answer to that is partly intellectual and partly feelings, and I think that no, I am not my mind, but I am the life behind it.

Lester: Yes, that is the right attitude to take. The mind is a composite of thoughts. Who thinks the thoughts? You do, see? So, you are other than the thoughts if you are thinking the thoughts.

Continue what you're doing, continue working to master the mind. The more you do it, the more you will see that you are not the mind, the more you will see what you really are.

You've got a wonderful method. Take full responsibility, then work to master the mind. If you can have pain in the body and not mind it by saying, "I am not the body," and the pain gets to be dull, what you are actually doing is moving out of that body. You're moving your center of consciousness out of the body. Most of us put our center of consciousness right within the body, and we are imprisoned by it. But it is possible to operate the body from outside the body, and this is what we should do. We should see the body as other than we. Then, as a puppet, move it around. And this practice will get you to the full knowingness that the body and mind are external to you and are at your command. And when you see this strongly enough, you'll throw the mind out. You'll work in the realm of omniscience, which is just behind the mind.

You won't need to think anymore. Everything will be known and perfectly in tune. Every action will be a right action, because you'll be initiating it from omniscience, which is perfect. The mind is imperfect, because it takes tiny bits of omniscience and lets them filter through it. Am I answering your question?

Q: Yes, you are. The thing, I guess, that has stopped me is my desire to experience supposedly some of the psychic phenomena that come with development. In my studying and reading, I became interested in astral projection, or the ability to see the aura, because I was a doubting Thomas. Something in me has grown that needs no proof, but still I would love to experience, just for the sake of experiencing, one of these things.

Lester: Getting interested in these psychic powers is a wrong approach. Being interested in the powers, one might develop the powers. Then, using the powers without having your understanding up to them, you will misuse them. You will use them too selfishly, and they'll boomerang and hurt you, your growth and the powers, causing you to lose the powers.

This happens to all psychic people who develop beyond their level of understanding. So, I suggest that you develop your understanding until all the powers naturally open up to you, and then if you choose to use them, you'll use them rightly, and you won't be hurt.

Someday, we all go back to recognizing that we are all-powerful, that all the powers are ours, and they happen with no effort. When you try to develop these powers, it's extremely difficult, because you need to use effort, right?

Q: Right.

Lester: The state in which all powers exist is the effortless state. And the reason for that is it's the ego concept with its concept of limitation that requires effort. In omniscience, omnipotence, we need no effort. If we are the all-powerful Self, there is no effort needed. It's also in the idea of letting go and letting God. When we let go of our little ego-self, then we can let any miracle be, and it is instantly effected without effort by just letting go and letting it be. Does that make sense?

Q: Yes, very much so.

Lester: So, developing powers isn't something we should strive for. And when they do come, should we get interested in powers, then we are interested in the external, illusory world. Powers are simply taking the external material world and working it short cut. We work the world miraculously just by eliminating time, effecting things instantaneously.

Q: When you say you picture a perfect body, what do you picture as a perfect body?

Lester: Well, I never suggested that you picture a perfect body. That's picturing the perfect trap and prison. There is no better prison than this physical body. However, if you're going to image yourself as a body, image a perfect body, an ideal body, completely free from pain, distortion, imbalance, etc. Can you picture that? It's hard for you, because you've experienced so much imperfection in body, but you can do it.

Q: I have personal problems, and if I could be just a little specific, I might get past this point. I had a patient yesterday who is a Jehovah's Witness, who would not allow blood to be given to him. They did the surgery supposedly to save his life, and throughout the surgery—which was at least three times longer because of complications—he lost at least half of his blood volume, which is close to the point of no return. I am in surgery, taking care of this patient.

Lester: Is it your responsibility?

Q: Yes. I have the problem of thinking, "Well, it's his business. If he wants to die, let him die." But I can't do that. Am I doing a wrong thing by using my desire? All I said was, "God, you take care of him, and I'll just be your helper." That's what I did.

Lester: If you did that, it works, doesn't it?

Q: It does work. Am I imposing my will on anyone when I do that?

Lester: Not when you let go and let God, you're not.

Q: I don't want to impose my desires on these people.

Lester: You are not imposing your will when you let go and let God. If you can do that, you're a great, great doctor.

Q: Thank you. Now I want to find out if I am doing that.

Lester: You know by experience. That man could survive even if he lost all his blood—if you let God take care of it. Everything is possible to God.

Q: That's what I did. I don't know how to pray. I don't know how to say the prayer for this patient.

Lester: Yes you do. Your prayer is, "Whatever is best for him should be." The prayer is there all the time; you don't have to voice it.

Q: That's what I've said, and I didn't know if it were sufficient.

Lester: It's sufficient. The prayer is there whether you voice it or not. He's alive, isn't he?

Q: Yes.

Lester: When a person decides to die, no one, but no one, is going to keep him alive. We can't keep anyone here who has really decided to leave. And you've seen the opposite, where the body has had very little chance of surviving, yet the person lived. See, it's the individual who's running the body who really makes the decision. We can only guide and support them.

Q: Is there a subconscious desire to leave?

Lester: Yes. Also, we all have preset the time when we're going to leave.

Q: Oh, we've already preset it. Can we change that presetting?

Lester: No, but you can transcend it. When you transcend it, you do not die. You consciously, and by choice, leave the body in a manner that you choose. You can't change the karma of the body. That's a law we set up, and it goes on and on. In trying to work out karma, we are creating karma. The only thing we can do is rise above it. When we get above it, if we want a body, we can make a hundred bodies. But when you get above it, you're not that foolish to limit yourself into a little physical body.

The most extreme limitation that you can impose upon yourself is the state we call physical. And when you get above it, there's no need for it. You've had your lesson. If you want a body, you'll use an astral body, which moves around instantaneously, and if it is damaged, you will instantly straighten it out. When you get above the physical body, unless there's a reason, and there could be, for you to maintain one, you won't maintain a physical body.

So, to answer your question, you can't change a preset course, but you can get above it to where the body becomes like a puppet to you. Everything in the physical is cause and effect, action and reaction, and this is called karma, the law of compensation. When we know this, it makes life easy, because we do not fight it. Now, this can help you in your profession. Everything is going to be exactly as it has been predetermined by us. We can't change anything in this life. We can just change our attitude toward it.

However, there is a free choice. It is to identify with this physical body or to identify with our real Self: that's the free choice. When you identify with your real Self, everything is perfect. When you identify with the body, you necessarily subject yourself to untold bodily misery. Worldly life necessitates pounds of misery for every ounce of pleasure. But we're so steeped in the misery, we don't know really how much misery we're in. We reach a tolerance point at which we can tolerate very much. I guess you know that from your experience.

So, the thing to do is to properly identify with the infinite Beingness that you are. Try to accept the physical state as an illusion until you actually see it that way. When you see it that way, you see it as a game, and you play that game knowing that it's only a game. Now, all these things cannot be done intellectually. You have to experience this knowledge. If you accept anything I say just because I say it, you're just harming yourself; you're working on hearsay. You must experience this yourself. You must prove it out yourself, then it becomes your knowledge and is useable. The only thing I can do is to point out the direction, the way, to get this knowledge.

Q: Other than what you've told us tonight, how can you heal yourself except with realization?

Lester: To relate things relatively, if a person can spiritually heal himself, he should; it's instantaneous. If he can't, he should do it mentally, which is from instantaneous to quick. If he can't do it mentally, he must do it physically: he must go to a doctor. So, we use that which is available to us. I suggest to people that they see doctors because that's the level of healing that they need, and it will help them. Doctors are necessary, as necessary as they are today. You wouldn't have this large medical field if it weren't necessary to help those whom the field is helping.

Q: I've read in so many writings that the state of celibacy is necessary for realization. Is this true?

Lester: This thing we call happiness is merely the infinite Beingness that we are experiencing to more or less of a degree. The real Self we are is infinite joy, and if we would take it only directly from where it is, that's all we would have.

But we miserly take it, in tiny amounts, through external means by assuming that we need something: we are not whole; we are not complete; we need something out there to make ourselves complete. And we create a want, a lack, which, when we fulfill it, the thoughts for it drop away—and when our thoughts drop away, we remain at that moment more in our real Self. And that's what is called happiness, joy.

So, any time we are seeking joy in the world, we are fooling ourselves into thinking it's out there, creating a need for it, satisfying it, and feeling a bit of pleasure, which is only a relief from the agony of a desire. But we are trapping ourselves into thinking that the thing out there gave it to us. What we did was to still the thoughts for it, create enough mental quietude to allow the Self to be a little more, and that's what happiness is.

Now we have to give up all that seeking for joy externally. So it is not only sex, but it is everything out there that we credit as giving us happiness. Point one. Point two. Giving it up and intensely wanting it can be as mentally disturbing as having it. What we have to do is let go of the desire for it, which seems impossible for most of us. So the best thing to do is, rather than fight it, be moderate and keep digging for the Truth until some day we get the understanding of what that joy was that we were having in sex.

And then we see that we are always in a state of joy that's higher than anything that sex ever gave us, and it's no problem to let go of it. Then, if you try to enjoy through sex, instead of it giving you joy, it takes a bit of it away, because you're limiting it through the sex act. So, the main thing is be moderate as much as you can. Stay away from it as much as you can, and, as you get your realizations, you'll get to a place where you'll let the whole thing go because you've got the joy all the time that you were trying to get through sex.

Now, the pleasure we get from sex is merely being more aware of our Self by the stilling of the thoughts. There are more suppressed desires and thoughts over the many lifetimes on sex than any other thing in life, so that when we satisfy ourselves sexually, we still the greatest number of subconscious thoughts.

Q: You mean we have brought thoughts into this life from past lives too? And we have to quiet all of them? *Mama mia*!

Lester: Eventually, you get to the place where you can drop the whole remainder of the mind. To sum it up, celibacy does not give realization. However, you won't get realization without it and also the dropping of all desire. But, as you grow, it gets easier, and you reach a point where it's very easy to let go of sex.

It's silly to tell someone to let go of sex who's so involved in it that he can't. A person like that has to be lifted to the point where he is able to let go of it. I guess there's another reason why people are down on sex. Originally, we created bodies mentally. In the Garden of Eden, we decided to do it the way the animals were doing it. And we got caught up in that. And it's a mess.

We are now on the way up. We'll reach a state where again we'll let go of the animal way of procreation, and two physical Beings will get together with one astral Being and create a third physical body into a family. And when we do it that way, we don't lose our memory of the past. And someday we return to that, here on earth.

And so, desire for sex is a thing that has really run us down lower than anything else. And, unconsciously, the race knows it and makes it evil. It's such a stupid approach we have to sex, "it's evil," and yet we all come in that way. But people don't see the overall reason why and therefore distort it. Eating food is evil if having sex is evil. The evil thing is creating lack and then a desire for something and keeping ourselves bogged down in this delusion. So I see food as being as evil as sex, if either one of them be evil. The thing to do is to attain the desirelessness state. No desire, no needs, and then you are in the happiest state.

Q: When I have nothing to do the rest of the day, I ask myself, "Well, what am I going to do? Want to go to a movie? No, I don't want to go to a movie. Want to go visit? No, I don't want to go visit. I don't want to do anything." So I force myself to do something to fill my time, because what am I going to do, sit?

Lester: Yes, and dig into yourself to learn more of what you are. The more you learn of what you are, the happier you will be, and, therefore, your restlessness will drop away. And this can be a joy beyond anything in the world.

Q: Then it's not necessary to be coming back and coming back? One can do it in one lifetime?

Lester: Anyone can do it in one lifetime. This is a great advantage that we have that we are not aware of. There is a small percentage of the worlds in the universe as difficult and as gross as our world. And because it is so gross and it is so difficult, the incentives to get out of it are the greatest. Therefore, we can go all the way back home from where we came—all the way into infinity—this lifetime.

Releasing Explorations by Hale Dwoskin

Are you your body? Most of us live like the body is the all of us when in fact it is the least of us. If you are having physical difficulties, you can use your mind to aid yourself in your healing. However, it is important to honor where you are. If you need external support, make sure you get it. There is no shame in that. The more we can accept our current level of understanding, the more we can move above it.

One powerful way to aid your body in the healing process is to do your best to begin by loving your body as it is. The more you love and accept your body as it is now, the more you allow universal energy to flow through that body. You can ask yourself, "Could I allow myself to love and accept my body as it is?" If there is any holdback or hesitation, you can follow up with "Could I welcome that?" "Could I let that go?" "Would I?" and "When?" Even simply fully welcoming the holdback or hesitation allows it to dissolve. Remember that letting go is just a decision that is always available to you if you are open to it.

Nothing we do in this book is meant to take the place of competent medical attention. We make no claims to treat, diagnose, or cure any disease.

There are two exercises that can help you support yourself in your freedom and in good health. First, allow yourself to recognize that you are not the body. The more you identify with your body, the more you will feel disturbed by anything that appears to happen to it. You can follow Lester's suggestion of saying to yourself, "I am not the body." You can also allow yourself to be both as identified with the body as you are and as free of the body as you are by using a polarity while focusing on a particular physical problem. "I am the body—I am not the body" or you can use "I am the [name a body part]—I am not the [name a body part]" is a good one. In fact, if you focus on a particular part of the body, it is often easier to see that as not what you are.

The second exercise is to allow yourself to see the problem as just a memory that you are constantly recreating in this moment, thereby missing your underlying perfection. You can explore this possibility by using these questions: "Can I allow myself to remember how I used to have this problem [whatever the apparent physical problem is]?" As best you can, allow yourself to see it as a memory. Then ask yourself, "Could I let go of wanting to have that problem again?" "Would I?" and "When?" As you catch on to this way of working with any of your problems, they will easily start to dissolve.

You can also use any of the following Holistic Releases.

I am the body—I am not the body.

The body is the all of me—The body is the least of me.

There is a body—There is no body.

That is my body—That is the body of God.

233

The World

Lester Levenson

This session is composed of aphorisms that were collected from various talks by Lester. Please spend some time pondering each aphorism before moving on to the next one.

We perceive the world through our physical body—more specifically, through our five physical senses. If we perceive the world and our physical body through our physical senses, then we cannot be the body vehicle that we are perceiving through, it being an instrument that we are using. Our prime object is to discover the perceiver.

Say to yourself, "I am not this body, I am not this mind—what am I?" In the background of all seeking and thinking, always keep this quest going. The more difficult the world is, the more incentive there is to seek the true happiness, the Self. When life is easy, the incentive is not as strong. This human, physical life that we are now in is the most difficult of all living that we will ever experience, and, therefore, it presents the greatest opportunity for growth and realization. However, if one does not seek the Self and goes along with the world, then one's delusion and ignorance increase, and that is the extra hazard of being in this difficult world. When things get worse, if you lose your head, the masters cannot help you. If you don't lose your head, you can see it as a motion picture and grow through it.

The world has a slave consciousness. Man is convinced that it is necessary to work for a living, and therefore it is. Were this not so, nature would freely supply all needs.

If you want to know how much hatred there is in the hearts of all Americans, look at the present conditions and the war. However, we are not going backward spiritually; we are advancing, in spite of what you see. We have been in a docile state of deep apathy, holding subconscious thoughts of hostility, and now we are moving up and out of it. This is shown by our ability to express our hostility. Expressing is higher than suppressing, and this is what is happening in the world. You see it throughout everything today. The people are growing.

However, the important thing for you to know is that there is nothing out there in the world but your consciousness. Let go of hostility and war and see the peace and harmony just behind it. A master, a Christ, sees no hostility and destruction; he sees the Truth. He sees God as All. Now, if God is All and God is perfect, where is there imperfection? In truth, in reality, there is none. You must get to see this. You have to start with the correct assumption that God is All and God is perfect, and if you look through that consciousness, that is all you will see.

We should not get too interested in this world if we want to know the Truth.

The more you want and have of the world, the more you let go of your limitless joy.

The things of man are not the things of God, and man wants foolishly to hold on to the things of man.

The world is nothing but a grinder-up of bodies.

Desires bring us here and keep us coming here until we tire of it and have no more desire for it.

To play with this world, to try to make it a good world—as is generally done in metaphysical teachings—is fruitless as far as realization is concerned. However, it is useful in giving us a life that is more conducive to seeking the Truth.

Accepting people's limited ideas of the world is injuring the world (and yourself).

Accepting worldly limitations adds your force to them by your validating them.

Education today is *mis*-education. We are taught limitation and illusion. The most important things are not taught. Colleges have no courses on the most important subjects: happiness, love, and the life-principle itself.

What we call knowledge in the world is ignorance. Everything that man is trying to learn is constantly changing; therefore, all of it is incorrect. That which is true never changes. The knowledge of your Self requires dropping all knowledge of the world.

The world authorities are generally those who don't know.

The more multiplex one is, the more multiplex is the world.

When we want to change the world, it is the ego playing God.

People set the vibration of a place.

The whole world is thrashing, dashing, gnashing, gashing, and slashing, which, in the end, results in ashing.

Exclusiveness is a blight on the world. Oneness is its salvation.

You cannot exclude even one percent of the people in this world and attain realization.

A frustrated person is one who attempts to do and carry out things by himself instead of letting the forces of the Infinite do it.

The real history of the world is not a series of dates, battles, and events. It is the continuous story of its spiritual growth. Someday, the history of this world will be rewritten correctly by a master, but not until the world wants it.

Clairvoyance and TV are similar except that clairvoyance is on a much higher frequency.

People are like dogs with a mean master: No matter how much the world beats us, we keep coming back for more.

The world has moments of pleasure with far more pain in between.

Chasing after joy in the world is an extremely frustrating thing. Has anyone attained full satisfaction in this world?

Never let anyone know or tell anyone your weaknesses. People accept us at our own values, and their mind goes to work to support the concepts.

Our vision of the world is our own. No one sees this world as any other sees it.

If the world pulls you down, it is because you have its negativity in you.

Weather is caused by the total of all peoples' consciousness.

The world beats you until you know your Self.

There is no such thing as a good world. It's the most extreme limitation man can impose on himself. It is the most hellish hell that he can live in.

The world is a grand graveyard: Everything in it dies or disintegrates.

If the world is real to you, you are all the time validating ego.

All knowledge of the world is knowledge of delusion and must be let go of for realization.

The highest enjoyment in the world is a mere pittance compared to your natural inherent state of joy.

The more real the world, the greater the misery. The more real the Self, the greater the joy.

There is much more to this world than meets the physical eye. That which the eye sees is the least.

The world is only God chopped up into little nothingnesses.

The world is one long misery when seen as world, but it is eternal joy when seen as your Self.

The world is powerful only because we have been in the habit of it for a long, long time.

Progress in the world lifts us from the physical agonies to the mental agonies. The world is a trap, attempting to trap Infinity into finiteness—an impossibility!

The true view of this world is intense joy. The deluded view is misery. See the world aright and have nothing but joy!

The absolute perfection is above the perfection of the world.

The only good world is a transcended world.

When you take your attention off the world, you can see what you are.

If you do not know the world is in you, how can you let go of it?

If the world is out there, what can you do about it? Any pleasure in the world is a momentary ego satisfaction.

The world is a limitation, no matter how high you go, until you see the truth of it.

People who have enough spiritual understanding don't need laws, don't need parliaments.

The only way to get a good society is to get the individuals composing it good.

All legislation is to control acts resulting from selfishness. When all are selfless, no laws are necessary.

In the not-too-distant future, the president will be the highest spiritual person in the country, the vice president the second highest, and so forth.

The world as world is one long sadness. The world as Self is one constant joy.

World equals misery; Self equals joy. The cause of misery is that you think the world is real. The cause of joy is the knowing that the Self is real.

In the world, we are seeking to know the truth about the world as we see it. This is tantamount to wanting to see the truth about a lie. There is no truth, no changelessness, that can be found in the world. *Only* within our Self can we find the truth of the world.

It should be obvious that, with all the tremendous increase in knowledge of the world acquired in the past twenty-five years, man has become less happy rather than happier. Any knowledge other than knowledge of one's Self is not right knowledge. It is because of the aforementioned that our authorities of today are of muddling minds, are constantly changing their knowledge and theories. Some day they will discover that they are about ninety percent wrong. Only the knower of his Self can be correct in the knowledge of the world. He can change the ninety percent to zero percent.

The world is a play act. You have written—in your imaginative mind—the script, the acts, and the actors, and you see yourself as one of the actors. Recognize this and dwell in your authorship.

The limiting of Infinity gives the appearance of matter and energy.

You have to master the world; otherwise, it is master over you.

If there is anything in the world we like or dislike, it is master over us.

Use the world to transcend the world. Look at your attachments and aversions to them and drop them.

Not seeing the world as it is is an aversion to it.

You have to start mastering the world, because you are convinced the world is master over you. You must see that you are the one who determines it. That makes you master over it. The next step is to become master over your mind, and then you are a master. (It's a nice feeling when you start mastering the world, isn't it?)

The world is a tremendous magnet.

Primarily, you have to unwant the world and want your Self.

You don't have to be subject to anything, because you are master of everything.

The truth is, we created the stars and the planets. The important thing is to run them. Don't let them run you.

Look at the earth's influence on you and undo it.

Rather than being locked into the world automatically, keep up your vigilance of remembering your true Self.

The world is a very good place for rapid growth, because your ego is being presented to you every time you talk to someone or someone talks to you. Daily, look at your ego motivations and let them go!

Every act in the world is motivated by your ego until, of course, there is no more ego. Then action goes on without ego.

After you scorch enough of the mind, the world doesn't trap you.

There is an immediate realization of the Self the moment one sees the unreality of the world.

When the eye sees the world as "I," that is realization.

Now you see the world as a very variegated variety. When you see the singular substance just behind it, you see the reality of it. Seeing the reality, you will see the singularness as the Self, your Self.

When you see the Self, the world does not disappear; your view of it changes. It will not look like it does now. You will see it as your Self.

The only reason people do not get realization is that they have more desire for the world than for realization.

It is the belief that the world is real that is the cause of one's difficulty in keeping out habitual thoughts. Were it not for this belief, realization of your Self would be easy. And this is your prime difficulty, this belief that the body, mind, and world are real.

Our pleasures must be taken directly, not attributed to things outside of ourselves.

Looking for joy in the world makes realization impossible. The source of that joy is you, and it is not outside of you.

Only desire for this world keeps us in the world.

You are causing everything around you, even when someone else seems to be doing it. When you realize this, you'll take responsibility for everything.

If you don't like the world, change your consciousness. That is all there is out there—your consciousness—and it's the only thing that you can change, the only thing that you should try to change. Make the world perfect by perfecting your consciousness and all will be perfect. The truth of the world is just behind what you now see.

Declare your mastership rather than be a victim.

The whole world is just a mere thought—think on that!

I and world, seer and seen, rise simultaneously, concurrently, codependently and necessarily coexist. The creation is instantaneous with the creator. Realize this. There is no world without the one who sees it. Realize the seer, within whom the apparency—the world—was imaged. The reality then is only the Seer.

Releasing Explorations by Hale Dwoskin

How much do you try to make the world real every day? We spend our lives trying to create changelessness where the only thing that is constant is change. If we would just allow ourselves to let the world unfold as it does and remain focused on the changeless background that we are, we would always be happy and free.

Allow yourself to look at your world honestly. See how much you have become the victim of the world by validating its reality over your own true nature. Make a list or just notice the particular parts of your life that are really pulling at your awareness throughout the day, either appearing as good things that you try to hold on to or as problems that you try to solve.

Engage in the following process to set yourself free. Remember, these things in and of themselves do not need to be gotten rid of or changed, they only need to be correctly seen. Focus on one item at a time, and ask yourself this series of questions: "Could I allow myself to dislike that as much as I do?" "Could I allow myself to like that as much as I do?" Keep going back and forth until you have neutralized your attachment and aversion to the item.

You can also ask yourself, "Could I allow that to appear as real as it does?" and then, "Could I allow that to be as unreal as it is?" Again, keep going back and forth between the two sides of the polarity until you can answer the next question in the affirmative. "Could I let go of wanting that to be real?"

When you are done, allow yourself to move on to the next item from which you would like to free yourself. As you go through this process, you will find that your desire to make the world real and give it power over you has begun to drop away. It will be replaced by the joy of being That which is always right behind all phenomena.

The more you believe the world is real, the more you are the victim of this projection. You can let go of wanting to make the world appear real to you by asking yourself, "Could I let go of wanting to make the world real?" "Would I?" and "When?" Or you can ask, "Is that real or is it merely imagined?" As you let this go, you see the dream nature of the world more, yet you still find that you naturally take care of yourself and your responsibilities with greater ease and certainty and less pain and suffering.

A Perfect Body

Lester Levenson

Should we try to achieve a perfect body? I would say yes, definitely yes, if you can't do it.

Q: If you cannot do it?

Lester: Yes.

Q: That's a contradiction!

Lester: No. Change your inability to being able. If you cannot perfect the body, you should learn to do so.

Although we should be able to perfect the body, once we are able to do that, then it is better to let the body be the way it is, healthy or sick, and not be affected by it. When one has enough understanding, no matter what happens to the body, it is all the same to him. I've given you an overall approach, and now I'll go into it in more detail.

If we want a perfect body, and we don't have a perfect body, it means that we don't have the conviction that we can make the body perfect. It means we are subconsciously holding in our mind a consciousness of an imperfect body. The body is an exact copy of the mind, the body being only our consciousness projected outwardly. We must change our subconscious thinking until we subconsciously have the conviction that our body is perfect. That will do it.

Now, is it necessary to have a perfect body? No, it is not. However, it is necessary to have a perfect understanding. To get this understanding, if you cannot have a perfect body, then learn to make your body perfect. When you can, then go beyond the necessity of a perfect body by getting the spiritual understanding of "I am not the body" and "The body does not affect me." This is a much higher state. In fact, this is one of the highest of states: to be able to maintain your equanimity regardless of what is happening to the body!

This body is not infinite. It's an extremely limited vehicle and is very, very delicate. Change the internal temperature twelve degrees and it dies. Put tiny amounts of chemicals (poisons) into it and it dies. Cut out oxygen and it dies. So, this body is an extremely limited vehicle. It is much better not to be the physical body, but to be what you really are and get out from under the fear of death, the basic fear behind all other fears.

The discipline of having an imperfect body and not allowing it to bother you is a very high spiritual discipline. Many fully realized masters go through life with a sick body, setting an example of non-emphasis on the body, because the body is a cage of limitation. We are not in the body, the body is in us. Our greatest limitation is, "I am this body." Not only is the body a limitation, but also associated with it are hundreds of other limitations.

So, although at first I corrected bodily imperfections instantly, I now prefer not to correct the body, but to have it touch me not—not even in the slightest—regardless of what is happening to it. This is something I started three or four years ago. I can tell you what happens when you do not identify with the body. I was just thinking of the time I was loading trees for firewood onto a truck, and one tree wouldn't go. I said, "I'll make this go," and I gave a tremendous push while I had my shoulder against a tree trunk. The tree went on, and I slipped a disc at the bottom of my spine.

The reason why I mention this incident is that it was an excruciatingly painful one. Immediately, I almost collapsed from the pain. Then I said, "Lester, be not the body." Now what happens is that the body doesn't bother me if I'm not the body. I was aware that there was a pain, but it was like a weak, distant pain, and it did not bother me. I could immediately load other trees. The body acted just as though it were not imperfect.

I've done that at other times. I once sprained an ankle and it swelled. That's painful too and, when I did not identify with the body,

I walked off as though the foot were perfect, yet there was a sprained ankle there. When I had that slipped disc, I'd awaken in the morning and, forgetting, I would not immediately not be the body, and the pain would be severe. To get out of bed, I'd actually have to fall out on my hands and knees. I remember doing this the first day or two. Then I'd shake my head and say, "Wow, what is this?" Recognizing the situation, I would say, "Oh, I am not the body"; then I'd stand up, move through the day as though the body were okay, and the body could do anything and everything. There was a weak, distant pain that I knew was there, but it didn't bother me. Now, this type of disciplining is excellent if one can do it. Be not the body!

Q: Wouldn't it be so much simpler to say, "The body's perfect," and then have a perfect body? After all, you control your body—why even have the pain or feel uncomfortable when you get out of bed?

Lester: Well, when I got out of bed, I was identifying with the body; that's why it pained so. But the moment I didn't, everything was all right. I'd stand up, and the body would do anything. Now, this is a test of your spiritual knowingness. This is much higher. This is being not the body.

Q: How can the body be imperfect when you said before that your body is a reflection of your mentality? And, if you know that there's only perfection, how can you have an imperfect body?

Lester: At first I identified with the body and then, after minutes, I did not. You want me to come down a step? Or do you want me to stay where I am?

Q: All right, go ahead and stay up where you are.

Lester: A perfect body is not the highest state. A body is a limitation even when it's perfect. It's a perfect body. It's still a body, but it's perfect. A higher state is not being the body but being the All. Ah, you're shaking your head now. Have I answered it?

Q: I'm beginning to follow what you're getting at.

Lester: So, again, it's a matter of level, but because we're now into a level that is high, I want to stay there. Be not the body! Be what you really are! Be infinite! Be the All! Perfection is not a perfect body. Perfection is absolute perfection.

Although you have a tendency to bring it down into perfect things, perfection does not relate to things. No thing is perfect. Everything is a thing of limitation, confined to form and space. So, the top state, the absolute, is a state of no things. It's just Beingness, or pure consciousness, pure awareness. That's not being a body, a thing. It's just Being.

So to sum it up, of course, we should have perfect bodies! If we have bodies that pull on our attention all the time, it's difficult to seek the truth. So, rid yourself of bodily demands. Make the body as perfect as you can. However, it is a higher state when the body does not affect us because of our not identifying with the body. Is it clear now, these two different aspects of body? It's great to make a perfect body. It is far better to be not the body.

Q: You see, it's very difficult for me to be Beingness or awareness without being something or aware of something.

Lester: You and most of us. But the top state is just Beingness, only Beingness, or consciousness, only consciousness. It's consciousness conscious of all consciousness. It's Beingness being all Beingness. And consciousness and Beingness mean the same thing at the top.

Q: Well, can't we enjoy the limitation at the time?

Lester: You can. You can if you choose, but that's not the ultimate joy. If you want more joy, don't enjoy the thing—be joy! Happiness is our natural, inherent state. We are the All. We artificially create a lack and then a desire to relieve that lack, which, when that lack is undone, we feel better.

It's like sticking a pin into yourself. It hurts, and you take it out and say, "Gee, that feels good." This is exactly what enjoying things and people is. We hurt ourselves by creating a lack and then remove the lack, the pain, and say, "Gee, that feels good. That makes me happy." Every time you feel happiness, you feel only your real Self, more or less. The happier you are, the more you feel your real Self, and you wrongly attribute it to things and people outside of yourself.

The mechanism of it is this: When you create the lack, you start up thoughts of I need this person, this thing, to make me happy. That causes a bit of pain—a need, a lack—which, when you are relieved of that thought of lack, you return back to being your Self, and this is what we call happiness. This is something very great to be achieved: to see that your happiness is inherent. That which you have been calling happiness is doing away with happiness, and then restoring it and wrongly attributing it to external people and things.

So, if you want to enjoy a body, that's your privilege. If you want more joy, don't enjoy the body, just be joy, which you naturally are. That's the natural state. It's not necessary to need things. When you see that you are the All, there's nothing lacking. So, take your joy directly, be your Self. That's being infinite joy.

Q: Now step down and discuss your experiences of changing your body, because, really, many of us are in the area where we don't quite understand this. Let's talk about myself, not "we."

Lester: Okay. What happened to me was that I saw that there's as much life in this body as there is in a piece of wood. It's composed of carbohydrates and minerals, the same chemicals as in a piece of wood; the only life in this body is "I." I put the life into the body. I saw that the body is my consciousness, and my consciousness puts the life into it. When you see that you make the body, then you can change it. You can mentally change it.

Now, the body we have now is the accumulated education, body-wise, that we have gathered up-to-date. This is my concept of a body, that's your concept of your body. It's deeply subconscious right now. This is why it's difficult to change the body. To perfect it requires a seemingly impossible letting go of all these past concepts of imperfection of the body. This, however, is the negative way of doing it—that is, of eliminating the negative concepts of imperfection. It's a difficult way.

251

Then there is the better way, the positive way, of putting in what should be there: a picture of a perfect body in your mind. Now, this picture of the perfect body must be put in with a willpower more powerful than the sum total of all the pictures in the past of an imperfect body. You must image the picture of a perfect body with a thought that's stronger than all the past thoughts. Does that make sense? This is the mechanics of it.

All right, now what is a powerful thought? A powerful thought is a concentrated thought. The more concentrated, the more powerful the thought. A concentrated thought is a thought without other extraneous thoughts present at the time. The very best way to get a most powerful thought is to let go of your self, your little self. Let go of your feeling: I am this person, I have this, I have that. Then say, "Yes, there is only perfection, and that includes this body." Let go of the world, let go of your thinking that your mind is your biggest obstacle.

Your mind is going all the time, whether you're aware of it or not. When you're not conscious of it, it's going on subconsciously. You've trained yourself to think, think, think. You've got the mind spinning with all these thoughts. You've given a lot of importance to this thinking. The importance of it is also subconscious, so it's not easy to let go of the importance of thinking. And this is an obstacle to your concentrating.

If you could let go of thinking, and in just one easy thought with no other thoughts around, think "I am perfect," you'd instantly have a perfect body. It'll take a continuous trying until you achieve it. An almost effortless thought is the way it is effected, because your mind is quiet at the time. And you might not even be aware of it when it happens. You might become aware of it later on.

I was just reminded of a case of a man who was in a wheelchair for many years, I believe ten. His house caught on fire, and he packed two bags, ran out of the house, and sat down on them. It was after he had sat down on the bags that he had realized what he had done. He had forgotten that he couldn't walk. See, when it does happen, you're accepting the positive so much that the negative is forgotten for the time being.

To sum it up, the thing that will effect a perfect body is a very strong conviction that, "My body is perfect." Saying it another way, it is a concentrated thought, which is a thought undisturbed by other thoughts at the time. And the feeling is a feeling of let go. You just let go and let the perfection be.

Q: Well then, what you're really saying is that when you see all-perfection, your thoughts are so based upon perfection, your body automatically takes that perfection.

Lester: Yes, if you see the all-perfection, then everything is absolutely perfect—everything.

Q: Then you cannot have an imperfect body.

Lester: Right.

Q: And this being very, very peaceful. If you go into psychosomatic medicine, they claim that the body difficulties are caused by turmoil in the mind. And if these are quieted, then the body may be corrected without any thought about it.

Lester: Yes, if you quiet the subconscious mind. You see, the body is working on automatic pilot. Everything happening in the body, we are doing subconsciously, automatically. So, you have to straighten out the subconscious thinking.

Q: When you were in New York and you accomplished much, did you do it systematically? Did you just see perfection so completely, or did you realize the power of your mind? Just exactly what method did you use?

Lester: Well, when I did it, it was almost like a byproduct. I sat down with a determination to get the answers to, "Who am I? What am I? What is this world? What is my relationship to it?"

In the process of which, I saw the perfection, and that this universe—including this body—was a product of my consciousness, my thinking. I therefore imaged the body as perfect, and instantly it was. Gone were the ulcers, the jaundice, the coronary trouble, and other imperfections. It was very easy. It was like an almost effortless thought.

There are different levels of healing the body. Spiritually, it's instantaneous. There's only perfection, and that's all there is, and it is instantaneous. Mentally, it is done from instantaneously to very fast, in days or in weeks, depending upon your mental concept of how fast you can do it.

Q: When you're using the word *body*, it also would include all our environment, wouldn't it? There's really no difference between our body and our environment.

Lester: That's true in the sense that it is all our consciousness, but I'm speaking specifically of the body, because we're talking on that. Actually, the whole material world and the body are very similar in creation. They are the physical out-projecting of our mind.

Have I answered all your questions on it? See, it does not help you much when I tell you what I did. You've got to do it your way. And, as I see it, your way is overcoming the accumulated wrong body-thinking of the past.

Now, this is a carryover from a prior life. This is how deeply engrained it is in you. If you can perfect it, good. If you can't, don't make a big issue of it, because it's better to live with it and not be it. Get your spiritual understanding. That's far more important. What's so great about the best of bodies? They decay sooner or later. The very best of bodies becomes awfully stenchy sooner or later when it starts decaying. So what's this big thing about bodies? Approach it from a higher point.

Q: As I understand it, if I have a sense of perfection, which would include my body, the body could not be imperfect.

Lester: That's correct. Get it! And when you get it, not only the body, but everything becomes perfect, which is far better than having just a perfect body. Then you have the whole universe perfect, and that's a very, very high state. To see the perfection where the imperfection seems to be is the highest state.

Releasing Explorations by Hale Dwoskin

If you believe that you can't have a perfect body, then allow yourself to let go until you can have the perfect body. Once you have achieved that, allow yourself to move above it to the state where there is knowingness that you are not the body. The body is the least of you, not the all of you. You would find this easy to do if you did not see the body as real but accepted it as an out-picturing of mind. As Lester used to say, this is either easy or impossible. It can be easy when you truly let go. It is up to you.

Remember, nothing we do in this book is meant to take the place of competent medical attention. We make no claims to treat, diagnose, or cure any disease.

You can allow yourself to see the perfection of the body if you also allow yourself to welcome and release the apparent imperfection. This simple exercise will help you do so. Focus on your body or on a specific physical problem that you believe you have and then use these questions to allow yourself to dissolve the picture of imperfection. First, "Could I allow my body to appear as it does?" Welcome this picture, knowing it is just a picture, as best you can. Then allow yourself to picture how you would like it to be. Go back and forth until both pictures dissolve and you are simply aware of the body as it is without wanting to change it.

If you do this exercise with an open mind and heart, and you accept at least the possibility that your body is just a picture in mind, you will find yourself dropping the pictures of an imperfect body and accepting the possibility of perfection here and now.

This next exercise will help you to start to recognize the body as a picture in mind. As you move through life, use these questions to stretch your consciousness beyond the obvious. Allow the body to be in motion, doing whatever it is doing, and then ask yourself, "Am I moving or have I never moved?" Another way to do this is to ask yourself, "Am I moving?" Allow yourself to feel, hear, and see what that perception is like. Then ask yourself, "Have I never moved?" Again, allow yourself to perceive what this is like as best you can. Go back and forth between these two perspectives and allow them to dissolve each other. You can take time out to do this exercise or simply occasionally do it throughout your day to interrupt the pattern of believing in the reality of the body.

You can also allow yourself to explore the question, "If I am not the body, what am I?" However the mind responds to this question, then ask, "If I am even more than that, what am I?" Keep going in this direction until the mind runs out of answers and you are at rest as the Presence-Awareness that you are. As you explore these questions, they will lead you to see that which is already aware of the body but not confined by it.

Growth Can Be Every Day

Lester Levenson

Most of you don't realize that every day you are presented with wonderful opportunities to make major steps in your growth. Were you to look at and see this, the goal that seems so difficult and elusive would soon be in your possession. Awaken to this fact and be done with worldly miseries.

To do this, you must accept the worldly happenings as they relate to you as your means of growth—yes, even as your teacher. You must look at all the unpleasantries; you must face them squarely with an objective eye, and you must seek and find their cause.

The method should be either or both of two approaches. Whenever someone or something bothers you and you are unhappy, or whenever you react to someone or something, ask yourself, "How and wherein did I cause this?" Look within your mind to find the past thought, now subconscious, that caused the event. Discover the originating thought in you, and you discover your mastership over the event.

The second approach is more readily available to you. Every time you react or experience something unpleasant, it is always because of some ego-motivation. Ask yourself, "What is my ego (selfish) motivation behind this? What, in this situation, do I want to be different from what it is?" When you discover it, drop it and be freer. Use your daily unpleasantries for growing freer every day. The more you do this, the faster and easier it is to do.

Either or both of the above methods will free you and return to you your mastership in a relatively short time. Make it a habit of using both, or one or the other, every day.

Whenever you're unhappy, do not look for escape from it via

distraction, doing something else, or seeking entertainment. This is the worst thing you can do. You will never be able to let go of or eliminate unhappiness. Either discover your mastership of the event or see the ego-motivation behind the misery, and thereby undo that particular unhappiness.

Almost everyone, when unhappy, looks for escape and calls the escape or relief from the misery happiness. This allows the unhappiness pattern to continue in the future. It postpones the time indefinitely as to when one will have to eliminate the unhappiness. Escape is the worst palliative in the world—worse than drugs. Every escape is a complete waste of time and a further continuing and holding on to misery. The more you feel misery, the deeper it becomes ingrained. Therefore, one should not escape from nor remain in misery, but should use one of the above two methods to get out of it permanently.

The rest of this session is comprised of a series of aphorisms collected from many different talks. Please allow yourself to read them one at a time, taking as much time as necessary to uncover their deepest import for you.

All unhappiness is caused by our trying to be limited, to be an ego. The more we are our Self, the happier we are. We will never be completely happy until we are completely being our Self.

Why waste time in entertainment, in escape? Looking to entertainment each time delays and pushes the goal a bit further away. Only a realized nonattached Being can enjoy things in the world without creating bondages and miseries.

What everyone is looking for in entertainment is escape from misery and the happiness of the Self.

Escaping misery keeps you forever miserable.

Problems are a constant reminder that we are in the wrong direction.

Every pain is basically a pain of limiting your Self.

A person cannot be happy if he has inner anxieties. Anxieties are expecting to happen that which you do not want to happen. Expect only that which you do want.

It's the ego-sense of being a separate individual that is the source of all trouble.

All unhappiness is separation. Limitation and misery are the same.

Misery is caused when an infinite Being tries to be a limited being.

If, when you are miserable, you would think and feel the opposite, that is what you would effect.

Misery is complexity. Happiness is simplicity.

If you see misery, it's your misery. When you see the perfection where the seeming imperfection seems to be, the misery is only an apparency.

The more miserable you get, the less you should look for an escape (socializing, entertainment). Rather, isolate until you see and let go of the reason for it, or move into your real Self. Never let go of—through escape from misery—a good opportunity to grow.

Misery is just the whip we set up to whip ourselves into happiness.

The more we move away from our Self, the more miserable we become, until finally we get so miserable that we cannot take it anymore, and then we begin to move back into our Self.

You create a lie when you say, "I don't have," and that starts the unhappiness of not having.

Any time you're miserable, you're dwelling in your ego. Just being miserable should be a realigner for you. Say, "Here, I am in the wrong direction," then change it, and you'll be happy again.

Anyone can feel happy; anyone can feel miserable. You don't have to see why—just change it!

Every worldly attachment is a dedication to misery.

Misery is the setting up of limitation.

Misery is to the degree that we think we are limited.

Every pleasure in the world has an accompanying pain, because there is associated with it the feeling that this pleasure may not be sustained in the future.

You turn your feelings on and, if you take credit for them, you can turn them off—that is, control them. However, be careful not to suppress them.

If you really see the reality of a problem, it is licked.

You can resolve any problem here and now.

Every problem is an ego problem. In order to have a problem, there has to be an ego-frustration.

Martyrdom can be ego.

Suffering is the opposite of godliness.

Suffering is not spiritual.

God is joy. Suffering is Satan.

The more you suffer, the more you will suffer.

Suffering karmically develops and leads to more suffering.

Suffering is good when it drives you to God, or to seek your Self.

Every time you feel miserable, there is present an excellent opportunity to make a big step forward.

The less we allow our Self to be, the more miserable we find ourselves.

Feeling sad about anything is holding on to it. Say, "This is something I have to let go of," and immediately you will feel better.

When you are miserable, you shouldn't try to escape it. Get quiet and go within until you see the reason for it, or better, be your Self.

If you will take full responsibility for feeling bad, you will feel like a master.

Every time you feel restless or unhappy, there is ego-desire behind it. If you can get it up into view, you'll let go of it with a chuckle. It's an opportunity to let go of something that's running you. Look for the ego-motivated desire, and, when you see it, let go of it and immediately feel lighter and happier.

Every time you drop ego, you experience joy.

Discover who the sufferer is; on discovering this, you find all joy.

Releasing Explorations by Hale Dwoskin

You can discover that in this moment, if you do not go into memory, there is no suffering and no sufferer. There may be strong sensations and circumstances that are not ideal for the body-mind however suffering is created only when we believe that there is a separate "me" that suffers. This separate individual is not real and has never been.

When you experience what you would call pain or suffering, allow yourself to discover who is suffering by asking yourself, "To whom is this experience?" or "Who is having this experience?" What may arise first is "me" or some intellectual substitute for the Self. No matter what answer arises, ask yourself, "If I am more than that, what am I?" Whenever your mind answers that you suffer, you can also ask yourself, "Am I that or am I that which is aware?" If you really look, you will discover that you are the Awareness, not a person who suffers. Keep going along these lines of inquiry until the illusion of suffering and a sufferer dissolves into the silence of the Self.

Another powerful way of letting go of any apparent suffering you are experiencing in this moment is to notice that all suffering is only an appearance on the surface of consciousness and at your core there is already perfection.

Diving into the Core of the Emotion

Now, if you look at any object and magnified it large enough, it would appear more and more like empty space. You would be looking into the gaps between the molecules and atoms. When you dive into the very core of a feeling, you will observe a comparable phenomenon: Nothing is really nothing there.

As you master the process of releasing, you will discover that even your deepest feelings are just on the surface. At the core, you are empty, silent, and at peace—not in the pain and darkness that most of us would assume. In fact, even our most extreme feelings have only as much substance as a soap bubble. And you know what happens when you poke your finger into a soap bubble. It pops. That's exactly what happens when you dive into the core of a feeling. Here is what you may experience: You receive some news that gets you upset. You start to feel a strong feeling of fear or grief, and you have the time to take a few minutes to release.

You sit down, close your eyes, and relax into the feeling as best you can. Then you ask yourself questions like:

What is at the core of this feeling?

Could I allow myself to go in consciousness to the core of this feeling?

Could I allow myself to dive into this feeling?

Could I allow myself to see past the surface of this feeling to what is at its core?

You will probably come up with your own versions of these questions as you work with them over time. You may picture yourself actually diving into the center of the feeling and / or you may find yourself merely feeling what is at the core. Once you start to go deeper, you may experience various pictures and sensations. You may also notice a temporary intensification of the emotion. So, keep asking yourself, *Could I go even deeper?* Cajole yourself to go even deeper beyond whatever picture, feeling, or story you may be telling yourself about the emotion.

Family Relationships

Lester Levenson

Why do we marry? Why do we have children? What are we seeking in marriage? In children? The answer to all these questions is: We want the greatest happiness. We believe that in marrying, and in having children, we will be happy. Were that true, all married people would be happy. A mere look at our institution of marriage belies this.

Wherein lies the fault? Is it in marriage? No, the fault lies within us. We wrongly look in the wrong direction. We externally seek happiness outside of ourselves, in others. We shall never find a continuous happiness with no sorrow so long as we look to others or to things outside of ourselves. A happy person is one who takes his happiness from within; he is happy whether married or single. Should we marry or should we not marry? That is a moot question. You will do exactly what you will do. You have predetermined precisely what you will do on this point. Therefore, the important question should be: How can I attain the ultimate happiness?

Marriage affords an excellent opportunity for growth and should be so used. One is constantly confronted with situations where one may increase one's love for one's family. Every day we should make it a practice of increasing our love, using all the situations we find ourselves in wherein we are not loving to the best of our ability by consciously increasing our love for the other one until it is a completely selfless love. When we reach the state of selfless love, we have reached the Godhead.

Q: What a difficult thing it is to be married, Lester.

Lester: Some people find it very easy. The difficulty is in us and not in marriage.

Q: It has a positive aspect, hasn't it? Isn't there a release from selfishness?

Lester: Yes. Marriage should teach us selflessness.

Q: So, in that way, there is a positive step, if it's handled correctly. It teaches love of one person, therefore you can enlarge it in the family and then on to a larger unit. Isn't that true?

Lester: Yes. It's a positive step wherein you're involved in a situation in which you can learn non-possessiveness. It's a very positive step in that direction. The thing we're looking for in a mate is the thing called love. Love is this Beingness that we are. Love is God. Looking for it in a mate, we never find it. However, if one is married, one should very definitely love his or her mate as much as possible.

When we learn how to love a mate properly, we can love others properly. When we realize what love is, and what we are really seeking, we stop seeking it externally in a mate or in the world, and we seek it within. The very best marriage is to marry God. Could you get a better mate?

Q: Should we be married?

Lester: I don't talk against marriage, I don't talk for it. I want you to have what you want for yourself. A married person can find God but has more obstacles than a single person. A single person can more easily concentrate on the path. A married person is forced to be concerned about his mate and children, if there are children. Now, most people who say, "I'll get married and continue on the path," almost invariably get so involved in their marriage they don't have the time nor the inclination for the path. So, in that sense, it's an obstacle.

Q: Unless you married someone who was searching for it also, wouldn't it be a very difficult thing?

Lester: Yes. The very best situation in marriage would be to help the other one get realization. Marry only to help the other one fully know God—that should be the basis for marriage. And the other one should do the same for you. It should be mutual.

Q: It should really be a spiritual state, not a possessive state?

Lester: Love is a freeing of the other one, not a possessing. That would be spiritual.

Q: How best could you guide children into the path?

Lester: The best thing you can do is to set an example. That's the very best way to teach children—by example. They want to be like their parents. So it always comes back to: If you want to help your children, you must help yourself. Then you'll find out you don't have to consciously do anything. Just help yourself, and you'll see them grow with you.

Q: We have two children, and they're really different: They desired to be our children, and we desired them, right?

Lester: Yes. We often choose parents who have characteristics similar to ours so that we can have a constant lesson in front of our eyes. This is why we find parents so difficult sometimes. If there's anything that I see in you that annoys me, it's because I have it in me. If I didn't have it in me, I couldn't even see it in you.

Because we choose parents who have characteristics similar to ours is one reason why people believe in heredity. (We only inherit our physical appearances.) Every child is so different from every other child. You parents know this, that each one is a completely different individual. And if the present environment and heredity had any appreciable effect, they would be very similar.

Q: A thought struck me that a child is born an absolute stranger to the parents. They don't know anything at all about that child. They are a stranger, and it is up to you to make them love you. It is the amount of love that you pour out that induces the amount that they can pour out, isn't it?

Lester: Yes, assuming that our memories are cut off, and we begin at the beginning of this lifetime. But I have to say no, if you take the history before this lifetime. We keep regrouping together. Attachments and aversions to each other keep us coming together lifetime after lifetime. An attachment between two individuals will bring them together again. Or, an aversion will do the same thing, because an aversion is a holding on by holding off. Attachment is holding them to you; an aversion is holding them away from you. But either way you're holding them.

Q: Lester, as a parent, am I loving the flesh or the spirit of the children?

Lester: You're basically loving your own ego.

Q: Because they're part of me.

Lester: Yes. You did it. You created them. You did that tremendous thing. And you want them to be a good example of you. See? Now, if we love our children, we free them; we allow them to grow, to bloom, and come out like a flower does. We don't try to fence them in. We free them and guide them and love them—unattached to them—knowing that they are God's Beings. They are just as much God as I am is the way you should feel. Also, they are going to go through life just the way they have set it out anyway. But you should strive to free them, to feel nonattached. This is a higher love than a love with attachment.

Q: Of course, as you say, you do have to lead them.

Lester: Guide them. And they'll ask you for the guidance if you just free them. But they resent being dominated and dictated to the same way you do, the same way you did when you were a child. They don't like to be ordered around, but they want to learn. They have a natural curiosity; they'll ask you. And if you can start from the beginning by freeing them from the first day, bringing up a child is one of the easiest things to do. They'll follow you. But when you start telling them from the first day what to do and what not to do, they behave like an adult does when being told what to do and what not to do. They resent it. They oppose it. Then, oppositional patterns are set up, and by the time they're able to walk around, they've got this oppositional pattern well developed.

That's what makes bringing up children so difficult. Because of all our attachment, we're trying to steer them, and they resist. We were trained that way; we train our children that way, and they will train their children that way, and it goes on and on. Training could be accomplished without opposition if it starts right. Show them the possibilities, the alternatives, and let them make the decisions. Then they're working with you from the beginning, and they don't develop oppositional habits.

Families are regroupings of people who have been together before. Strong loves and strong hates bring us together again and again. Our attitude toward relatives should be the same as that toward all Beings. The first place to practice love is at home with the family. We should try to love our family more and more by granting them their right to be the way they are, more and more.

It's a great thing for spiritual growth to resolve relationships with parents (even if they have passed on). Parents present excellent opportunities for growth if and when we try to resolve our differences until there is only a feeling of love with no attachment. Family is excellent for bringing up to us all our reactive automatic behavior, because that is where we developed most of it. Giving unselfish love to a child will develop unselfish love in that child this lifetime, and will condition the child for a most happy life.

The main thing that a child wants from us is love, and we cannot fool a child. Children know our feelings, and that is what they read. We fool ourselves with words, but we don't fool them. When children are contrary, it is because they are seeking to get attention from their parents. In early years, this meant survival: If I am approved of by my parents, they will take care of me, and I, the helpless child, will not die. A child tries to be good to get approval. If that's impossible, he becomes bad in order to get attention. This attention subconsciously implies approval. It becomes an aberrated pattern of behavior.

If you can get to see your parents the way they really are and then love them the way they are, you would be accomplishing tremendous growth. You behave most automatically with parents. You'll find your parental behavior patterns applied to the world. You carry on the automatic behavior patterns set up before the age of six for the rest of your life (unless, of course, you change them).

Normalize your behavior with your parents and family. You've got to see your parents the way they are and accept them that way. Nothing should be blamed on your parents. No matter what they do, you should accept responsibility for what you are. Total nonreaction to parents is close to realization. It doesn't matter how we act as long as the feeling within is love. The attitude is more important than the act. Use this with family.

If we were capable of selflessly loving, instead of being in conflict with children, there would be complete harmony. But it is only because we have lost sight of what selfless love is that we are in this difficulty of opposition between parent and child. Parents want to do wrong, yet want their children to do right. This makes the parent look dishonest in the eyes of the children; it disconcerts them, causing rebellious feelings. A child will learn no better than the parent's example.

Our responsibility toward children, because they cannot take care of themselves, is to feed, clothe, and guide them until they are old enough to take care of themselves. But after children become adults, we should let go and let God take care of them, even though they seemingly can't take care of themselves. They need to learn that they too are taken care of if they take responsibility for themselves, or, better, if they surrender to God. The only real difference between children and adults is size and experience.

When parents say "don't," they are instilling inhibitions. When parents say "do," they are instilling compulsions. Both cause feelings of inability in the child. Children we see as an extension of our ego. We should see them as individuals and extend to them the rights we do to individuals.

If you want to help your child, help yourself. Every child is a whole, complete, infinite individual. Seeing truth doesn't belong to married people or single people. It belongs to those who seek and discover truth. Married people can get realization if they are determined to get it. The only happy couples are those with an understanding of truth. They know that their joy is within and not in the other one.

What people are really looking for is love of God. Not knowing this, they look for it in a mate. Once you get the taste of God, it's easy not to marry. You feel no need for a mate. Being married to God, you reach satiety. It's an obstacle to have a mate. It's an added obstacle to have a child. It doesn't have to be; it can be an aid to growth, if we so use it. There is no one married whose unhappiness does not come from looking to the other one for happiness. The only ideal marriage is when each marries to help the other one grow spiritually. The top attainment is to have nothing but love for each parent, each sister, each brother, and each child. Resolve this and you will resolve your relationship with the world.

Releasing Explorations by Hale Dwoskin

How do you feel toward your family? More pointedly, do you have only feelings of love for your family? Congratulations, if you do. You have let go of a lot of attachment and aversion to your family. This will really support you in your self-recognition. If you have any other feelings besides selfless love for them, I highly recommend that you allow yourself to deepen your love for them. As Lester said often, "The freer you are with your family, the closer you are to freedom."

If you do have any feelings besides love for your family, I suggest that you set it up as a goal to continually deepen your love for them until that is all that you feel. A goal many have found helpful is: "I allow myself to love and support my [mother, father, sister, brother, husband, wife, or lover] exactly as they are." And / or "I allow myself to want for them whatever it is that they want for themselves." Remember to release your thoughts and feelings to the contrary to these goals until you experience unconditional love as best you can.

Here is another great way to both increase your love for your family and free them and yourself. When you notice that you are having less than pure love for a family member, ask yourself, "Could I allow myself to love them as they are as best I can?" "Would I?" and

"When?" If you really want to stretch, you can ask yourself, "Could I love them because they are the way they are?" "Would I?" and "When?" As you find yourself saying yes to any of these questions, you are dissolving the barriers to love.

You can also ask yourself, "Could I welcome [however you feel about them]?" and then ask yourself, "Could I welcome the love that is at my core as best I can?" Each time you ask these two question in succession, you will find that the love that you are will shine through more and more.

Lastly, you can explore these statements with an open mind and heart: "I am you—you are me. There is only One. There is no you and there is no me. There is only One." As you hang out with these statements you will find that you are drawn into the living Awareness that is pure love and unity.

Is There a Difference between Worldliness and Spirituality?

Lester Levenson

What is the difference between the divine and the worldly, the spiritual and the material? Is there a difference? Is there a difference between being spiritual and being in the world? There is a tendency for us to separate the two. That is a gross error. There is no difference between the spiritual and the material when we look at it from the viewpoint of truth.

The difference is in our outlook, in the way we see the world. It's the way you look at it, that's all. You may look at it from the ego point of view, or you may look at it from the Self. A realized person sees the world only as an out-projection of himself; therefore, it really is his creation. And as an out-projection, it's like a cinema screen out there with this whole universe projected on it and which, at will, could be changed or withdrawn. To the one who doesn't see the truth, this cinema—this moving picture—seems not self-created and, as such, one makes himself subject to it and becomes a slave to it.

A master is very much in the world; a master has his feet firmly planted on the earth, but he sees the basic substance just behind the apparent world as his very own Self. And when he does that, everything is in harmony, everything is perfect.

It's not a matter of separating one from the other, or having one or the other, it's merely seeing the truth of the world. When one does, one is realized. When one doesn't, one is forever shadowboxing with his self-created world of opposition. Both see the world. The master sees the Truth just behind it, and there's nothing but harmony! The unrealized one sees separation and opposition, and there's much disharmony. The unrealized person sees it as a thing running him; the realized person sees it as his own projection; therefore, he can run it, and it cannot run him. Being a master over it, he resides ever the same, in peace and tranquility, and lives in complete ease all the time.

We must, in our everyday lives, be in that state of tranquility, and, until we can be in that state while in the details of daily living, we haven't reached the top. So, there are no two categories, the world and spirit; it's all one and the same. It's just a matter of the way we look at it. We should strive to get to the place where no one and nothing can perturb us.

When you get to that state, you are at the top. You are in the world, and nothing and no one can disturb you in the slightest. Develop this. Make this a practice. Make this your way of life. Do not react to people; do not become angry, jealous, hateful, and so forth. Remain ever the same, ever the same. No matter what happens, no matter what goes on, you really are ever the same, serene and poised.

Q: But, Lester, when I look at the world, I see differentiation.

Lester: Anytime we see any difference, or a difference between the spiritual and the worldly, it's because we don't have enough understanding of the spiritual as yet. We are separating. The highest state is when we are in the world and in spirit at one and the same time, and there is no difference. When we're there, we don't see it as world and spirit. We see it as one and the same thing. We see a Oneness; we see it all as our very own Self. Or, if we want, we see the whole world as being within us, as a dream is within us in sleep. No matter what happens in the dream, we remain the same. We see absolutely no difference in anything; there's a singular Oneness throughout everything. Nothing changes. Ever-the-same is our feeling.

This can be used as a yardstick to know how far we are on the path. Is everything ever the same? Do things really not change? It is a little shocking when we start examining it from this point of view. How far am I on the path toward seeing the sameness, the Oneness, the no-otherness, the nothing but God, God in all, the

God in everyone? When you accomplish that nonduality, you lose the feeling of "I." If you want to recognize the "apparent" others, you use the word *we*. But more than that, you would rather talk about yourself in the third person.

That is the feeling a master has, and he talks that way. Certain masters will not speak of themselves by name. They'll speak of themselves in the third person as their disciples do. For instance, if everyone called me what Ken jokingly calls me, I would talk about Father Divine. Instead of saying "I," "me," or "Lester," I would talk about him [pointing at himself], Father Divine. That's just the way you feel when you're in the state when all is one and all is the same. You don't identify yourself with just your body. I've been emphasizing this point, because quite a few were asking questions and talking about the two—the world and spirit—not knowing that, in truth, they are one.

Q: There is no difference?

Lester: Right. It's one and the same, when you see it aright. If you see it through illusion, if you see it incorrectly, you'll see separation. You'll see the differentiation that this is spiritual and that is worldly, that this is divine and that is mundane.

Q: The "I's" are our ego?

Lester: Yes. The "I's" are a condescension on the part of a master in order to communicate with the apparent egos. A master sees nothing but masters—specks of infinite light, all looking alike: blazing, effervescent, radiant Beings, points of Beingness all being one. This is the way a master really sees everyone. He doesn't see people the way we see them.

Q: Does he see them as different shades or all one shade?

Lester: Identical points of light, of one ocean of light—brilliant, effervescent, emanating—with center everywhere and circumference nowhere. Are you trying to imagine what it's like?

Q: Well, I had an experience of seeing something like that, and it's a light like a bright sun.

Lester: Yes. A bright, blazing sun. masters can see nothing but a master in us. At the same time, they can go through the pretense of seeing it otherwise, by saying, "Harry, yes, you do have problems," or, "Harry, you do have a body, and you do live in a house." But, as they say it, to them it's like a dream voice talking, or apparently talking, and it's all an apparency. It's a pretense. They're actually pretending, as their view of the omnipresent, infinite One never changes.

Q: They are pretending a duality then, actually, where we're more or less living it?

Lester: Yes. However, we're pretending it too but we don't know that we're pretending it. A master pretends it, and he knows that he's pretending it. We are ignorant of the fact of our pretense.

Q: In that way he's coming down to our level?

Lester: Yes. And he does it only to help us.

Q: Well, why can't I, as a human being, say, "I will play a game of baseball"? When I say I'm a baseball player, I can make myself subject to all the rules. But I don't have to play baseball. So, why can't God say, "I will play the game of being Bob"? And then he puts himself subject to the limitations of Bob as he defines it, as when I play baseball, I make myself subject to the rules.

Now, why can't God, to entertain himself, be a Bob or be a Lester, and be limited, in a sense? The thing is, if I play baseball, I limit myself to all the rules of being a baseball player. Well, then I will play baseball and have a good time and be Bob.

Lester: God can, and does, but he never forgets he is God! Do you never forget?

Q: Therefore, I am God who is playing Bob, and, for the moment, I forgot?

Lester: You only are if you know that, not if you state it. Stating it, lip service, doesn't equate with knowing that.

Q: I agree absolutely.

Lester: So, theoretically, you are right. Now, the important thing is to carry it out practically, to know your Beingness in God while you are playing the game—to know that you are God and that you are pretending to be limited as a body and so forth.

Q: And any time I don't want to, I don't have to play, and I don't have to take that particular step of being limited, because I am the creator of the game. I make the rules, and I don't have to play any more than I have to play a baseball game. I can quit just like that [finger snap]!

Lester: That's the way it is. All right now, when you don't really know that you are God, you can discover it by tracing the source of "I." If we trace the source of the ego, "I," we'll discover it's the infinite Being. If you'll trace the source of the mind, you'll discover the same thing. The infinite Being is putting this pretense of limitation, ego, and mind over itself so that we don't see this statement of Truth: that this world is only God playing a game of apparent limitation. The way to discover it is to seek the source of the ego, "I," and, if we stay with it, we'll discover that it is really the Infinite I that I am.

Q: Well, according to you, if I play the game of ball looking up to God, then I don't have it made. If I do anything at all looking out from God, then I know who I am. But if I play the game looking up to God, from the outside, then I don't know.

Lester: You are very right. Translating that into Christ, if I look up to Christ, or believe in Christ, that isn't it. I have to look out through the eyes of a Christ. I have to believe as Christ believed; I have to be as a Christ. I'm just taking what F said and putting it in a biblical way.

Q: It's in what you say. I read it in the Gita this morning and also in what you say, so you get your stuff from a good source.

Lester: I always start with stating that this knowledge is not mine. It is Truth: I can't make it, I can't unmake it. I can recognize it or not recognize it. That's the choice that we have, to recognize the Truth or not to. We can't make it, we can't do anything to it—but we can recognize it.

Q: All the books that I read say the same thing: Patanjali says it, Yogananda says it, the Gita says it, and the Vedas say it. They all say it.

Lester: And they said it a thousand years ago, a million years ago, a billion years ago, a billion, billion years ago; and in the future they'll say the same thing. Because Truth is that which never changes; It is changeless. The basic Truth will never, ever change in all eternity, and you can know this for the entire universe.

If somebody comes from a planet billions and billions of light years away and tells you otherwise—no matter how high he looks, acts, and talks—if it doesn't fit in with what you know of the changeless Truth, you can be sure he's wrong, even though he's acting and looking like a god.

Do you know what I'm saying? Even if an angel tells you something, if it's not in accordance with Truth, reject it, because there are so many high-appearing Beings that look like gods that you can be very easily fooled—until you know the Truth. Truth is the same throughout, from infinity to infinity.

Q: We're trying to get ahead as quickly as we can, and we listen and read, and we think the right thing to do is to be on the path—but I go to church, and I see a priest or a monk up there, and he's been struggling on the path for twenty years. How can I make it quickly when I see in front of me someone who has been on the path much longer, and he's struggling?

Lester: All right, look at it this way. If you want to go from Los Angeles to New York City and the direct route is not known to you, you start probing. You might go up to Washington State first, then cut eastward, then come down to Nevada, then go up to Montana. However, if you know the direct route, you take the direct way and get there much sooner. Probing may take you a whole lifetime. Going directly, you could do it in three or four days' time.

Q: Don't say another word to me, because I got the answer.

Lester: All right. Now, the priest or monk doesn't see the direct route, and he's probing and he's learning bit by bit. He'll get to New York eventually if he keeps trying and wandering all over the United States.

Q: But doesn't each of us have different abilities? One person gets over something very easily, very quickly, and someone else has a problem that's deep-seated, and it's been with him a long while, which takes a very active struggle to get over?

Lester: Yes. However, quickness of realization is determined by the intensity of the desire for it. How far have we gone in our desire for it? If we've gone very far, the realizations come fast and easily.

Q: And we stick by them then?

Lester: Yes. They really stick with you. I say to you: I'm not teaching you. You're getting something you've known. You are doing it; you're just re-remembering things you've always known. I can't give you this knowledge; no one can. I just suggest, and you open yourself up to that which you already know, have always known, and always will know, subconsciously.

Q: In other words, you just read a page of your true Self. Well, it's Self-realization, actually.

Lester: Yes, and this is also true: If you haven't grown much, or as much as someone else, you can go way beyond that one if you have a very strong desire for it. Only a very strong desire for full realization will give it to you this lifetime. Anyone who has only a desire for Truth will get full realization quickly. You can override your past conditioning when you want to. How long should it take an infinite, omniscient Being to know that he is omniscient, omnipotent, and omnipresent? How long should it take him to do that?

Q: One realization.

Releasing Explorations by Hale Dwoskin

Allow yourself to explore the possibility that there is nothing separate from the Truth of who you are. The more you explore this idea, the more it will dissolve the illusion of a world that is separate from you, revealing that which is beyond the world of ideation.

The following exercise can be done as you appear to move through life or you can take specific times to explore it as a way to open to Awareness. Allow your body to be in motion as it is, and then allow yourself to shift gently between the two following perspectives, engaging yourself as fully as you can in each. Let yourself hear, see, and feel what it is like to explore the statements while you go about your activities. "I am in this scene—This scene is in me." As you do this, you will move beyond the usual boundaries that appear to confine you.

You may also want to explore the following Holistic Releases.

I am me—I am blazing, effervescent, radiant Beingness-Awareness.

I am here—I am everywhere and nowhere.

I am in the world—The world is in me.

All about Love

Lester Levenson

I thought tonight I might talk on the subject of love. *Love* is one word I don't often use, mainly because it's so misunderstood. I also believe that only through growth do we understand what love is. Defining it, we just add some more words to the usual words, and it doesn't really convey the meaning. But love is an absolutely necessary ingredient on the path. If we ever expect to get full realization, we must increase our love until it is complete.

Now, the love I talk about, of course, has nothing to do with sex. Sex is a body gratification. However, most of us confuse it and tie it in with love. When you see what sex is and what love is, you'll see that they are two different things. They can be tied together and also they don't have to be. The love that we talk about is the love of Jesus Christ. It's the love complete, which expressed in the extreme is, "Love thy enemy."

I think the best definition of the word is, "Love is a feelingness of givingness with no expectation of receiving for the giving." It's a very free giving, and it's an attitude that is constant. Love doesn't vary—not the type of love we're talking about. The amount we have, we apply to everyone. We love our family as much as we love strangers. This might sound odd, but this is the truth. To the degree we're capable of loving strangers, to that degree we're capable of loving our family.

The concept of possession is just the opposite of the meaning of love. In love, there is never a holding on to, a fencing in, or anything like that. Love has a sense of freeing the ones we love. When we are giving in our attitude, we want the other one to have what the other one wants. I guess the best example of this type of love is the love of a mother for a child. A mother will sacrifice and give everything to the child, without considering herself.

There are other definitions for love. I think acceptance is a good word. When we love people, we accept them as they are. If we love this world, we accept the world the way it is. We don't try to change it, we let it be. We grant the world its Beingness the same way we should grant every other person his or her Beingness. Let them be the way they want to be; never try to change them. Trying to change them is injecting our own ego. We want them to be the way we would like them to be.

Identity is another definition. Love is a feeling of oneness with, of identity with, the other one or all other ones. When there is a full love, you feel yourself as the other person, and you treat the other person just like you treat your own Self. There's complete identity. A constant state of gratitude accompanies a state of complete love. We are thankful for everything. We even thank God for the bad as well as for the good. To understand this requires reaching the state of high love. Only then does thanking God for the bad have any meaning to us. The practical aspect of this is that the more we practice being in a state of gratitude, the more loving we become.

Try this and learn the truth of it. Love is not only a feeling, love is a tremendous power. This is so little understood in the world. We have an example of this type of love being expressed today by Martin Luther King. No matter how much he's attacked, he will give out nothing but love to his attacker. He teaches nonviolence. And the greatest demonstration of this type of love was Mahatma Gandhi's winning a war against Britain. He did this without any arms and through his teaching, when he said, "The British are our brothers. We love the British. Nonresistance to the British and to the British soldiers, only love for them."

Gandhi well understood this and was able to win over enough followers in India to make this effective. The power behind love, without question, is far more powerful than the hydrogen bomb—that is, once you know what love is. Love is the most powerful force in the universe when expressed as love really is, not as we have been taught to think of it. It is said that God is love, and I add, "One with God makes a majority."

One individual, with nothing but love, can stand up against the entire world, because this love is that powerful. Love is nothing but the Self that we speak of. Love is God. When we are only love, we are God. To quote the Bible, "God is love. God is all powerful." So, there's some authority for what I'm saying besides my saying it. Love will give not only all the power in the universe, but also all the joy and all the knowledge.

Now, how do we make this practical? The best way of increasing our capacity to love is through wisdom, understanding. Also, we can do things in our everyday life that will increase our love. The first place to practice love is at home, with the family. We should try to love our family more and more and more. I think everyone knows the wonderful experience of love, of loving one person. Can you imagine what it's like if you loved three billion people? It would be three billion times more enjoyable! Home is the first place to keep trying to increase our love for the ones around us by granting them their Beingness. That's the most difficult thing, I believe, to do in a family, especially if the other one is a child. But every child is a whole, complete, infinite individual and a child of God. Next, after loving the ones in our home, we should try to love our neighbors, then our larger group—our state, our country. Then we should try to love all people all over the world.

Q: The Russians?

Lester: Even Russians.

Q: The Chinese too?

Lester: I heard Oral Roberts say something on that some Sundays ago. He said, "People ask, 'What would the attitude of Jesus be toward the communists if he came back today?'" And he answered, "He wouldn't be the way people expect. He wouldn't have anything against anyone. He would not hate the communists. He would talk against doing wrong, doing evil, but he would never say anything against any human being."

I believe that if we understood the power of love, and that if the majority of Americans loved the Russians, Russia would be won over by the Americans without any arms. After we learn to love all the people in this world, there are many more people outside of this world. I think loving all the people in this world would allow us to meet with our brothers and sisters of other worlds, because in this universe there are many, many mansions—many, many places of abode. And because of our inability to love on this planet, we have cut them off.

So, to come back to the point of being practical: The more we develop love, the more we come in touch with the harmony of the universe, and then our life becomes more beautiful, more bountiful, and more delightful. It starts a cycle going where you spin upward. Love begets love. Love falls in love with love! There is another thing. If we want to be loved, the way to get it is to love. It is not only the very best method, but it is, I think, the only method.

To receive love, we must love, because what we give out must come back. Looking for love without loving does not bring love to us, it does not satisfy us. This is a basic error in many, many people's thinking. They go through life wanting to be loved, never feeling that they are even when they are really getting the love. The feeling has to be in us. If I love you, I feel wonderful. If you love me, you feel wonderful. It's the one who loves who feels great. So wanting to be loved is getting into a direction that can never be satisfied. The happy one is the one loving, the one giving. Blessed is the giver because he's so much happier.

Love should be felt equally for all. When we say we love one person more than another, if we would trace it through by going inwardly, we would find that the one we love more is a person whom we think we need, who has something that we would like to have. Therefore, we say we love that person more.

Actually, love cannot be chopped up. If you want to test your own state of love, look at your enemies. This is the real test. Or, if you don't want to go that far, look at strangers. Examine your attitude toward strangers. It should be one of: they are me, they are my family. Every mother is my mother, every father my father, every child my child. This is the attitude we achieve through understanding. This is the real sense of the word *love*.

Q: Lester, it seems to me you're talking about love as giving, giving of yourself and so forth, and yet the conflict that I have occasionally is that it seems that as you give of yourself, people tend to take more and more. And eventually, if you don't put a stop to it, they bleed you dry emotionally, mentally, financially, and they use you as a crutch.

Lester: That's impossible, if we feel the real love. If we have the correct attitude of love, that doesn't happen. What you're saying, I often hear. What is needed is for us to know what real love is. The givingness is an attitude. We can always maintain an attitude of love. Most people who give are not giving lovingly. They're giving because of the recognition they think they will get for giving: "Look at me; I'm doing good," or "I may get my name in the paper," or something like that. You see, that kind of love will get us into trouble. People will drain us on that, because we're looking for something in return. We're looking to put ourselves up in the process; therefore, they'll pull us down.

Q: Don't you think it's easier to love somebody five thousand miles away than somebody next door to you?

Lester: The easiest thing in the universe to do is to love everyone. This is what I think. This is what I've discovered. Once we learn what love is, it is the easiest thing to do. It takes tremendous effort not to love everyone, and you see the effort being expended every day. But when we love, we're at one with them. We're at peace, and everything falls into line beautifully. The main thing is to know love in the sense that I'm defining it, then those things don't happen. But when we love in the sense that humanity understands the word, then you're right. But I don't call that love.

Q: What do you call it? Or do you have a name for it?

Lester: Selfishness, actually. We are doing things really to help ourselves. And yet in the real love, in the spiritual love, there's no self-abnegation. We don't have to hurt ourselves when we love everyone, and we don't. When we love, there's a feeling of mutuality. That which is mutual is correct. If you love, you'll hold to that law, and therefore people won't take advantage of you.

If you are loving, you're applying the most powerful force in the universe. But it's the love of a Jesus Christ I'm talking about, not the everyday selfish love. Practically speaking, if people are trying to hurt you, and you just feel love for them—if they continue, you will see them hurt themselves. If they continue further, they'll hurt themselves more. They won't be able to oppose you anymore. But we have to practice this love that I'm speaking of, not the love as we have known it.

Q: It's a basic attitude. It's nothing you physically or even mentally do—

Lester: It's a constant attitude that evolves in us when we develop it. However, we should try practicing the love, as I said before. First, on our family. Grant everyone in the family their own Beingness, if you can. If you can't, keep trying—keep trying until you can. Then apply it to friends, then strangers, then everyone. By doing this, you will develop it, although it isn't something you can turn on just like that.

Q: In a way, all of us have it, but it's just layered over by many attitudes?

Lester: Yes, it's smothered by wrong attitudes. Now, this love I talk about is our basic nature. It's a natural thing. That is why it's so easy. The opposite takes effort. We move away from our natural Self and smother it with wrong attitudes.

Q: Isn't love almost like a selfishness—because when you love somebody, it's such a wonderful feeling for you?

Lester: Well, this is a matter of semantics. The way you put it, yes, but not in the general sense.

Q: I know when I love somebody, I feel so good. It's such a wonderful feeling.

Lester: It's true after you discover what love is. It's the greatest thing in the universe. It's the thing that everyone wants only because it's his basic nature in the first place. Every human being is basically an extremely loving individual.

Q: To understand this thing of joy, is it the same type of thing as when your mind becomes stilled in one avenue of thought, of acceptance of the other person, and therefore the mind is stilled?

Lester: Yes. The more we love, the less we have to think. If I'm not loving you, I have to be on guard. I have to protect myself. If I'm not loving the world, I'm always protecting myself from the world, which causes more and more thoughts. It puts me extremely on the defensive. Subconsciously, it builds up year-in and year-out, and then I'm a mass of thoughts protecting myself from the world. Now, if I love the world, the world can't hurt me. My thoughts get quiet; the mind gets peaceful, and the infinite Self is right there. And that's the experience of this tremendous joy.

Q: In other words, it's not the object that brings this out. It's the quieting of the mind that actually lets the Beingness come through a little more, and that really is the love experience, isn't it?

Lester: Yes.

Q: The light shines through!

Lester: Yes. What he is saying is that we take our infinite Beingness, our infinite joy, and we cover it over with thoughts. We take the natural state, which is unlimited, and we cover it up with thoughts of limitation. The thoughts smother this infinite Self that we are. It smothers the capacity to enjoy just being. And so all we need to do is to quiet the thoughts, or rid ourselves of all thoughts, and what's left over is the infinite, glorious Being that we are, which is our natural state.

Isn't that odd? That is our natural state. That's the way we were, that's the way we're going to be. We are actually that now, but we don't see it. This infinite, glorious Being that we are, being absolutely perfect, can never change. It's always there. We just don't look at it. We look away from it. We look far away from it. What we should do is turn our mind inward and begin looking at it, and the more we look at it, the more we see it.

Everything seems to point to the same direction, does it not? That happens as we get more understanding of what life and the universe are. Everything fits together more and more, and gets simpler and simpler, until there's just one absolute simple called God. God is simple; everything else is complex. The greater the complexity, the further we are from God. God is One and only One—One without a second.

Q: If someone else has a desire, and there's a feeling that if I went along with him that I might lose something, then that isn't love. But if my love is complete in the sense of whatever they wish I wish, then I wouldn't be afraid?

Lester: Yes. There's a word for it today: togetherness. It's a very good word. Doesn't that fit what you're saying? Togetherness?

Q: The thought occurred to me that when I know my Beingness, I can't get hurt, so how can anybody else hurt me?

Lester: That's true. It's impossible to be hurt when we love fully. We only feel wonderful when we love—in fact, we feel the greatest!

Q: If you feel a sense of togetherness with one more than another, then you begin to separate?

Lester: Yes, it is not full love. It's partial love, and the more partial it is, the less good it feels. When we love fully, we love every being. We have nothing but a tremendously wonderful, warm attitude that everything is fine; every person is just right. We see only perfection, and that's the way we see the world. When we hate, we see the same world in just the opposite way.

Q: When you speak of giving, are you speaking of giving things or spiritual understanding?

Lester: Love is an attitude of givingness. When things are given with this attitude, it is love. If I give you something because I want you to like me, that is not love. That is trying to bolster my ego. The greatest givingness is giving understanding, giving wisdom. If I give a meal to a man in poverty, four hours later he needs another meal again. However, if I give him the principle of how to produce a meal, he will never go hungry again.

Let me end with a quote: "Love is patient and kind. Love is not jealous or boastful. It is not arrogant or rude. Love does not insist on its own way. It is not irritable or resentful. It does not rejoice at wrong but rejoices in the right. Love bears all things, believes all things, hopes all things, endures all things."

Releasing Explorations by Hale Dwoskin

Think of the last time you felt really loving or in love with a person, a place, or a thing. Now, allow yourself to imagine, as best you can, magnifying this love until it encompasses all supposed others, all places, and all things. This is a little sense of the love that you are and that is always available to you in every moment. Every moment we are either choosing to embrace the love that we are or we are resisting, denying, or ignoring it. What do you choose?

You can easily increase the awareness of the love that you are by doing this exercise. Think of a person—any supposed other. Start with someone who you already feel some love toward. Ask yourself the following question: "Could I allow myself to love this person as much as I do?" Allow yourself to feel the love that you feel for them as best you can. Then ask yourself, "Could I allow myself to increase my love for this person as best I can?" Allow yourself to increase your love for them to the best of your ability. Continue with the second question until you feel you can go no further and are at rest as the love that you are.

Repeat this procedure with another person. Keep this up until you have done it with everyone you know, including the people whom you love the least. Also make sure to include yourself in the list of people on whom you do this exercise.

You may also want to explore the question: "What is love?" Whatever answer arises, ask yourself, "If it is more than that, what is love?" and, "If it is even more than that, what is love?" Continue along this line of questioning until you are at rest as love and the question no longer arises.

Karma

Lester Levenson

For those who are here for the first time, our method is one of question and answer. The reason why we use question and answer is that it's one of the very best methods of teaching Truth. The most effective teaching is individual teaching, rather than group or mass teaching. The knowledge we're after cannot be picked up intellectually, cannot be gotten from books. Were it so that we could get it from books, all we would need to do is to read the books, and we'd have it.

The only really effective teaching is accomplished by the teacher getting the pupil to experience the answer. It's only when we experience the answer that we really understand. This experiencing is also called realizing.

Do you have a question? No? If you don't have any questions, I can always speak on any phase of the subject that you want.

Q: I'd like to know a little more about how karma works, and why it works. I'd like to know what puts it into effect, what starts the wheel. You mention that it's the thought. Knowing that these things do come back to us, naturally we want only good things to come back to us, so we want to send out the right thoughts.

Lester: The word *karma* is a Sanskrit word meaning action. Its general use means action, and the reaction to the action. Other explanations are cause and effect: what you sow, you reap; what you give out, comes back to you. Karma is initiated in thought. Thought is the cause, and action is the effect. When we create a desire, we want something. The desire initiates the thought of wanting something. Wanting something causes us to act to get that something. That something does not satisfy us, and therefore, we increase the desire. That goes on and on and on, and we become bound by desire, never able to satisfy it. If our desires were capable of being satisfied, we would have no desires, right?

Q: Would you say that again?

Lester: If our desires were capable of being satiated or satisfied, we would soon lose all our desires. They would soon be satisfied, and we would have no more!

Q: Which is the state to which we should attain?

Lester: Yes, we should attain the state of no desire, no longing. Then we are happy always.

Q: I understood you to say that karma is a law of action and reaction and could be used—not in the sense of punishment for a wrong deed, but as a reward for a good one.

Lester: Creating things we don't like we call punishment. Creating things we do like we call reward. Creation is initiated in the mind. The mind doesn't know good or bad; it just creates. When we create things that are distasteful to us (and we don't take responsibility for the creation), we say we're being punished.

What is karma? To every action, there's an opposite and equal reaction. It's called the law of compensation. It is initiated in the mind. Every thought we have creates a vacuum, and nature immediately moves to fill that vacuum. The pace at which nature fulfills it is also determined by our thought, and every thought is initiated by a previous desire. Since a desire is not real, but is an assumed lack, an assumed agony of need, it can never be satisfied, and it actually becomes stronger the more we try to satisfy it. The only way we can be happy is to let go of all desire. Then we become perfectly content.

Q: So it takes the two. The thought alone without desire won't do it?

Lester: Without a desire, would you have a thought?

Q: Never.

Lester: Correct. You wouldn't have any thoughts without desire.

Q: Well, there are intellectual desires, aren't there?

Lester: Yes, but they are desires. Otherwise, there would be no thought. You desire to be heard; you desire to communicate with people. It might not be a desire for ice cream, food, for things that the body needs, but it might be a desire for approval. So, desire initiates the whole cycle.

Way back in the beginning, it started with a thought of lack. Then there was a desire to fulfill the lack. The desire caused more thought. The thought caused action. Since the action does not fulfill the desire, we increase the desire and action, keeping it going until we are apathetically spinning in an endless cycle, with satisfaction impossible. All our present thinking is initiated by something from the past. Our total feelings now are all from the thoughts and actions of the past. So, all thinking is now motivated by something that has already happened. Action and reaction go on and on that way, and we are caught. It's almost impossible to have an original thought anymore, every thought being based on past thoughts.

Q: So, then, it all started way back when?

Lester: It's beginningless, and it's endless. I'll take you a step higher. Let us look at the example of the rope being mistaken for a snake. You're walking along the road—there's a rope on the ground, and you think it's a snake. Karma is in the realm of the illusory snake. When did that snake begin and when will that snake end, so long as you think it's a snake?

It's beginningless, and it's endless, because, in reality, it never was—it was always a rope. If you are in karma, it is a forever thing. If you are not in it, it never was. Does that make sense? Karma is beginningless and endless. Hence, it's impossible to work out karma. Some schools of metaphysics teach that you must work out your karma. While you're trying to work it out, you are creating new karma for the future, so, it's impossible to work it out.

Well, what can we do? Awaken from the illusion, and you'll see the Truth! See the snake as the rope! Once the rope is seen as real, the snake no more is. When we see the Truth of our Being, all this action and reaction turns out to be a dream-illusion and therefore, as such, cannot touch us anymore.

Q: Didn't you say we become the observer? I understood that the cycle still must be performed, regardless of enlightenment. Is that correct?

Lester: No, that is, once your understanding is full—from that moment on, there's no more karma. When I say, "Be the witness," that is still in the realm of duality, witnessing the duality, but it's a giant step forward. It's a method of letting go of the ego-sense of being the doer. It's a mode of behavior that's very conducive to growth.

However, when you are fully realized, you'll look at the world, and you'll see only a singular Oneness in everything and everyone. And you'll see that it is all nothing but your very own Self. And the Self is only the Self. So, what happens to the world is that you see it as it really is. You look at it as the rope instead of seeing it as the snake. Then you are out of karma, and there is no more karma.

Now, what's a little confusing to you, are statements that have been made at different levels of approach. Things at one level seem to contradict things at another level. However, when the Truth is seen, all contradictions vanish. So, from the highest point of view, when you see who and what you are, there is no karma. When you see your real Self, there's only Beingness; action and reaction are only apparently going on.

Q: Let's say I'm driving out onto the freeway, and I see a guy coming, and I step on the gas and get in front of him. What does this do to me? Is there a reaction coming back from this?

Lester: In this dreamworld, to the last ounce, there's action and reaction.

Q: One of the big things with any human, and I know I am no different, are thoughts of sex. This is quite a strong interplay and quite a strong force. How does this all get worked out?

Lester: It's one of the most difficult things to transcend. However, it's possible and it's relatively easy to do it, once you recognize that all that joy that you're seeking through sex you can have all the time—but much more so—once you're out of the trap of desire. That's why I say, "Get to the higher place where, in order to have sex, you give up joy." Then it's an easy thing to let go of.

Meantime, moderation is the best guide. Happiness is only your very own Self; happiness is your basic nature. You don't need anything external to have it. But you think you do, because you've covered over this happiness with layers and layers of limitation: I must have this to be happy, I must have that to be happy. And this has been going on for a long time, but the more you see who and what you are, the less desires have a hold on you.

Q: You have shown the way or method for me by which I have realized that there is something greater than sex. I have now realized that sex is actually a giving up of something, giving up of a higher feeling for a lesser feeling. It's much easier to understand in that light.

Lester: Sex will keep you earthbound. It's necessary to get above it. Having sex will not prevent you from moving toward realization, but while you are enmeshed in it, you are a slave to it and can never get full realization. You are making the physical thing the joy, and it isn't. The real thing is that you are that joy, only a million times more so! As high as the feeling is that you get from sex, you can go way, way beyond that feeling in joy and have it twenty-four hours a day. And it is this unlimited joy that you are really seeking, but you sacrifice it for sex.

Q: When we do things and realize that they should not be done, can we dispose of them by doing the opposite?

Lester: Well, if you're doing the opposite, you're involved in action again, creating the opposite for the future.

Q: You just have to be desireless?

Lester: Yes, that's it! Being desireless, you will see who and what you are. You'll see that you're above all this illusion of karma, and then it can touch you no more.

Q: When you do see that, the release is so tremendous, it's like a sex release.

Lester: Much greater, much greater. I'll have to get some testimonials for you, I believe. [laughter]

Q: If you drop the desire for something, will it still come your way?

Lester: No. The desire is the cause for it. You can mentally undo karma by mentally undoing desire. Karma is caused by desires that remain in the subconscious mind. Dropping desire drops all thoughts of it. If you take desire out of the subconscious mind, the seeds of karma are no longer there. This is the fastest, the very best way of undoing karma. If you want to undo karma, do it mentally. Why experience it again and again and suffer it? If you let go of things mentally, you let go of them forever; then you don't have to experience them. As Jesus said, "Whosoever looketh on a woman to lust after her hath committed adultery with her already."

The act originates in the mind. Every negative thought, every bad thought we have, creates karma that we don't like, and we call it bad karma. If people only knew this! It doesn't matter whether we carry out the act or not. The seed is sown in the thought.

The remainder of this session is composed of aphorisms taken from various other talks by Lester. Allow yourself to take as much time as you need pondering each one before you go on to the next.

Karma sows the seeds of its own destruction.

What we go through is determined by what we have gone through. This is the law of compensation or karma. In between physical bodies, we choose a certain part of what we have been through to go through the next time around. We set up similar situations, hoping that this next time we will transcend them. You always get another opportunity, ad infinitum.

Bad karma keeps us so miserable with negativity that we change our bad karma to good karma, and that turns out to be a golden chain instead of an iron chain. Freedom is above karma.

Whenever we move up, something happens to test us. What actually happens is that we subconsciously feed ourselves more karma, because we have become stronger and can face it.

Karma is nothing but the accumulated past habits of thought that are going on subconsciously.

Karma is the conglomeration of all the subconscious thoughts running you. Get rid of these thoughts; quiet the mind totally, and there is no karma.

Where is karma? It's in the world of illusion.

Anything karmic is really comic.

Karma is a harmer. It is a bondage maker.

We hurt ourselves when we judge others, because it is karmic and returns to us.

The fastest way out of karma is to grow.

Karma and reincarnation are part of the illusion and have no part in the reality. Past lives should not be gone into as it is playing with the unreality, making it seem more real.

Get to accept karma. The idea that you can fight it is contrary to the accepting of it. If you accept it, your fears, frustrations, tensions, miseries, etc., are alleviated, and you are no longer holding on to it by attempting to avert it. Since there is nothing you can do about it, you just let it be. Everything this body is going to go through, it will go through. Understand this and remain as you really are—free.

You can't change what the body will go through. That was determined by you by prior action. However, you can choose not to be that body, but to be your Self.

The ego doesn't like to hear that it doesn't have freewill. But the ego itself is a product of karma.

Examine karma, and you will discover that karma and destiny are one and the same.

Acts performed with no interest in the fruits thereof produce no karma.

If action is being done without attachments and aversions, there is no karma being created.

Once you reach the state of nonattachment, you can enjoy the world and do it without creating any karma.

It is when we rise above karma, good and bad, that we move into being our real Self.

How can an infinite Being be subject to karma, karma being an extreme limitation?

Get above karma; don't work out karma.

Karma comes to an end when one recognizes that it is all in his mind, and he is not his mind.

There's one act that will do away with all karma: be your Self.

All actions that the body will perform you have already concluded before it came into existence. The only freedom you have is whether or not to identify yourself with the body and its action.

If an actor plays the part of a king or a beggar, he is unaffected by it, because he knows he is not that character. In exactly the same manner, we should carry out our part in the world—and whether we are king or beggar, we should be unaffected by it, knowing that we are not that character but are a grand and glorious Being, our very own infinite Self.

Releasing Explorations by Hale Dwoskin

Letting go of desire is the key. The more you let go of desire, the more you are free to just be in and as this moment, free from anticipation or dread. There is nothing wrong with having, as long as you recognize that everything is on loan from God or the One. Thank you, God, for all your bounty! If you desire anything, desire for things to be exactly as they are and for you to wake up from the illusion of "me."

Because desire is what motivates all thought, allow yourself to start exploring the underlying desires that are motivating your thoughts. As you move through life, occasionally pause your mental activity long enough to ask yourself this question: "What is the desire that is motivating these thoughts and feelings?" If you do this with an open mind and heart, the motivating desire will present itself and you can let it go. In order to support yourself to let it go, ask yourself,

"Could I let go of wanting [the desire]?" "Would I?" and "When?" This is especially helpful when you find that you are feeling disturbed or your mind is particularly active.

The more you let go of desire, the quieter the mind will become and the more you will rest as the freedom that you have always been.

Growth and Receptivity

Lester Levenson

Happiness per se is not necessarily an indication of one's state of realization. Aborigines and natives are as happy as we are and sometimes more so. We who are supposed to be at the upper end of civilization, as a whole, might not be as happy as they are. Their enjoyment is mostly through the physical senses. Our enjoyment is more through the mind; hence, we are capable of more joy.

However, because this allows more joy, it therefore allows more misery. Many of us think that the things we do that give us a state of happiness are giving us spiritual growth and therefore are the right things to do. This could be true, and it could also be false. The happiness we get from a new realization is definitely growth. We are delighted in the new revelation, because we have become a little freer and therefore permanently a little happier.

However, the happiness we get from avoiding or escaping unpleasantries is not growth. Rather than furthering our growth, it keeps us bound to the unpleasantries we are avoiding. Until they are faced, looked at, and dropped, they will remain in our subconscious and emerge from time to time until we finally drop them. Therefore, in order to be undone, they must be faced and not avoided. Then no escape is necessary. However, it's really true that the greater our growth, the happier we are. We gain an accumulative total happiness that doesn't vary from day to day. It is freedom from the constant nagging of our compulsive subconscious thoughts. It's a sense of well-being, a sense of security, of peace. Even when things are outwardly being expressed against us, when the world seems to turn against us, we still feel a greater peace within than we did before.

It's that inner state that should be used as a measure of growth. A miserable person can, for the time being, for the moment, be laughing happily. But you cannot use that as an indication of that person's constant state of freedom. How can we tell a person's state of freedom or happiness? By checking when everything is against one. Use this as a method for checking yourself. When things go wrong in the world, then check your state of happiness.

Q: Aren't we inclined to be almost irritated when we see someone else who is happier than we? Maybe it's a little jealousy?

Lester: Yes, it is called jealousy, and when we see one who's happier than we are, we don't like it. Sometimes we attack that one indirectly, even if that one is our mate. This goes on between couples as they grow. When one moves ahead, the other unconsciously resents it, does things to try to undermine the first one. It's motivated subconsciously, but sometimes it does become conscious; even when it is conscious, we sometimes don't understand why we're doing it.

The reason is that whenever two people get together, the higher one automatically tries to lift the lower one up a bit, and the lower one tries to bring the higher one down a bit. They move toward each other. This is an unconscious behavior that goes on whenever two Beings meet. To come back to what I was saying before, the stability of one's peace is the best measuring stick for one's growth: peace under circumstances not ideal, and peace under circumstances in which the individual is being tried. If you maintain your peace while everything out there is going against you, then you really have it. This peace that I'm talking about is the real happiness, and it can be measured by its imperturbability.

If a person cannot be disturbed in his peace, he's got it! He has let go of much ego, because only the ego can be disturbed. The Self of us can never be disturbed. And when we abide as our Self, we allow the whole world to be as it is.

If you want to know your state, check yourself under adverse conditions. Measure your growth by the bottoms, not by the tops. You'll find that your growth goes in cycles, up and down, but that the bottoms keep rising. You should get to the place where the bottom is happiness, and that makes the top even higher—a state of serenity, tranquility, bliss—all with a deep, imperturbable peace.

Q: Where is this bliss, joy, and peace felt?

Lester: People feel it in different places. Actually, it's at the very center of your Beingness, wherever that center may be. This is the first time in this series that the group has reached the state of spillover joy. During each series of the past, we had gone from a low point at the start to a very high point at the end.

Q: Do you know why?

Lester: Yes. This is something I'd like to explain to you. Why go down? We're supposed to be intelligent people. We know the way, why go down? That's somewhat stupid when you know how to be high and happy the way you feel now; in fact, it's stupid not to be the way you are now all the time.

The reason why you go down after I leave you is that you have not undone enough of your unconscious thoughts. I direct you toward the infinite Being that you are. As you see it, you undo the contrary thoughts and feel freer and higher. After I leave, the remaining unconscious thoughts of limitation re-emerge, take over, run you, and you feel lower. What is necessary is that you continue to eliminate the unconscious thoughts until there are no more, until you are totally free. Only then will you be satisfied.

I'm pointing out now what you need to do to further your growth. The intellect is excellent for growing and is necessary at the beginning. It sets you in the right direction, it takes you forward. Then you reach a place where it can take you no further. So, what do you do? Do you stop at the top of the intellect, or do you go on? I'm saying let's go on! This doesn't mean let go of your intellect, forget it, or suppress it. No, I'm saying go beyond it. I'm suggesting another giant step forward.

I'm trying to get you to see what this next step is by first telling you what it is not. It is not intellectual. Intellectually, there's nothing more I can give you. What is it? It is becoming aware of your Self by actually experiencing your Self. I could lead you much higher than we've ever gone before if you would draw it out of me. This would help you to experience a higher state than you have ever known before. Then the experience would be your knowledge, and after you experience it, it would leave you with a stronger desire for freedom, a stronger incentive to move faster toward the goal.

Now, I don't want to talk in riddles or intangibles. What is it that will draw out more than the intellect has drawn out so far? It's your state of receptivity. It determines the amount of the power that flows into you. Stated another way, it is letting go of your reservations. As you become more receptive, more of the power flows through me into you and lifts you to the place where you experience your Self. I, Lester, do not do it; it flows through me to the degree that you receive it. It can help lift you to a higher state; by experiencing that state, you definitely know it. You better know that "Thou art That."

Q: How do we do that?

Lester: Greater acceptance of the direction coming through me, and of the fact that happiness really lies within you and not without. The direction up to now has been to quiet the mind by looking at and letting go of subconscious thoughts. As you let go of these thoughts, you become freer, your mind is quieter, your real Self is less obscure, and you're more able to be the real Self that you are. Also, the more you have this experience, the more you are capable of being drawn into your Self by the power flowing through me into you. This could go on to the ultimate.

You have quieted the mind to quite some degree; there is much more to be done. That's why I asked last time, "Who can sit down and immediately quiet his mind and have no thoughts come in?" If you can do that, you're a master. To the degree you can quiet your mind, to that degree, you are a master. But everyone is quieter now than they were. Our next step is to get even quieter. And I say we're not going to get it through intellectualism any more, through bandying words up and back. We're going to get it through a method that directly helps you experience the quietude of your Self.

Q: When you quiet your mind and no thought comes in, then what happens? Is it a blank?

Lester: No, it's not a blank; you have no mind to go blank! You're in the realm of all-knowingness: you don't have to think anymore, you just know everything, and everything falls into line perfectly—every moment. You operate on a feelingness, called intuition. Everyone in this room has experienced it at times. Mind is nothing but the total bundle of your thoughts—a small part conscious, the major part subconscious and held out of view. Mind is not complicated when you see what it is: it's simply the totality of thoughts.

Q: Isn't it true that subconscious thoughts are thoughts that are not being thought of at the moment?

Lester: No, they're being thought of at the moment, but they're not consciously being thought of. They're subconsciously being thought of at the moment.

Q: So that's the difference between conscious and subconscious thoughts?

Lester: Yes, subconscious thoughts are active right now, but we're not looking at them. Are you consciously pumping your heart? Breathing? Running that chemical digestive factory you have? Are you doing these things consciously? Well, then you're doing them subconsciously.

Q: I didn't have that in mind, exactly.

Lester: I know, but I want to show you how all the thoughts on the body, even though you're not conscious of them, are active right now. There are many, many thoughts connected with running a body; there's a lot of action going on there. They're active right now, even though we're not conscious of them.

Q: That's automated; that's what I call automation.

Lester: Right. But who is now running the automated action? We are. It was originally useful in that we didn't have to consciously operate the body. Then we lost sight of the fact that we threw this onto automatic; therefore, it is now running us. It's difficult to change it, because we have made it unconscious. As we become aware, we see this and then we change it. We become free of it; we reestablish our control over the body.

Our object is to let go of unconscious thoughts, these habitual things of the past that keep us automatically bound. Every habitual thought is a bondage that takes away a certain amount of freedom, happiness. We must let go of all these old habit-thoughts until we are totally free of them. Then we are liberated, fully realized masters.

Q: That's why some words will trigger us. If we hear a certain word, we fly into a madness, or, if we hear something else, we feel good.

Lester: Right! So, our object is to let go of all these subconscious thoughts. We have done a beautiful job so far, through using the thoughts, the mind. Now I'm suggesting that we move on, that we get the mind yet quieter by doing that which does it directly—that is, by experiencing your Self. It can also be done in meditation. I ought to redefine the word *meditation*.

When I say meditation, I mean holding one thought to the exclusion of other thoughts, and that one thought should be a question. As other thoughts drop away, the mind gets quiet and concentrated. When the mind is concentrated, you will experience your Self, and it will answer any and every question. It will answer the questions that we need to have answered to show us the way out of the bondages. Now, in meditation, the moment you sit down to quiet the mind, it seems to get noisier, which is natural; the thoughts come up for us to drop, to let go of. And each time we let go of one, that's one less that we have to let go of.

As time goes on and we keep dropping these thoughts, we have less and less to drop. Someday, the mind becomes quiet enough so that we fully see this infinite Being that we are; then, in one lump sum, we drop all that is left. And when there are no more thoughts, we are free, and there is left only our infinite Self.

Q: My mind keeps getting noisier and noisier.

Lester: No, it is just that you are looking more at your subconscious thoughts. You don't get more thoughts, you just become more aware of them. The unconscious thoughts that control you will come up. Every time you meditate, this happens. Through practice, some day you will be able to hold one question, one thought, without other thoughts coming in. When you get that far, you are moving rapidly. When you have dropped all subconscious thoughts, then you know what God is, that your Beingness is he.

Q: I'd like to identify the feeling in meditation. Is it similar to a feeling you get while listening to a fine piece of music?

Lester: Yes, it is one of the nicest and quietest feelings you can have.

Q: Then the process of meditation, as I'm seeing it now, has not at all to do with thoughts, but with identifying with this feeling and allowing it to expand.

Lester: Yes! However, this nice feeling is accomplished by quieting the thoughts. Someday, the meditative feeling will be far more enjoyable than the music was.

Q: I feel that it would be such a tremendous welling up that you would almost explode!

Lester: Well, you won't explode, because you take it on as much as you can accept it. There is such a tremendousness in us that, if it came all at one time, we just couldn't take it.

Q: Is meditation related to receptivity?

Lester: Definitely, yes! The better we are able to meditate, the more receptive we are; and the more receptive we are, the better we can meditate. I'm stressing meditation with the hope of helping us to become more receptive. We should let go of the queer ideas we have about meditation. You don't have to be a Hindu or a yogi; you can be one hundred percent American and be a very good meditator.

Meditation is simply holding one question or thought to the exclusion of all other thoughts—and when that question or thought is on your Beingness, that's right meditation. Before we attain good meditation, we have to work to let go of extraneous thoughts that come in while we're trying to hold one question. Then that one question will be answered, whatever that question is. "What am I?" is the final question. When we get the full answer to that, we are in the ultimate state.

Q: Don't you automatically try to answer that when you ask yourself the question?

Lester: Yes, you do, but your mind cannot. The mind can never give you the answer to the question, "What am I?" Why? Because realization is elimination of the mind, and the mind posing the question is not going to eliminate itself. It's almost like saying, "Eliminate yourself." The mind does not want to eliminate itself. Therefore, when the mind poses the question, "What am I?" the mind will never, in all eternity, give the answer.

This is another reason why the intellect can take us only so far. The mind cannot give us the answer, because it itself is in limitation, in finiteness. The answer is in infinity. The mind can pose the question, "What am I?" and when the answer comes, it's from beyond the mind. It's only by quieting the mind that you will be able to see who and what you are. The mind is the blinding cover over this infinite Self that you are.

Q: But underneath it all, I'm trying to find something to hang onto here. Is it this glow, this feeling?

Lester: Yes. If you will examine the glow, you'll discover it to be a feeling of "I"-ness, of Beingness.

Q: Assuming this feeling that we all get occasionally is our true Being shining through—even though it's a very small part we're experiencing—this is the constant experience we should attain to, right?

Lester: Yes! Make it nothing but that, and that is it. Then there's nothing but the experience of "I, I, I, I, I" all the time, and you are there.

Q: Up until now, I've only had an intellectual understanding of these things, and this is the first concrete experience I've had.

Lester: Well, that's not really so. There was always a feeling of experiencing when you got a realization.

Q: Well, that's what I'm finding out. I've now identified with this glow, this feeling.

Lester: Yes, the glow is the experiencing and is higher than the intellect. It's simply experiencing.

Q: That's the way I want it, because books make it sound awfully complicated. How does that fit in with the Self-Realization Fellowship teachings?

Lester: SRF teachings will say the same thing from a different approach. Their approach is for the majority of seekers. Christianity is in the realm of love, devotion, and surrender to God. So are the SRF teachings. Instead of working so hard to eliminate the ego, they say, "Just surrender to God."

If you really surrender, it's only surrender of the ego. "Thy will, not my will" is simply surrender of the ego. SRF directs you to quiet the mind, mainly through meditation, so that your infinite Self becomes obvious. Its main teaching is its methodology, called Kriya Yoga, an integral method that can be used by everyone. If you understand the overall picture, you'll see that there's no disagreement. I'm trying to get you to quiet the mind, to let go of the mind. Their teaching will end up doing the very same thing, and it's a good balance to have our intellectual, wisdom way and their devotional, love, and surrender aspect. However, you can't really have one without the other. So, approaching it from both sides is beneficial, and we should use every aid possible.

We need it; we're in an earth period that is extremely low. We're having opposition going on all day as long as we associate with the world; therefore, any aid that is helpful should be used. When it comes to aids, there is no greater aid than the actual, wonderfully exhilarating experience of being your Self. Be more receptive—surrender your little self and allow the power of your real Self to flow until it, the power, is the only power flowing through you. Glory in that power! Remain in that power! Remain and abide as your infinite, glorious Self!

Releasing Explorations by Hale Dwoskin

What are you meditating on? Most of us are meditating all the time without realizing it. Another way to look at meditation is that whatever the mind is focusing on is a meditation. Whatever we meditate on, we are focusing our power on and it therefore increases. What most of us are meditating on all the time is our problems or limitations and therefore they increase. If you honestly examine what you focus on all day, you will see that what I am saying is true.

I highly recommend that you start tipping the balance of meditation to meditating on the Awareness or on questions that will lead you to recognizing that which you are. As you tip the balance in the direction of meditation on Truth, the power of the Truth will be more and more active in your awareness and it will increase exponentially.

Allow yourself to take breaks throughout the day to just stop and rest as the Beingness that you have always been. You can use simple questions like "What is actually here now?" or "Am I?" You can also use any of the self-inquiry questions that have been discussed throughout this book. As you allow yourself to rest, you will discover that the more you rest, the more you find yourself staying at rest, even when the body is in activity. This will increase until you discover for yourself that you have always been that which is perpetually at rest despite all the apparent activity.

The Quiet Meditative State of Beingness

Lester Levenson

Man may be divided into three general categories of havingness, doingness, and Beingness. The lowest of the three is the havingness state. Man thinks that if only he could have, he would be happy. "If only I could have a million dollars, I would be the happiest person in the world! If only I could have a strong, healthy body. "If only I could have. . . ."

The next higher state is a doingness state. Instead of saying, "If only I could have," we rise to the place where we want to go out and do, and we are capable of doing things in the world. There, we are more interested in doingness than we are in havingness.

The highest state is the Beingness realm. This is the state that I'm trying to get you into. Beingness will have no meaning until you experience it. Only then will you know what it is, and you will want Beingness more than anything else in the world. This reminds me of something one of you said to me. "We visited a friend we hadn't seen for over a year. She's very interested in metaphysics. While we were visiting her, she said, 'Let's cut out this talking; let's meditate. Why waste time talking?'"

She had already experienced this realm of Beingness. When you're up there, it looks silly to talk. Why talk? Why not just be?

Havingness is the category that roughly ninety percent of us are mostly in. "Oh, if we only could have those almighty dollars, more and more of them, or a million of them, then we would be free and happy." But what is the experience of those who do accumulate a million or more? Are they happy? No, they have many, many problems and are loaded down with non-freedom, more unhappy than happy.

The proof of their not attaining happiness is their compulsive drive to get more and more, even though they cannot use up the amount already accumulated. Were it true that material things brought happiness, the wealthy would be so overhappy that they would be incapacitated by it, and the poor would be so miserable that life would not be worth living.

The next higher state is the doingness state. Here we are the real doers in the world, and here are the leaders. Here we are found as big businessmen, small businessmen, big politicians, and small politicians, people in the arts, and professional men. ("Men" includes men and women.) Here we are out on our own, more independent than the jobholder. Are we happy? No? Happier than the jobholder, because we're more independent, but still not free. We are yet compulsively driven.

I think the proof of this is the number of actors and actresses who, on attaining the height of fame and fortune, find themselves so unhappy that they commit suicide or go through life frustrated. We come now to the only state that can give us happiness with no sorrow—the state of Beingness. Beingness is the highest of the three states, and it is the very highest state possible. In the ultimate state, we are Beingness, being all Beingness. Stated another way, it's Awareness, aware of all Awareness. When we are just that, when we are only that, that's the highest state. It is in this top state of Beingness that we reach our ultimate of perfect contentment, perfect satiation, perfect joy, perfect peace. It is the state of highest felicity.

There's no giving up of anything on this path. You always take on more. Those who tell me, "Well, I don't want to give up" are refusing to hear what I have been saying. But why don't you hear it? It is very subtle ego-sabotage, saying, "I don't want to grow anymore."

When this happens, I should present it to you so that you may see the ego-sabotage. Then you may let go of it and go further. We're moving toward an infinity, and until we are absolute and infinite, we should keep moving—if we want the ultimate happiness, and who doesn't?

We will never be fully happy until we reach that state. The ultimate happiness and your Self turn out to be one and the same thing. There will always be a subconscious, below the surface, a nagging that pushes us on until we achieve it, until we are there. What the world today calls happiness is escape from misery, alleviation of misery. The relatively small amount of happiness the world has is only relief from misery. All entertainment, all socializing, is relief and escape from our thoughts! Look at, examine, and discover this. Stop chasing rainbows!

In the havingness state, one has the least happiness; in the doingness state, one has more happiness; in the Beingness state, one has the greatest happiness. I can't tell you what it is; it's an experience, and you just must experience it. The best way I can help you to experience it is to get you to do that which will put you into that state. It is a very deep, quiet, meditative state; it's a state wherein we let go of thoughts. Through my helping to guide you in such a way that you may fall into it, you can experience and know what this state of Beingness is. That guidance is to lead you into right meditation and to support you while in it.

My object is to try to show you how to get a deeper and deeper feeling of this state of Beingness. Now, some of us have gone very deep into the state of Beingness and know what it is. Yet, if I asked you to describe it, you'd have difficulty; you couldn't tell what it is. You could talk around it, describe it by saying it's nice, it's peaceful, serene, delightful. But what is it? You can't put it into words. It's like trying to explain to someone what an orange tastes like; you just cannot do it. Once one tastes the orange, then one knows. It's the same with this deep meditative state of Beingness. Once you taste it, you know it. And after you have tasted the deep state of meditative Beingness, you will want it more than anything else in the world.

You should meditate at least one hour in the morning and one hour before retiring. The morning meditation sets you in a mood and prepares you for a better day. The evening meditation helps undo the turbulence of the day and carries you through the night. You'll find yourself sleeping better. Increase the length of your set time of meditation until the meditative state stays with you all the time, until it remains with no effort. When you want this more than anything else in the world, you've gone deeply into your Beingness, into your Self.

This experience is so far greater than anything else you've ever experienced, you'll just prefer it to anything and everything else. Then you'll see and know that this is what you've been blindly seeking for in the world—looking for it through indirect means, through external means—and now that you've discovered that it's right where you are, you don't have to have anything, you don't have to do anything. You only have to just be what you are. It's your natural state!

I have not spoken about ways and means of meditation. I haven't been asked questions on it except, "What is meditation?"

Q: Do you want questions on it? Is that what you want?

Lester: That is up to you. I know that some of you joined Self-Realization Fellowship and are beginning to get some of the methods. SRF's root teaching is meditation: how to meditate and how to do those things that will prepare you for meditation. It has many methods and means of helping one meditate better.

When thoughts come into our mind unwanted, when we cannot keep them out, we are far from being free. When we, at will, can cause thoughts to enter or not enter, then we are free and a master over mind. Until then, the mind is the master, and we are the slave; we are victims of our thoughts. We are actually being pushed around like automatons by our habit-thoughts.

People talk to us, and it's just as though they are pressing our automatic buttons. They praise us, and we go up; they berate us, and we go down—like an automatic robot—and we think we're free-willed! Anyone who goes up on praise and down on condemnation is behaving like a robot, because whether I praise you or condemn you, I don't do a thing to you but send out tiny bits of sound, energy, and you give it enough power to make you happy or miserable, making you nothing but an automatic robot.

Now, an easy way to become master over your mind is through meditation. It's the practice of quieting the mind by seeking that which we really are. This we should do until we reach the goal. Our direction from here on in should be learning how to meditate better. I can give far more potent guidance while you're in the meditative state than I could through my voice, but you will never know it until you experience it. The help you've gotten so far is small in comparison to the help you can receive when you get quiet. Then I can communicate to you directly, Self to Self. Then I can help you be your real Self—and not only I but also the masters. Whether they're here in body or not, this is exactly what they do.

When we are quiet, They come in, and they help establish us in our Self. And by our experiencing it, we go deeper and deeper until it's complete, until we're in the quiet, meditative state twenty-four hours a day, regardless of what we are doing. In this quiet state, you never lose consciousness. When you go to sleep, you're fully aware that you're sleeping. When you are dreaming, you're fully aware that you're dreaming. Should you decide to cut the dream, you can cut the dream. The same with the sleep. Or, while you're fully awake, if you decide to go to sleep this moment, you go to sleep this moment.

This is not giving up anything. This is becoming a master over the three usual states that we all go through every day: the waking state; the dream state; and the deep, dreamless sleep state. I am summing up what has happened since I started with you. First, we worked to increase our havingness, then our doingness, and now we're with the top state of Beingness. The Beingness state should be developed from here on in. Any questions about what I've been saying to you? Is it understood?

Q: The main purpose of meditation is to learn to quiet the mind?

Lester: Right. Purely, simply, and wholly to quiet the mind until it's totally quiet. When it's totally quiet, that's the goal. Every thought is a thing of limitation, is a cover, a veil, over our infinite Beingness.

When we remove all the veils, there's nothing left but our infinite Beingness. The veils are only our thoughts. Mind is not mysterious—except when you don't understand it. When you understand, it's nothing but thoughts; it's as simple as that. It's the sum total collection of thoughts that is called mind. Stop the thoughts, and there's no more mind action. Meditation is simply a method of quieting the thoughts, and meditation should be continued until all thoughts are quieted.

The all-quiet state is such a tremendous state that it can never be put into words. The words *ecstasy, euphoria, bliss, nirvana,* don't describe it really; they allude to it. But, as I said, when you once experience a certain depth of meditation, you have experienced the greatest thing you ever have experienced in your life. And you will want to repeat that experience, want to establish and maintain it so that it is all the time. This experiencing turns out to be only your very own real Self, now called happiness—and indulged in very minutely.

When you gain this beautiful depth of quietude, don't spill it out in conversation. You don't see how much you let go of this beautiful quietude when you pour it out, lose it, in conversation. You get involved in thoughts, and the thoughts take you away from it. Then you have only the memory that it was a nice feeling. That feeling should be maintained, sustained, and retained. The best way to do this, after group meditation, is to go right home with it.

If you obtain it by yourself, remain by yourself. Just keep quiet; stay in it as long as you possibly can, until you become fully established in it all the time. Then it's all right to talk; you won't lose it. But as it is now, you let go of the depth of quietude you get in meditation when you talk to people. You just waste it. It's so valuable to get that feeling. Hold it and develop it further and further, until it is there all the time. You'll know when the state of Beingness is complete: when you see yourself as all Beingness.

First, we get a little of this beautiful state of quietness, peace, serenity, tranquility; then, as it develops, we begin to see more and more that we are all Beingness. In the beginning, it might be a flash, or for a minute, or five minutes; each time the concept will stay longer and longer until it's the only thing. Then you see yourself only as Beingness being all Beingness. Then you'll know what God is; you will know your real Self.

Q: This whole thing is like trying to tell somebody what the orange tastes like?

Lester: Yes, but most of us have experienced this quietude of Beingness to a degree, so it has a certain amount of meaning. To the degree that each one has experienced it, it has that much meaning to him. Then I add to it by saying: someday, you're going to have such a tremendous experience of just Beingness, that, after it, you will want only to reestablish it permanently. Everything else in the world becomes secondary to it. You also recognize that what you have been seeking in the world is right where you are. It's not out there—it's within, right where you are. It's your natural, inherent state. It's your Self, and it's all the glory of gloriousness.

Q: Can this state be reached without direct conscious effort toward finding out who you are?

Lester: Yes, in a slower way, by seeking God through devotion and self-surrender. Surrender yourself wholly and completely unto your God, and you will reach it.

Q: I am trying to understand where I am now.

Lester: Okay, I'll tell you where you are now. You are at that place that's equal to how well you can remain quiet. To the degree that you can remain quiet, imperturbable—to that degree is your growth. In meditation, how well you can keep your mind on one thought without other thoughts coming in shows you how far you've gone. Your mind is much quieter now than it was when I met you. Are you aware of that?

Q: Well, I'm experiencing thought, so I can't see it.

Lester: There are indirect ways of telling: how easily you're disturbed by others, how much you react to what people say, and so forth. When your mind is really quiet, it doesn't matter what people say about you; you don't mind.

Q: But you already are that which you are seeking. It's just a matter of knowing it, isn't it?

Lester: Yes, it's a matter of re-remembering it, recognizing it. We have to experience it to recognize it. Meditation is the way to experience it. Right now, we're convinced that we're limited to being our body. That's the biggest lie of all lies; we're infinite! It's just a wrong perception, a wrong seeing. It's an illusion, it isn't real. The reality is that we are the Beingness behind the body.

Q: What we really should do when we get into meditation is to see what we are and not see the limited being, to get away from the sense of limitation?

Lester: Yes, let go of the concepts of limitation. By so doing, you experience Beingness more and more until you experience only the Being, You, just behind the body and mind.

Q: Our thoughts of limitation are what's restricting us from seeing what we are?

Lester: Yes, our thoughts, which themselves are limitations. Not our thoughts of limitation, but our thoughts—every one of which is a limitation.

Q: How do you differentiate between consciousness and thought?

Lester: Consciousness is general awareness. Thought is awareness of a particular thing.

Q: To me it means more if, instead of using the word *meditation*, you would say, "I want you to begin getting rid of your sense of limitation and get a feeling of being All—that you are all knowledge, all consciousness."

Lester: That is what meditation does and achieves.

Q: I have to put it into words, and I suppose you know it instinctively.

Lester: No, I put it into words. I define meditation as keeping your mind on one thought. Now this makes sense to you: hold one thought such as, "What is God?" Just stay with that thought and only that thought, and keep other thoughts out: that's meditation.

Take another thought, "What is this world?" and just hold that thought, "What is this world? By golly, what is it?"

You keep questioning, "What is this world?" When there is only one thought, the mind is quiet. When the mind is quiet, the answer comes from beyond the mind.

Q: You are not saying what we have been taught elsewhere, to think about a rose and not let any other thought come in. You're really saying, "Think about God," or about "It."

Lester: Yes. The very top question is, "What am I?" When the answer to that comes fully, that's it. By holding that question in your mind and awaiting the answer to it, you are doing the very best of meditation. No matter what method one uses, no matter what path he takes, in the end he gets the answer to, "What am I?"

But know this: the mind will never give you the answer. Any answer the mind gives has to be wrong, because the mind is an instrument of thought, and every thought is limited. Therefore, you mentally pose the question, and you await the answer, and it is from beyond your mind, from your Self, that it comes.

Q: Because you already know, so you just stop the nonsense?

Lester: Yes, you stop the nonsense of not knowing.

Q: And, in recognizing, "I know, I know," I'm getting rid of being limited.

Lester: That's it! That's the whole thing in a nutshell. As you said, you already know it, and you just let go of the thoughts contrary to it until this knowingness is self-obvious. This is called realization or revelation.

Q: Is Beingness no thought of consciousness?

Lester: Beingness, when complete, is without thought. However, Beingness and consciousness are the same, which one cannot intellectualize on, but which one can experience. Beingness and consciousness are the exact same thing. That's why I said if you want to know a cow, be a cow. If you want to know what a tree is, be a tree.

And you can, because you are. How better can you know something than to be it? The real answer will come when you get there; then you'll see that Beingness and consciousness are the same. Don't intellectualize on it; do it. Be it.

Q: It's awfully blah when, in meditation, nothing comes.

Lester: It shouldn't be blah, because, as you're doing it, you're quieting thoughts. The more you quiet thoughts, the happier you are.

I think by now we can all examine and know what our joys really consist of. If we're listening to music, our mind gets concentrated only on the music. All the other thoughts and problems of the day are let go of, and so the music seems beautiful. If we're thinking of the one we love, the same thing happens: our mind is only on that person, and all the other thoughts and troubles drop away, so loving that person is beautiful. It is really the dropping of our discomforting thoughts that makes the focus of our attention on something external seem so wonderful.

Q: I must express a thought I just had when you were talking. In other words, it's like all the electricity going one way, with no side issues, no interference. When you listen to music, you think about nothing but the music.

Lester: Yes, all other thoughts—bothersome limitations—are let go of for the time being, and you feel your real Self much more. You'll never know the real beauty until you see the beauty behind the beauty, the source of the beauty.

Q: Which is "I"?

Lester: Yes, your real Self.

Q: I now know what you're talking about when you use the word *meditation*.

Lester: When you develop it, it leads you into the most beatific, blessed state; into nirvana, tranquility, and serenity; into your quiet meditative state of knowing what you are—You, the real Being of the universe, being your infinite, glorious and magnificent Self.

Releasing Explorations by Hale Dwoskin

The Beingness-Awareness that you are is always the most intimate part of every experience. Without Awareness there is no experiencing. We get so caught up in changes in the body-mind-world that are appearing in or on this Awareness, that we miss the natural beauty and bliss of pure being.

A great meditation to do is to simply take a break from outside activity and pay attention to what is aware. You can do this by simply watching what is appearing on the surface and then allowing yourself to simply dissolve into the space or emptiness that is between every appearance. It feels like simply opening and sitting back into what is as it is. You may also find this happening spontaneously as you explore what you have been learning in this book.

You can also use this question as you move through life. If you are getting lost in a train of thought or in a feeling, ask yourself, "What is deeper than that?" and "What is even deeper than that?" Keep going with these questions until you are at rest as the silent Beingness that you have always been. This exercise will help you to start living more of the time as the Beingness that you are, rather than only when you are in what you call meditation.

You may also want to explore this question: "Where does the surface end and the core begin? Where does the core end and the surface begin?"

Meditation

Lester Levenson

The greatest thing, and the most difficult thing, we have to do is to drop the mind. It's a junkyard full of refuse from ages past, a refuse of thoughts of limitations: I am a limited body; I have troubles. All thoughts contain limitation. We pile them up in the thing we call mind. Mind is nothing but the total accumulation of all these thoughts. So, mind is nothing but a junkyard of limitation.

All right, so how do we get rid of the mind? By quieting it. When we quiet the mind, we discover our infinity. The more we see our limitlessness, the more we recognize that junkyard called mind—and the more we let go of it—until we go so far that we drop the whole remaining mind at one time. However, before that, we keep battling the thoughts as they come up. As the thoughts come up, we let go, let go, let go, until we let go of enough of them so that the Self that we are is obvious. Then it takes over and takes us all the way. The greatest thing is quieting the mind, which is eliminating thought, eliminating the mind.

Meditation is necessary. This is the major point I'm stressing: meditation. Learn how to meditate. The deeper one goes, the more one discovers the innate joys to which there are no limits. No matter how joyful you get, you can always go further. If you were a thousand times more joyful than you are now, you could still go on and on and on in joy. Joy is unlimited because we're infinite. But the major thing to accomplish is the ability to control the mind, to meditate, to drop into peace at will.

A man can control a whole nation, and if he cannot control his own mind, what kind of control has he got? He is a victim of his own mind. Rather than being in free control over his thoughts, he is an effect of them. He is actually pushed around by past habits. He is no master. Only he who can control his mind is a master, a master not only of himself, but of anything and everything he does. Meditation is the way.

The remainder of this session is composed of aphorisms collected from various talks by Lester. Allow yourself to spend as much time as you need pondering each statement before you move on to the next.

Meditation is directed thinking.

Meditation is putting your mind on the way to find God.

Meditation is looking for the answers in the right direction.

Meditation is basically thinking in the right direction and holding to it so that other thoughts keep dropping away until the mind is concentrated. When the mind is concentrated, the answers become obvious to you.

Concentration is holding one thought to the exclusion of other thoughts that will lift one and help one grow.

The ability to hold one thought concentrates the mind so that it can crack the secrets of itself.

Meditating to get the mind quiet is good. Meditating to let go of ego-wants is better. Meditating on "What am I?" is best.

Meditate, actively seeking.

Meditation should be on "What am I? What is God? What is the world? "What's my relationship to the world? What is the substance of this world? What is infinity? What is intelligence? Where is this world?" Or you can also meditate on some of the statements you've heard, like, "I'm not in the world, but the world is in me." Question, then ask, "How come?" Try to see it. Try to see the meaning behind these statements of Truth.

We get to see the perfection by looking in the direction where the perfection is. Now, the perfection isn't out there; we know that. The perfection is in here where we are, where the "I" of us is. So, first we have to direct our attention inwardly. We should pose a question and hold it until the answer comes. When the answer does come, you know, and you know you know. To get the answer to, "What am I?" it is necessary to still the noise of the mind, to still the thoughts. The thoughts are the noise. The thoughts are concepts of limitation, and there are so many of them that they're constantly bombarding us, one after another all the time. Keep on dropping them until the perfection is obvious.

All these extraneous thoughts wouldn't come in if we weren't interested in them.

We must learn how to quiet the mind. We can never learn how by constant conversation. The less conversation, the better.

Meditation does not have to be formal to be meditation. It can be any time one gets quiet and seeks. Some of us find it is easier to meditate when it isn't formal, because sometimes we unconsciously have objections and resistances to formal meditation. However, we should work to drop the objections and resistances and be free of them.

Reverse your negative thoughts as they come into mind. Let go of negative thoughts by reversing them, and then, eventually, let go of all thoughts.

What you gain remains. Even though you've undone one thought, one idea, there still remains multitudes of thoughts, and so another one comes up. Undoing one limiting thought doesn't undo all the subconscious thoughts. What remains must be let go of. By dropping a tendency or predisposition, you drop all the thoughts motivating it.

Everything that everyone is looking for through work is far better gotten through meditation. Meditation will sooner and better get you what you want than working in the world, for it will.

It is the doorway to the Infinite when you go inward. When you go outward, it is the doorway to limitation.

Internalize your attention. All externalized attention is wasted.

What you do to yourself, being your own doing, can only be undone by you.

God is known only through your effort and direction. Look concentratedly within for the kingdom of God.

With meditation, you will discover that you've covered up your unlimited Self with your limited ego.

Meditation is the road to omnipresence.

Meditate to get into the practice and habit of meditation. We should meditate as much as we possibly can. Meditation is getting the mind one-pointed in the direction of who and what we are. It's taking the mind away from the worldly things and focusing it on the direction that we're in. The more we do it, the more we like it. And the more we like it, the more we do it, until it becomes a thing that goes on effortlessly all the time. No matter what you're doing, that meditation continues in the background. Then you are really moving. Until then, you're not moving very rapidly, because most of the time you're in the world and in the direction of limitation.

There's only one way to get to the high state and that is by quieting the mind. The method of quieting the mind is meditation. It's very difficult: the moment you sit down and want to quiet the mind, up pop the thoughts. Well, as the thoughts pop up, keep knocking them out, putting them out, dropping them, until you reach a state where you can sit relatively quiet. Then you begin to like meditation, because it's a deeper experience of your real Self.

Once you like it, the main obstacle to the practice of meditation is eliminated. But you should never stop until you reach the place where meditation is delightful. Then you will go on with ease.

The most effective meditation is when you are by yourself. Group meditation is for beginners, for the purpose of accustoming one to meditation.

Meditation really should be communing with your Self.

You'll see your Self to the proportion that your mind is quiet.

The way to get rid of the ego is to get the mind so quiet that you can see what you are. Then you know that you are not the ego, and you drop it.

Intense meditation will get you to your realized teacher, to your master.

To expand out from being just a body is so difficult because of the state of the world today. We do need the help of the masters to lift us, actually to help pull us right out of it. They cannot do that unless we are receptive. We cannot be receptive unless our mind is quiet, and our mind becomes quiet through meditation.

Just go into meditation—get quiet and expect that higher help, and it will come. God and gurus are constantly helping us.

If we just get quiet, with their help, we are lifted into experiencing our Self.

Meditation has to get to the point where it is the most important thing. However, even a little meditation will go a long way, especially if it is concentrated.

Spiritual things are spiritually discerned. Spiritual knowledge does not come down to a lower level. We have to raise ourselves up to it. We raise ourselves in meditation. Meditation should be used to get higher understanding by raising ourselves up to where higher understanding is.

Meditation is wonderful. Things happen in meditation that never could happen while you are talking or active.

You can make the mind quiet by the desire to discover what you are. When the interest in knowing what you are becomes stronger than the interest in this world and body, then you discover You. Desire—intense desire for it—is the key.

The concept of meditating by making your mind a blank is in error. You cannot make your mind a blank.

Meditation is a steppingstone to the knowledge of the answer to "What am I?"

Someday, the most delightful thing you will know of will be meditation.

Meditate until it becomes constant, i.e., until it continues in back of the mind regardless of what you are doing.

There is a meditation of just getting quiet. Just get quiet, not in a passive way, but in an active way of just being. It's awfully nice to just be and be and be. It's a tremendous experience. It's a wonderful feeling of just being. However, don't stop there. Keep dropping ego until there is no more.

You'll reach a point where you'll like meditation better than anything else, because you'll reach a point where you're being very much your real Self.

That is the greatest of all joy which you formerly thought was external in the world, in your wife, in your children. You'll see your wife and your children as nothing but your very own Self; you'll see that. And the joy will be direct and constant all the time.

The answer won't come from reasoning. It will come from quiet meditation. Someday, some time, it will come. It will just present itself to you, so simple, and you'll say, "Oh!"

Meditation is thinking, but thinking on one thing so that other thoughts drop away. When you are intensely interested in one thing, other thoughts drop away.

The quieter we are, the more we are the Self. When meditation becomes constant, all the time, even though we are outwardly active, we go through life and work automatically, all the time remaining in our real Self.

The mature seeker of the Self starts with, "The reality is that I was never bound. I was always free and perfect," and takes off from there.

Just look at what you are instead of what you are not. When you discover what you are, you simultaneously discover what you are not and drop it.

Say, "I am not this body; I am not this mind," and stay with it.

Seeing that you're not the ego, you're letting go of big chunks of ego.

The depth to which you go in meditation determines how much you wipe out the ego.

Depth of meditation is the degree of quieting the mind.

The longer you can meditate, the deeper you can go.

Once you reach peace, then find out what you are.

Getting the good feeling is good. The higher you go, the better the feeling is. But when you look for the good feeling as the end, then that is the end. Growing is more than dropping into the good feeling of the Self; it is dropping the non-self, the ego.

Enjoying meditation is a step, but don't stop there—go beyond it. You have got to get the answer.

One could possibly meditate forever and forever.

Meditation in itself can get to be a trap, can be used as a crutch. You've got to get realizations.

When you get full realization, you're in the meditative state all the time. Actually, meditation is the natural state.

Constant meditation is a constant remembering of God, of Self.

Meditation is extremely difficult at first, but it gets easier as time goes on. Then one day you'll say, "This is great! This is what I want!" Then you do it all the time. Then you're really on the spiritual path.

With complete concentration, dwell upon your Self. Turn the mind back upon the mind to discover what the mind is, and then go beyond the mind and dwell in your Self. Each one must experience it. It's a perception, but it's not really a mental perception. You get recognitions, revelations, and realizations by keeping the mind pointed in one direction until it gets very quiet, until other thoughts drop away. Hold one thought until it takes you to the realm just behind thinkingness. The answer is there. We call it an experience, a revelation.

We must learn to quiet the mind so that when we sit down, we let go of the world. Only then do we really begin to move at high levels on this spiritual path. We've made this world a better world; we've made this dream a happier dream, but we're almost as bound as we were before. We have replaced bondage to bad things with bondage to good things. Now we must learn to let go of thoughts, all thoughts. The way is through meditation, right meditation: quieting the mind, stilling the thoughts, and, finally, eliminating all thoughts.

In group meditation, support is lent one unto the other. The power is multiplied, and you can get more deeply quiet as time goes by. But the very best meditation is when you are by yourself, and you need no group support. Then you are not confined to any time period. You get with it, and you might stay with it five, ten, even twenty-four hours. And this should happen. When you get to like it so much that you stay up all night continuing it, it has become more interesting than sleep. Then you've got the momentum going. Then you'll get to see and be your real Self.

A way to dominate the mind is to drop into the Self. You reach a place where it's so delightful you just don't want to do anything but remain in it. It gets to be very easy. Once you get to the point where it's easy, then just continue it. Stay with it until you go all the way. By the constancy of it, each day, you get quieter and quieter, and then the Self, as you see it, keeps scorching the ego, which further quiets the mind.

You know, it's said that your spiritual growth really begins when you are able to drop into *samadhi*. I don't like to say this, because it's discouraging to some people. *Samadhi* is complete absorption in your thought. It's total concentration.

Meditation at first is holding the thoughts on God, Self, to the exclusion of other thoughts. When one is realized, meditation is the awareness—not of anything by anyone, but only the current of awareness where there is no otherness and no action, yet is compatible with the full use of the mental and physical faculties.

At the end of the road of meditation, you discover your grand and glorious Self!

Releasing Explorations by Hale Dwoskin

When these sessions were written, Lester felt that meditation was the highest path to freedom. As he worked with people and meditation, however, he discovered that for most it was not enough. He had students who could easily meditate eight hours a day or more yet who would plateau and not keep moving forward. That is why he started looking for a better way to quiet the mind. This was the inspiration for the creation of the Sedona Method. The Sedona Method is like meditation in action. It can easily be maintained whenever the body is awake throughout the day. It is a form of self-inquiry that is uniquely suited to the Western mind.

All the releasing explorations at the end of the sessions in this book are based on the Sedona Method, so you have already been starting the exploration of this wonderful tool.

Here is yet another one that will take you even deeper.

As you have probably heard and even felt many times, you are already the freedom or Awareness you are seeking. Lester also used to suggest that we reason from freedom as opposed to from our belief in being a separate individual identified with the body. You can let go from freedom as opposed to toward freedom. This will help you to dissolves feelings, thoughts, problems, and limitations with even greater ease than you ever have before.

As you simply allow yourself to perceive whatever appears to be limiting "you" from the perspective of that which has never been limited, all else dissolves revealing profound peace, light, love, and clarity. As you see it from this perspective it becomes more and more difficult to hold on to what, just a moment ago, may have seemed to be an unsolvable issue or an unreleasable limitation.

Releasing from Truth also profoundly shifts the way you perceive and experience all that appears. Here are a few questions you can use to start exploring this for yourself.

Does Awareness have a point of view about _____?

Does Beingness have a problem with _____?

Does Beingness see that as a limitation?

Is Beingness in any way limited by that?

Does Beingness know any limits?

As you ask questions like this, check to see if you can actually look back at the body-mind-world from the perspective of, or as, Awareness as best you can.

As you keep releasing from this perspective, you discover that there is no such thing as an enlightened person. There is enlightenment perceiving the appearance of the personal. We call releasing this way the Free Way.

The Game

Lester Levenson

Since we have such a large and mixed group, I don't know how to start. The best thing is to do that which is best for the greatest number. There really is no mass teaching that is very effective. Teaching, in order to be really effective, must be on an individual basis. The power of the teacher when focused on a group is not nearly as powerful as when focused on an individual.

The power used by the guru is more intense with the individual—it's dispersed to the group, it's not concentrated. When the guru works with an individual pupil, all the power flows through to the pupil to lift him to the place where he sees the Truth.

Now, each individual has a particular thing that he or she is seeking and needing at the moment. When I answer an individual on the point that he is asking, usually there are others who have the same question and who can benefit by it. Therefore, in general, I like to answer questions. But, if you want, I'll give you a short synopsis of the subject.

Basically, we are all infinite, perfect Beings. I assume that most of us accept this, at least theoretically. We are told this by the scriptures, especially the Hindu scriptures. The masters tell us this. I come along and say the same thing. But why don't we express this infinite, perfect Being that we are?

The reason why we don't express it is that through the habit of lifetimes, we have played a game of limitation. We have played it so long that we have completely forgotten that we have been playing a game of limitation and that our real basic nature is infinite. We do not look at this infinite Being that we are. We continue, every day, every moment, looking at this little puppet that we set up called the body, and assume that we are that body. So long as we keep looking at this body as being us, we are stuck right there. We cannot see our infinity, we don't know that it is, and we go on and on, lifetime in and lifetime out, assuming that we are a body.

We have done this for so long that it takes a super will to move in the opposite direction, to look at and see the infinite Being that we really are. This super will can take us away from assuming every moment that we are a limited body. If we would do it for just one second and see this infinite Being that we really are, we would use that second to undo much limitation. But first we must assume that we are infinite. Then we must start undoing the limitations.

We must actually accept that we are not this body, that we are not this mind, and, until we do that, we have absolutely no chance of getting out of this trap called "The Game of Being Limited Bodies."

So, as the scriptures say, "Thou art that." Be still and know it. Every thought we have is necessarily a thought of limitation. Let go of thought—get still. The methods are, as we know, to get quiet. Quiet the mind. The moment the mind is quiet enough, this infinite Being that we are becomes self-obvious. So, the method is very simple: quiet that mind enough so that you see this infinite Being that you are.

Now, the moment you see it, the moment you see this infinite Being that you are, you'll immediately go to work to undo the remaining thoughts that you are not it. And when there are no more thoughts, there's only the infinite Being left. Very oddly, what you are seeking is the very closest thing to you. Every time you say "I," that's it. When you say "I," you're talking about the infinite Being. When you say, "I am a body," you're saying, "I, the infinite Being, am a limited body with a limited mind." It's really as simple as all that. But simplicity does not mean it's easy to let go of the habits that you have been hanging on to for eons.

This that everyone is seeking, the thing that everyone calls happiness, is nothing but the infinite Self that we are. Everyone, in his every act, is seeking this infinite Self that he is, calling it by other names: money, happiness, success, love, etc. Having been told this—and, again, we've been told this many times before—why don't we just be what we are and stop trying to be what we are not, a limited body? Can anyone answer that? Why don't we stop being limited?

Q: Because we can't.

Lester: You mean an infinite Being can't stop being limited?

Q: Because we don't want to.

Lester: Right. We don't want to!

Q: The infinite Being doesn't want to?

Lester: Yes. I, the infinite Being, think I am a limited body, and I've been doing this so long that I, the infinite Being, don't want to let go of constantly assuming I am this limited body. Does that make sense?

Q: Yes.

Lester: Every time you say "I" without going any further, you're talking about the infinite Being that you are, but you immediately add to it "am this body." If you would only just say, "I, I, I," from here on, you'd get full realization, because, as you're saying, "I, I, I," you're concentrating on "I" and not saying "am a little body with needs."

So, there's no one who is not every moment experiencing the infinite Being that he is. As long as he experiences an "I," he is experiencing this infinite Being that he is. However, you don't want to see that. You want to be the body.

So, what is required? First, saying to yourself, "I am not this body, I am not this mind; then what am I?" If we reject this body and mind enough, what we are becomes self-obvious. We can never become an infinite Being, because we are that. We can just let go of the concepts that we are not it. We can just let go of the concepts that we are a body, a mind.

The first thing needed is the desire to let go of this limited being-ness that we think we are. A very strong desire to be the infinite Being that we really are is the only thing that we need to get there quickly. But we don't want it. If we really wanted it, we would have it. There is a difficulty, of course. And what is the difficulty? It's the habit; it's the unconscious habitual thinking. It's the mind. So we attack it by attacking this unconsciously always-thinking mind.

The mind is the only cover over the infinite Being that we are. We must stop thinking long enough to see what we are, and that "long enough" can be just one second. If you would stop thinking for one second (thinking includes the unconscious thinking too), if you would stop thinking for one second, the tremendous liberating shock of seeing what you are would cause you to use this infinite power that is yours to scorch the mind. The mind can be scorched in large amounts, each and every time we will—just for a moment—drop into that unlimited state of no thinking.

I guess the next question is how do we create the desire for it? If the desire is strong enough, anyone can see and fully be the infinite Being in a matter of weeks, months, a few years. If anyone of you had a strong desire to see this infinite Being that you are and just kept that desire only, in a few months you would see and remain as the infinite Being that you are. You would stop imagining yourself to be a limited body.

The key is desire. When you desire to be a body beautiful, a body healthy, all these thoughts prevent you from seeing the infinite Being that you are. You simply must exchange all your desires for the one desire to discover your infinite, real Self. I'd like some questions now on what I've said, so I can get closer to your wishes.

Q: While doing "What am I?" I looked at the stars, and I got an idea that I could be the stars. Then I talked to someone else, and they said, "No, you don't do that." And I thought, "Well, for God's sakes, I am going to find out how to do it!"

Lester: We are talking about a method called Self inquiry, which is really the very top method. The final question we all have to answer is: "What am I?" And when that answer comes, that's it. So why not pose that question at the beginning?

When you pose the question, "What am I?" whatever answer the mind gives cannot be right, because the mind is the cover over your real Self. The mind is the thing that limits you. The method is to hold only the question "What am I?" If another thought comes in, quickly stop it by saying to yourself, "To whom is this thought? Well, to me. Well, what am I?" And you're right back on the track.

Q: I see. Thank you.

Lester: Now, there are just a rare few on our planet who can successfully use that method. Therefore, I suggest we use it this way: always seek the answer to "What am I?" No matter what you do during the day—whether in meditation, reading, and so forth—in the back of your mind, always keep that question poised and posed, ready and waiting for an answer. "What am I? What am I?"

I use "what" rather than "who," because "who" is a personal pronoun that tends to lead us into being the body. "What" is more impersonal, but this question should always be held. No matter what path we follow, no matter what method we use, we should always hold in the background, "What am I?" And if we do that, eventually we must see the full answer. Did I answer your question?

Q: Yes, you did, thank you.

Q: Lester, pertaining to that, how many times does one ask the question?

Lester: Every time a thought, a stray thought, comes into the mind, we must say, "To whom is this thought? Well, it's to me. Then, what am I?" This will have to be repeated after each stray thought.

Q: But if no thoughts come, then it's not to be said?

Lester: Right.

Q: You wait then for an answer.

Lester: Wait to see. You don't wait for an answer, an answer would come from the mind.

Q: You wait to see?

Lester: Yes, you wait to see. The Self becomes self-obvious. All of a sudden it's there, and you realize it has always been there, that you have been looking away from it by deluding yourself into thinking you're a body, a mind. And then you see yourself as all Beingness. You become every person, every animal, every insect, every atom in the universe.

That the Beingness of the universe is only your Beingness is what you discover. It's there; it's there right now! But you are looking away from it all the time. When the mind is quieted enough, it's there. It's the "I" that I am—that's it. There's nothing closer to you than that. Most of the time you are seeking it out there, through a body, and it isn't out there. It's the "I" in here that is the infinite Being.

Holding only that question is not easy, and therefore I suggest holding it in general. Get in the habit of always seeking what you are, no matter what method you're using. And when quietness of mind comes—to the degree that there's no other thought on your mind but "What am I?"—this stilling of all the other thoughts makes your Self self-obvious. It's right there where you are, wherever you are, right where the "I" is. So, again, hold that question—no matter what method you use—until the answer shows itself, until it becomes obvious.

Q: It seems very hard.

Lester: It's hard to let go of the habit of thinking every moment that you are a limited body. We're just bombarding ourselves all the time with the thought: I am a body, I am a body, I am a body. This goes on all the time, so that we don't see the infinite Being that we are. It's a constant bombardment of: I am a body with involvement. Meditation is an attempt to quiet the mind by holding one thought so that other thoughts die away. By holding that one thought—if we can get to the place where just that one thought is there—that's enough quieting to see the infinite Being that we are. There isn't a method that doesn't try to effect the quieting of the mind so that the infinite Being that we are can become self-obvious.

Q: When you say "self-obvious," what does your real Self feel like?

Lester: When you get toward the end, as Vivekananda said, you see that there never was anything but "I" all alone. Now, if there's nothing but "I" all alone, then "I am everything, everyone" is your feeling.

You look upon every other body as equally your body. You see everyone as you; just as you see your body as you, you see everyone as you. The feeling is indescribable. It's such an intense experience, far beyond anything that limitation today will allow, that you'll never know it without experiencing it. But, from the level where we are, it's the thing we call happiness. It's joy unlimited, infinite joy. At first it comes on as an elation: it's overwhelming; it's hard to contain. It gets to be uncomfortable. You get slap-happy, punch-drunk, ecstatic; it gets to be annoying.

And then you work at it until it falls away, and what's left is a very deep, profound, delectable peace. It's a peace that is so much better than the extreme joy that you had before that you don't look for that joy any more. The joy state is not the ultimate; the ultimate is the peace state. Every one of us can get a taste of it at times.

Q: Then it's possible to come across this and then lose it?

Lester: Oh, yes. Many people do. The first time we really drop into it, we are not able to maintain it, because the habit of thinking takes over again. And the moment we're thinking, we are thinking we are limited. Every thought must be a thing of limitation. Let go of the game of being limited; let go of the world.

Don't try to control it. Don't try to enjoy it. Take all your joy from within. Then, what was formerly the game assumes a sameness picture. Everything becomes the same. If everything is the same, and it is in the absolute Truth, where can there be a game? If you get caught up in a game, you're caught up in an eternal illusion. The game will never end. And if you're in the game, you're away from your infinite Beingness. There is always a certain limitation in the game that will always keep you from being fully satisfied.

So, there is a step above the game of playing we are bodies, and that step is where everything becomes exactly the same. And that exact sameness is only you, your Beingness. There's an infinite

Oneness left, and that infinite Oneness is you and is your Beingness. It's Beingness being all Beingness.

And there's no separation; there's only Beingness, being all Beingness. Now, of course, it takes experiencing it to really know what this Beingness is. I am convinced that the best description of the top state is Beingness being all Beingness.

Q: How can I increase my desire for it?

Lester: Only you can do it. No one can do it for you. This is the unique thing about it. You have to do it. The grace we hear of is always existing. It's the inner Beingness that we are making us uncomfortable until we reestablish the original state. Desire for happiness is the grace. It's always there. All we need to do is to recognize it and take it.

Q: How does God get made into man? Isn't it somehow sacrilegious to try to change back?

Lester: No. Anyone who tells you that doesn't want you to attain the top state. But it happens this way: It's like going to sleep at night. You dream you're born into a little infant body; then you are a week old, a year old; then twenty, then forty. And you dream you have problems and problems and problems. Remember, this is only a night dream. This goes on and on, and you get so tired of it that you dream the body dies. Then you wake up.

Where did you ever change yourself while in that dream? You didn't! You say it never was; it was all concocted in my mind, right? That's exactly how we do it in this waking state. This waking state is a sleep state. We are totally asleep to the reality of this infinite Beingness that we are. We are no more awake to the Truth right now than when we are asleep at night. We are just dreaming that we are awake.

Actually, this is a sleep state that we need to awaken from—and, when we do, then we say, "Oh, my gosh, it never was! I never was a limited body! I was always that infinite Being that I am!" So, we mentally create a dream called the waking state of the world. However, it's just a dream-illusion. But to recognize that it's a dream, you must wake up out of this state. Does that make sense? So, the answer to "How did we do this?" is that we are dreaming it!

Q: Deliberately?

Lester: Yes, deliberately. You see, we start off as infinite Beings in a passive way. We go down to the bottom—that's where we are now— then go back to the top and again see our infinity. But after going through that, there's a positive knowingness of our infinity, whereas before it was a passive knowingness. It's something like this: "Perfect health" is a meaning—lesser to someone who was born perfectly healthy and stays that way all his life. He doesn't positively know what it is. And yet, it's a nice state when he's in it. But he's passively healthy; he cannot fully appreciate it.

However, if he got very sick and was on the verge of dying for many years and then reestablished the perfect health state, then that perfect-health state would be far more meaningful to him than it was before he got sick. And this is the silly thing we do to ourselves: We go from infinity down to where we are and back up to infinity with a positiveness of knowing the infinity that we are. But we pushed, on the way down, in a way that we lost sight of what we were doing. And if we look within, we'll discover this.

Q: That's the first time I've heard a sensible explanation of the whole mess, the first time it's ever been explained why we've been pulled down.

Lester: Okay, now go back up.

Q: Is there one person doing this?

Lester: There is one Beingness doing this. I think the best example of this is that of the ocean and the drops. We, the ocean of Beingness, imagined little tiny circles around parts of us that we called drops; and this drop says, "I am separate from that drop and separate from all the other drops." It's an imagined circle around part of the ocean calling itself a drop, but, actually, every drop is the ocean. It has all the qualities of the ocean: it's wet, it's salty, it's H_2O, and so forth.

I think that example might make sense. Or it's like a comb, and each tooth says to the other, "I am separate from you." It's all one comb, and we are the teeth saying that we are separate, when, in actuality, it's just one comb. Remember, you are the one infinite ocean of Beingness. It is the "I" that you are. Seek it, see it, and forever hold it!

Releasing Explorations by Hale Dwoskin

Would you rather play the game of limitation or would you rather be free? That simple question is a key to dropping our obsession with being limited body-minds. If you think you are your body-mind and the stories that you tell yourself and others about being that body-mind, then you would rather play the game of limitation. However, if you begin to recognize that you are not now and have never been that body-mind with all its limitations, then you have begun the process of waking to your true nature. You would rather be free.

At first you may only want this freedom a little. But the more you taste it and live it, the more you will choose it over the game of limitation.

As you move through the game of life, whenever you find yourself taking it seriously or getting caught up in your story or your problems, ask yourself, "Would I rather play the game of life or would I rather be free?" When answered honestly with the response, "I would rather be free," this simple question will cause you spontaneously to drop your identification with the you that appears to be playing the game, as well as with your problems related to playing it.

If you find that you would rather play the game at that particular moment, then let yourself play it full tilt, doing your best to recognize it as a game. This will weaken your attachment and aversion to the story that we call the game of life.

Realization by
Dropping the Unconscious

Lester Levenson

Our subject is called many things by many schools. I like to call it happiness. That which gives you the ultimate in happiness is the discovery of the Truth of you. Then you get to completely know you—you reach the ultimate joy, the peace of satiation. You discover that you are the All, and that your former worldly search was your trying to find your real Self in the world. There you never could discover the real you, the consequence of which was that you were never satisfied.

You are this thing called happiness. Your basic nature is infinite joy, far beyond anything your mind could comprehend. That's why everyone is seeking happiness. We're all trying to return to that wonderful inherent state that, when discovered, is ours all the time. However, we do not find it, because we are looking away from rather than toward it. We must look within. Basically, we are infinite Beings. We have no limitation, we have all knowledge; we have all power, and we are omnipresent, here and now.

There isn't anyone who doesn't possess these three things. The difficulty in discovering our purpose and goal in life is that, because we are infinite, we can make ourselves infinitely small. And this is exactly what we have done. We have achieved the extreme in limitation. We couldn't be much more limited than we are right now. In this universe, which is infinite in size, and in the three worlds, we are at the most extreme end of limitation. We have imagined ourselves, and frozen ourselves, into physical bodies; and because of so many millennia of looking at ourselves as bodies, we have become convinced that we are these physical bodies.

Beings are capable of seeing all realms that are denser than theirs. In the subtlest realm—the causal world—Beings can perceive the denser astral and physical realms. In the astral world, Beings can perceive the denser physical world, and, because we are in the physical realm and cannot see a denser realm, we are in the densest, most limited realm possible. The physical body being the most extreme end of limitation possible to us, we feel cramped: we hurt, we reach out. We try to express our freedom in the physical world. We try to eliminate time and space, to go faster and farther.

I'm pointing out how far we have gone in accepting limitation since we came into a physical body, and that this is the reason why it is so difficult for most of us to discover the Truth of ourselves, which is we have no limits. However, there's an advantage to being in this very limited state. Because we are so cramped, we have more of a desire to get out of it than we would if we were living in a harmonious heaven where everything was easy and immediately available— where life does not prod us into trying to get liberation.

We have a very distinct advantage in being here. We are forced to seek a way out. We are trying in many ways and with many methods to get free. No matter what the methods are, they all must end up doing the very same thing: freeing us of our concepts of limitation. The methodology must quiet our mind, must do away with thoughts. Every thought is a concept of limitation. When thoughts are undone, what's left over is the infinite Being that we are.

Unfortunately, we set into motion an automatic way of thinking called the subconscious mind. There, we relegate thoughts to the background and let them operate without needing to pay any attention to them. And we have lost sight of them. In the beginning, it was an advantage in operating a physical body, because originally we had to operate every part of the body consciously—every cell, every organ—and to eliminate all that attention, we put it on automatic control via the subconscious mind, and the subconscious mind is the real difficulty when we try to let go of thoughts.

It's difficult, because we are in the habit of not looking at it. Not looking at it, we don't see it. Since we don't see it, it goes on and on, lifetime in and lifetime out. We are so married to our thoughts that we never even think of divorcing them. And, until we do, we will continue, blindly attached to physical bodies and, in the overall, having a miserable life.

For every ounce of pleasure we take, we get pounds of pain; and it must be that way, because the pleasure we are trying to get is by seeking our very own Self externally in the world and through the body. And it just isn't there. The methods to be effective must be in a direction of first quieting our thoughts, then actually getting rid of our thoughts. Make a conscious effort to bring up subconscious thoughts and, when they are brought to the conscious plane, drop them. When they do come up, because they are very limiting and very negative as a whole, you want to drop them—and you do.

After you have dropped an appreciable number of them, then you can drop thoughts in larger amounts. To drop thoughts in larger amounts requires dropping the tendency or predisposition that has evolved from the accumulated thoughts on that one particular thing. Dropping the tendency or predisposition, one drops all the thoughts that caused that tendency or predisposition. In this way you may, at one time, drop a large accumulation of thoughts.

For instance, if one has a tendency to like sweets, one could bring up from the subconscious one thought at a time and continue letting go of them until there are no more. This takes a lot of time. However, if one drops the tendency itself, then all the subconscious thoughts that make up that tendency are dropped, and one is totally free from desiring sweets. Later, you reach a point where you can drop all the remaining thoughts at once, because having infinite power, you will have reached the point where you can see that you have this infinite power, and you then can use it to wipe out the rest of the mind. That is why it is sometimes said that realization is instantaneous.

When you get that far, that you can see that the power is yours, you wipe out all the remaining thoughts at once. Then you are *totally* free; you've gone all the way. When this happens, you don't become a zombie, and you don't disappear or go up in a flash of light. What you do is let the body go through that which you preset for it; and when you reach the end of the line of the action for the body, you will leave it with joy. You will leave it just the way you leave and let go of an old, worn-out overcoat.

You will never die. People around you might say so, but to yourself, you don't die. You consciously drop the body the way you would drop an old, worn-out overcoat. But, again, you won't do this until you run the course that you preset for it.

Now, I tell you this so you won't be fearful of dying if you get realization. So, attaining the ultimate state is not disappearing into a nothingness—it's a moving out into your omnipresence and letting go of confinement to only a physical body.

Now, to do this, you must have a strong desire to do it. The only thing that keeps you from being the infinite Being that you are is your desire to be a limited physical body. When your desire shifts into wanting to get free of the extreme limitation, it's a start; but to go all the way, you must have a desire to be totally free that is more intense than your desire to be a physical body. The reason why so few of us make it is that most of us have a stronger subconscious desire to be a physical body than we have a conscious desire to be a free, unlimited Being.

Until you confront this and see what your desire really is, it is impossible to achieve total freedom, total realization. You should dig into the subconscious to bring up your desires, because, unless you see them, you can't let go of them. The only reason why you are limited to the physical body is that, subconsciously, you have a strong desire to be this limited physical body. When your conscious desire to be free becomes stronger than your subconscious desire to be a physical body, then you'll quickly achieve your freedom. And therein lies your ultimate happiness. I think that is an overall presentation of the subject. Now, if you have any questions, I'd be very happy to do what I can to answer your specific questions.

Q: How do you dig into your subconscious?

Lester: Good question. You do it by first wanting to do it. It's very difficult when you begin, but as you do it, the more you do it, the easier it becomes. You can actually reach a place where it becomes easy.

Practice will do it. By practicing bringing up subconscious thoughts, the more you do it, the more you're able to do it.

There are many aids to doing it like "Get to the place where no one and no thing can disturb you." When someone disturbs you, and you don't know why, the thought is subconscious. Bring up the thought. By constantly trying, you will develop the habit of actually getting it up; you'll see that there's a limiting thought, an ego or selfish motivation behind it, and you'll drop it.

Q: Is just seeing the subconscious thought or motivation enough?

Lester: Just looking at it is not enough. You must consciously drop the thought or consciously will out the tendency or motivation. I'm assuming you'll want to let go of these thoughts, because they're all limiting and negative. One reason why we don't like to dig them up is that we don't like to see how awful we are. But there's nothing good or bad; there's just moving in the right direction or the wrong direction. When we move in the wrong direction, we move toward more limitation, and that's so-called bad. But everything is experiencing, and when we don't judge ourselves, we move much faster.

Q: When we don't judge ourselves?

Lester: Right. When we don't judge ourselves. Whatever comes up, so what? To get this far in your limitations, you have run the gamut of everything bad. It'll come up, but it's from past experiences.

Also, when you wake up, you'll discover that you never, ever were apart from your real Self, which is whole, perfect, complete, unlimited. All these experiences were images in your mind, just like in a night dream where you imagine everything that's going on. But while you're in a night dream, it's real to you. If someone is trying to kill you in a night dream, it's real; you're struggling for your life. But when you wake up from that dream, what do you say? "It was just a dream; it was my imagination." This waking state is exactly as real as a night dream. We're all dreaming we are physical bodies; we're dreaming the whole thing. However, in order to reach this awakened state, it is first necessary to drop a major part of your subconscious thinking.

Q: How do you see it when you come back after realizing it is a dream?

Lester: You see it like you now see a dream you had last night. You see it as a dream, and that's how important it remains to you. The before and after picture is simply point of view: before, you thought you were limited to a body, and all these bodies and action were so real. After, you see it as a dream, like a moving picture. When you see characters on the screen, you can lose your awareness of yourself by identifying with one of the characters on the screen, and you'll emote with him and feel unhappy.

Q: But you don't have all the desires that you had before?

Lester: You have no desires, because you wake up to the fact that you are infinite, you are the All, leaving nothing to desire. Desire limits you. "I don't have the All, therefore I must get it, and I create desires to get it." So, desire is only a limitation. When you see the full picture, you naturally lose all desire; there's nothing to desire if you are the All.

Now, practically speaking, if you choose to go along with the dream, you can act out a desire for the time being, and then act as though it's being satisfied. However, it's just an act, and you playact.

Q: How does the mind distinguish between bad and good?

Lester: By saying, "This is good and that is bad."

Q: Is that an individual thing?

Lester: Of course. What's right in one country is wrong in another; what's right to you is wrong to someone else. It's a very individualistic approach. Of course, there's some general agreement on right and wrong; we generally agree we shouldn't kill each other. So, right and wrong is a very individualistic standard. If you need a right and wrong, doing that which helps your growth is right; doing that which hinders your growth is wrong. That should be the right and wrong.

Q: Do we learn the right from experiencing?

Lester: Yes, you learn the right by doing the wrong. [laughter] Right? And also by experiencing the right. Unfortunately, most of us do it by actually doing the wrong thing. We learn to keep our hand out of a fire by burning it. This is what seems to prod us more than anything else—the hardships of life. We all want to get away from the misery of it, don't we? It should be the other way, that the wonderfulness of the right way should be the attractiveness of it. When you do get that far, then your growth is very fast, and you're approaching the end of the line.

Q: What did you mean by, "After you're realized, you live your life out as you preset it?" What does that mean?

Lester: We preset the behavior of this physical body before we enter it to put us through experiences that we hope to learn from.

Q: Knowing that you would attain realization this time?

Lester: No. Knowing that in past lives you subjected yourself to the law of action and reaction, cause and effect, karma (they're all the same thing), and that you want to continue that game. You did certain things when you were in a physical body before, so next time you want to set up similar things in a hope of undoing some of the things you don't like and instigating the things you do like. But you cannot change anything that the body was preset to do by you.

You're going to do exactly what you preset for that body before you came into it. There is no freewill in worldly living. However, there is a freewill. The freewill we have is to identify with the real Being that we are, or to identify with the body. If you identify with the body, you're in trouble. So the freewill is one of identity. Knowing this, it makes life much easier; you don't fight it. You aim for proper identity.

Q: The desire for bliss, would that be enough to start your search for happiness?

Lester: Sure.

Q: If one is sincere and isn't succeeding, will a guru help them?

Lester: A realized teacher is the greatest of all help, but he can't help you any more than you will help yourself. This is most important: he cannot help you any more than you will help yourself. When you try to help yourself, he joins you and helps you to a realization that you're ready for.

Q: He helps?

Lester: He helps you get a realization that you're ready for. If you're tapped on the chest, and you get cosmic consciousness, it's because you're ready for it. Of all help, a guru's is the greatest, because he has gone the direction, and he can help you go the same direction.

Q: How is it that when you see the dream structure of Maya and you see the real Self, then all of a sudden you're caught in the dream again and you believe it? What happened?

Lester: It is possible to see your real Self and fall back into the world. Why? Because you have not let go of the subconscious thoughts, "I am this physical body; this world is real." You must go into your subconscious and make conscious all these thoughts and drop them. Or see your Self to the degree that you see that your mind is external to you—something that you created—and then you just wipe it out.

If you can't wipe it out, and very few of us can, keep picking away at it; keep bringing up the subconscious thoughts and dropping them. Or you can make it ineffective in large chunks by willing out tendencies.

Take a particular tendency like smoking. If you've been smoking for years and years, you have thousands of little desires to smoke. The tendency is strong. However, you can say to yourself with willpower, "This is ridiculous! I am through with this!" and never again have a desire for a cigarette. That's getting rid of all the thoughts of desire to smoke by willing out the tendency. That's one chunk: smoking.

Q: That's one chunk; the whole bit clear back?

Lester: Complete. I've seen many people do this on smoking with no problem. They just made that decision, and that was it!

Q: And that's how you get rid of each thing that's bothering you?

Lester: Yes. If you're jealous, look at it. If you're disgusted enough with being jealous, you say, "Finished! Done! It is gone!" and you can undo the whole thing. That's letting go of a huge piece of mind. That's letting go of many, many thoughts of jealousy that you've had in the subconscious mind. It takes some maturity to undo that tendency.

Q: And it won't come back if you really do?

Lester: Right. If you, with resolve and determination, really drop it, it's gone. You can try it on smaller things first, and when you succeed, then go to something larger. Do it on one thing. Then you can do it on two, then on all. Do that which you can do. Keep doing this every day, and it won't take you long.

Make this a way of life. Grow every day. Every incident is an opportunity for growth. Everything you're experiencing is an experience of limitation. Every annoyance you have is an excellent opportunity to transcend that. Develop the habit of digging into your subconscious for the causative thought of the annoyance and then dropping it. Daily striving assures quick arriving.

Releasing Explorations by Hale Dwoskin

Are you willing for this world to be just a dream—a dream that never was? Most of us, even when we say that we are interested in freedom, spend much more time trying to prove the reality of the dream than the reality of Awareness or Beingness. We would rather know that we are who we think we are—our limitations—than face the possibility that who we think we are is only a lie—an erroneous belief about something that never really was.

If you want to recognize the Truth of who you are, choose to look honestly at what is actually here now. Truth is not based on memory. If you do that, you will see that what you thought you were never was, and what you are is and has always been.

Allow yourself to review what you call "your past" and allow yourself to reflect on one incident at a time. It does not matter whether you label your memories as positive or negative. Both have an equal hold on your consciousness. Then ask yourself this question: "Did that really happen or was that merely a dream that never really was?" This question can allow you to wake up spontaneously to the dream nature of what we usually call reality.

If a memory seems real, as opposed to being only a dream, you can ask yourself, "Could I let go of wanting to make this memory real?" "Would I?" and "When?" This will help you to let it go and allow it to be as it truly was—just a dream.

This process may seem difficult at first. But if you stay with it, it will get easier. Ultimately you will recognize for all time the dream nature of what we called "real" and that which is now and has always been: the one true changeless reality.

You may also want to explore the following question: "If nothing I experience is real, then what is real?"

The following process will assist you in applying what you have been learning in this book and in all areas of your life.

Triple Welcoming +

This process is used in most of our courses to address the spins of limitation that prevent us from recognizing that we are Awareness. This can be used any time you would like to go from being lost in a story or a belief in an old identity to resting as the presence, love, and joy that you are.

What also can be "done"—or may simply happen spontaneously—is that these habit patterns from the past can be welcomed fully as one vortex of energy spinning in or on the presence of awareness that you are. This naturally causes them to dissolve.

Triple Welcoming is a three-step process that may happen spontaneously or with our apparent help. You can "use" the following process for any resistance, issue, problem, belief, or feeling that you would like to release.

Step 1: Allow yourself to welcome the pictures, sensations, and sounds that arise in, or as, this pattern. Welcome as well the labels, stories, judgments, and conclusions—concepts that arise with, or as, this spin of energy.

Step 2: Allow yourself to welcome any desire to do anything with this spin or issue, including wanting to get rid of it or change it or wanting to hold on to it or make it real, as well as any attachment or aversion to the issue. You may even recognize that wanting to do something is simply part and parcel of more of the same spin.

Step 3: Allow yourself to welcome any sense that this whole spin or issue is personal—about you or who you are—any sense of me, mine, them, or theirs.

Optional Step 4: Allow yourself to welcome what is beyond the spin or what the spin is appearing in or on.

When we welcome all three aspects of the spin, it feels as though it breaks free inside, and often we actually experience a spinning sensation as it naturally and effortlessly spins itself out of existence. We are simply noticing the spin that was always there. It is as if we suddenly felt the spin of the earth. The earth spins at over 1,000 miles an hour at the equator and is spinning around the sun at 60,000 miles an hour, yet we do not feel this because we feel attached to the earth as we have felt attached to, or part of, these internal spins.

Simply allow the whole spin to have its own momentum. As this happens, the spin stops being fed by "you," and it dissolves on its own accord. At any moment, you may notice that this whole spin has no center or is about no one.

I highly encourage you to explore this for yourself as you explore this book and in your life as best you can without expecting any result. Everyone who has explored this application of the 5th Way has been amazed by its power.

Here are some questions you can use to explore Triple Welcoming +.

Could I welcome [whatever the issue is] and whatever it brings up inside?

Could I welcome any wanting to fix, change, control, or do anything with or about that?

Could I welcome any sense that is personal, about me or who I am?

Could I welcome the freedom which is beyond [the issue]?

Why Not Go All the Way?

Lester Levenson

You've been given the direction on how to go all the way. So far, none of us have taken it. We've gone to the place where life is nice, easy, and comfortable; we're satisfied, not totally, but satisfied enough not to go all the way. Is it that what I promised you would be there is not enticing enough? Maybe it wasn't made promising enough? Was it? Why shouldn't you go all the way?

Q: Well, I'd like to go all the way, but it's always over the next hill. I get to this point, and it's not there; and I get to the next one, and it's not there.

Lester: Not really, because it's right where you are. Over the next hill is where it isn't. Right where you are, where the "I" of you is, is where it is.

Q: How come we don't know it?

Lester: Yes, how come? That's what I want to know.

Q: That was my question.

Lester: Yes, but what is the answer? I say it's silly not to, because once you do, you'll never, ever have a moment of unpleasantness ever again. It becomes impossible to be unhappy. What's wrong with that? Why don't we do it? I would say you don't believe it enough. You don't believe that you have no limits, you don't believe that life can be, every second, ecstatically happy. You don't believe that it can be totally effortless; you don't believe that you can do things mentally. Or is it that we keep procrastinating? I say that if we really do want to go all the way, we do it. So, again, why don't we go all the way?

357

Q: Well, I think in my case, I've probably hypnotized myself into believing the opposite. I've associated with the finite me all my life, in all my conscious awareness, to the degree that it is real to me.

Lester: Oh, then to you the infinite would do away with finite?

Q: Yes, because the finite is what I believe in; it's real to me. What you say about the infinite has infinite possibilities, but until I can totally accept that, it's like when you touch a light bulb and it burns you and somebody says, "Now touch it and it won't burn you." It's difficult to overcome your subconscious reaction not to touch it.

Lester: Well, let me tell you then, that the infinite includes the finite and is the basis for it. You see, you can hold on to all the finite you want when you're infinite; you don't have to lose a thing.

Q: Then I'd be glad to give it up for the infinite.

Lester: Give it up? Maybe this is what's bothering us—that we're afraid we're going to give up our bodies, that we're going to give up our families and homes. It doesn't happen that way. When those who did go all the way achieved it, they did not abandon their bodies, homes, and families. They only abandoned their former feelings of bondage and attachment to their bodies, homes, and families, and in place of it felt free.

Q: If there's happiness greater than what I've experienced in a body, to heck with this!

Lester: Well, again, you do not give up your body. Your happiness gets more intense the more you move toward total freedom, until it reaches a point where you just can't contain it anymore. Then you resolve it into a very beautiful peace that is never, ever again disturbed. And that peace is really far more delicious than the intense joy was. Then, when you choose to be active in the world, you'll never, ever lose that background peace; you will feel it all the time. And you are free to do anything in the world: you can act angry or scared, be poor or rich. You can do anything you want, but you do not disappear.

Q: It doesn't affect you?

Lester: The world can never, never touch you again, because you have imperturbable peace.

Q: I understand.

Lester: So then, why don't you come along?

Q: I am. Whenever I identify my source of income with the effort I exert in my business, I say to myself, "You're a stupid idiot. This isn't the source of my infinite supply." However, I'm not strong enough just to say, "Well, this isn't it; I'll do it the other way," because I think *What if it doesn't work?*

Lester: You would have exactly what you had before you tried it. However, you expect it not to work if you say that.

Q: Yeah, but that's where the hang-up is. Maybe it's lack of faith— not that it hasn't worked for you, but whether it'll work for me, I am not convinced. If you could only help me, just one little infinite bit of strength that you could give me—

Lester: Oh, now wait a minute. You have the support, and I've given you many directions, any one of which would take you all the way. I could give them to you again.

Q: That's like the sign "San Francisco." I'll bet there are probably a hundred signs that point the way to San Francisco, but if I get to the sign and sit down underneath it, it would take more than just knowing where San Francisco is—and that's where I bog down.

Lester: Right, you don't take the direction; you look at it and sit down. Now, the direction: get to the place where no one and nothing can disturb you. This would have taken you all the way.

Q: Yes, but that's like going to the moon.

Lester: It is easy, if you would do it. It is your decision to be disturbed or not to be disturbed.

Q: That's quite a challenge!

Lester: Do you want more? I'll give you new ones.

Q: Yes.

Lester: Be totally selfless. Be interested only in others; have no interest in you yourself. That would take you all the way. If we would be totally selfless in our behavior—act not for ourselves but for the other ones—this would do it rapidly.

Q: I don't mean to be argumentative, but this is really a nitty-gritty.

Lester: I'll give you another one: Get to the place where you have no more desire. Keep letting go of desires until there are no more, and that's it! You don't like that one either, do you?

Q: Well, part of it. I've got a lot of things I'd like to let go of.

Lester: If anyone would carry that through until there are no more desires—and it's just letting go of them as they come up—you'd go all the way.

Q: Lester, what about the one that you and I discussed, about the mind? You see everything out there in your mind, right? So that's where everything is. So, that thing out there is just your mind. When you discover this, you change your mind, and it changes out there.

Lester: Yes, that would take you there.

Q: What about no attachments and no aversions?

Lester: That'll do it too. That will take you all the way. But why haven't we used these things? They are not new to us.

Q: That's what I'm earnestly trying to decide for myself. This is ridiculous; all this intellectual knowledge that I've acquired and what little I've actually done with it. It's alarming. I said, "How many people have their own private master in their family?" You've given us all this stuff, and I say, "It's my responsibility what I do with it. Why haven't I used it?"

360

Lester: Yes, and your private master is you! This is important: Your private master is you!

Q: Isn't there only one, anyway?

Lester: When you see what you really are, you'll see the Oneness and no more otherness.

Q: I try to squint, and no matter how I do it, I still see separation.

Lester: That's the way you are approaching it, with squinty eyes. You won't look at it full view, wide open, because you are afraid you're going to disappear. So what you have to do is dig down within, pull it out, and see it. Once you see it, you'll naturally let go of that fear.

You're also afraid you're going to lose your individuality. Your individuality is something you'll never, ever lose. It's with you through eternity. The "I" that I am is never, ever lost. What happens is that we just expand it to include more and more until it includes the entire infinity. I say you're afraid of losing yourself, your body, your mind, your family, your business, and all your little things. You're subconsciously afraid you're going to lose them. If it were conscious, you'd look at it, drop it, and be free.

Q: Well, you reached me when you added those other things. The physical body attachment I don't see, but when you included my family and my business and these other things—

Lester: Do you want me to show you how attached you are to that physical body? Just imagine, don't do it, but just image throwing your body over a cliff. Can you now see your attachment to the body?

Q: Yes. But do you have to have that desire to get rid of it?

Lester: You don't get rid of it; you see what you are, and then you'll see that you are not the body, that the body is one infinitesimal part of you.

Q: Why can't I go all the way?

Lester: Because you're afraid that if you do, you're going to disappear. Does anyone feel that? That you'll disappear if you go all the way?

Q: I'm afraid I'd lose my mind. [laughter]

Lester: You actually do lose your mind, and then you reestablish it so that you can communicate. It's far more difficult to reestablish the mind than it was originally to let go of it, because the mind itself was such a clamping down of you, you don't want to come back to it. But you will; you'll start thinking again. The only difference in the before and after picture is that now your thinking is unfree, determined by subconscious, compulsive thoughts. In the after picture, there are no more subconscious, compulsive thoughts. Every thought is totally free and without any conditioning by your tendencies and predispositions.

That leads me to another great one: Rid yourself of all your tendencies and predispositions, and you will go all the way. I have never talked much about miracles, have I? I don't feel as though I'm imposing on you now, as I used to feel, were I to talk about miracles, because, having moved up, you are more able to accept them. When I first moved to Sedona and lived by myself, most things were done by thought, and I was unaware of it. However, others began to come in, and it was because of them that I became aware of these unusual things. To me they were natural, but not to the others.

I might have told one or two of you about the teleportation incident. This one is interesting, because it involved two others—one who is following this path and another one who is not. The first one is F and the second one is D, the son of T, whom you all know. He came to Sedona from Phoenix and asked me if I would take a walk; naturally, he chose a direction uphill. We walked a mile and a half uphill, F, D, and I, and when we got to the end of our trip, we sat down to have our sandwiches. We had only a pint-sized canteen of water for the three of us, and we drank most of it on the way up. We had left only about an eighth of an inch of water in the bottom of this pint canteen, hardly enough for half a cup.

But the three of us were thirsty, and so I let go with the feeling

"Everything is perfect!" I received the inner knowledge that the water was abundantly there. Then I asked, "Do you want a drink, F?"

"Sure," she said. I gave F a cupful. Then D drank a cup, then I. We kept drinking until each one was satiated. We each had seven drinks! I curiously looked into the canteen and the same amount of water was there as originally, just about an eighth of an inch on the bottom of the canteen. We then started the downward trek for home. I was so tired that I felt as though the body would not walk anymore. I just let go, and I said, "Oh, Lord, there must be a better way!"

And the thought again came to me: "Everything is perfect." As I thought *perfect*, we, the three of us, had one step up there, and the next step was down near my home, where the surroundings were similar to the place we had left so as not to make it obvious to D.

F caught it and said, "Lester, we teleported!"

I said, "Oh, you're crazy, F, you're imagining it," because D's mind was in a turbulence. I could tell by the frown on his face. For his sake, I had to again say, "It's your imagination, F," and shut her up. F knew.

Later, when she was alone without D, I said, "What made you think we teleported?" And she laughed. She said, "Don't you remember, on the way up, D and I were collecting rocks, and in several places we put them on the left side of the road on the way up (the road was cut into the side of the hill). I wanted to pick up those rocks on the way back, but we bypassed all of those places.

Now, to do these things, it takes a mere effortless thought: you surrender, let go, and have a thought with no effort, no drive. It's the easiest thought you could have. And then it happens.

During the early days in Sedona, I was living this way, unaware of it. To me, it was natural. Whatever I thought, I expected. It seemed natural, just the way everyone thinks he lives naturally. It is really the natural way, and it is meant for us to live that way. Although, if we did, we wouldn't fit very well into our present society, would we? So, if you want to stay in communication, you go the way of people. Miracles are just this dreamworld effected immediately.

And miracles don't necessarily mean spiritual development, because the majority of people in the universe use these things. They use them on other planets where they're not necessarily more spiritually advanced than we. It is their natural way of life. But the easier way to live is purely mentally—mentally do everything. You people should be able to do all this.

Why not go all the way and have nature serve you? Why do you do things the harder way? I think it's because you're afraid you're going to disappear. I'm saying to you, "Look, I have been through these things. And I still have a body here. I didn't disappear."

Q: Can you demonstrate your infinity for me too?

Lester: You must demonstrate your own. You have had ample witnessing of these unusual things. If I do it for you, that would mean you can't do it. I just finished saying that you can do it! It's surrendering, then mere effortless thinking! You have the feeling that it is not I, but the Father who worketh through me. I can go on and on. I'm trying to entice you.

When I moved into the mobile home on my grounds, a girl, now living here in Laguna Beach, asked me, "How often do you fill that butane bottle?" (It was a five-gallon bottle.) I said, "Every month." Then I remembered it had been eight months since I had last filled it. Becoming aware of it, I let go of it.

When I was trying to show F how to conserve water, I let her take charge of and keep filled my fifty-five-gallon water drum alongside my mobile home. It took care of all my needs, including a shower every morning. The reason why I wanted her to take care of it was that I wanted to show her that you can live on very little water. But I lost track of time, and when I brought it to her attention, she laughed. It had been four months since she had filled it last. I kept using the water, and the tank wouldn't empty out! When we opened it and looked, it was still full after using it for four months. It never would have emptied out if I had not let go of it.

Q: "Had not let go of it." What do you mean?

Lester: Let go of it by letting it be "normal."

Q: You thought again of it as being a limited thing?

Lester: No, I let it be as usual, or as is normal to people. I want to remain in communication with people, and I choose to live like people live, because if I live in an unusual way, I'm out of communication. It even scares people.

Q: This wouldn't scare anybody.

Lester: I know by experience that it scares people. When it first came to me while I was living in New York City, some people wouldn't come near me because of these things happening. What's wrong with this way of life? Why won't you take it? It is yours for the taking. I hope to allure you by making it so tempting that you will go all the way. Look at the difficulties you go through to make a living. Ask yourself, "Why don't I go all the way? Why don't I take things directly, just for the thought of them? Why don't I express my total freedom?" And maybe the answer will come up, and you'll see what you're doing to hold yourself down.

Q: One reason is that we are so used to being hamstrung that we don't realize that we can get out of it. I was just thinking of the motel, of getting it sold, and then I thought, "Do I really want to leave it?" And I know I upset it every time.

Lester: That's true, and that is why I'm telling you of the easy way. Your habit of thought runs you the hard way. One way to undo all habits of thought, which are in the subconscious mind, is to see that you are not the mind, and you will scorch it.

Q: Tell us a little more about scorching this mind, which I have found out is most important.

Lester: I see you've gotten a realization just recently.

Q: That's right.

Lester: And yet, you didn't carry through on it. With that realization, you should have continued and said, "I can do it; I am infinite!"

With that infinite power, you just pass your figurative hand over the mind and it's finished. It's just a mental wipeout that you do, and that's it. You know how long it takes? Less than that [finger snap]! Less than a second. When you get your full realization, it's instantaneous. Before that, you play around, dropping a little bit at a time. This goes on and on, year in and year out, until you decide to let go of the whole thing. Then you've got full realization. It really comes instantaneously when it comes. You will it. Will is your power. You turn on your will so strongly that you just undo the whole mind, and you are totally free.

Q: It just doesn't make any sense at all. It's just as though you're handing me all the money in the world and saying, "Here!" and I'm sitting and saying, "Why don't I take it?"

Lester: Yes, why don't you?

Q: What's wrong with me?

Lester: What is? That's the big question. What is wrong? I know you think that this is possible, otherwise you would not have listened all this time.

Q: It's the intellect that's in the way.

Lester: That is it. Why not wipe it out? The intellect is the mind. We have to see we're not the mind, and that it is external to us, and then just make it ineffective. Just like that; that's the way you'll do it.

Q: You said something the other night, Lester, which was a help to me and that was, "I am going to put Lester to bed." So, I've said this to myself several times. "I am going to have him do so and so." And he's been doing so and so.

Lester: I always think that way. I'll send Lester and this body around and make it appear to be doing things. After I got the realization that I am not the body, it was years before I could use the word "I." People would laugh at me, because I'd talk about Lester. I would talk about "him," and sometimes I would say, "It, Lester," or "Lester, he."

I couldn't say "I" even though I was being corrected. Why? I was not this body. I could talk about this body, but it was so obvious and glaring that I was not this body that I couldn't say I was this thing, anymore than you could say you were your car. Because you are carrying yourself around in a car, would you call yourself the car? In the same way, you'll look at this body. (This body is a car-case, a carcass.) I say you're silly to not take the All.

Q: I think there's a stronger word than silly.

Lester: Yes, it's really stupid. He led me to say it. [laughter] It's so stupid not to go through life with everything you want, with nothing but extreme joy, peace, and loveliness every moment when that is your inherent state. It takes no effort to be what you are. It does take extreme effort to be what you are not: a body with trouble, sicknesses, and needing this and needing that. It takes effort to be what you're not, but to be what you are takes as much effort as you women would need to be a female and as much effort as you men would need to be a male. It takes no effort to be what you are. And yet you persist in using effort to be what you are not. It's really stupid!

Q: Well, I persist in using effort to try to be what you say I am. I keep working at this thing of being effortless. Does that make sense?

Lester: No, does it?

Q: Not to me.

Lester: Right. There's something wrong there.

Q: What did I say?

Lester: You're using effort in trying to make yourself effortless—that's impossible! It's a contradiction. You've got to stop using effort. You've got to let go and let be. That's what is meant by "Let go and let God." You are it, you're the god—let go and let your Self be. However, it seems to take much effort, because you are using tremendous effort to hold on to and maintain your non-self, your ego, and there is where your effort is. It takes no effort to be what you are—the Self.

367

Q: If I could arrive at the dreamer instead of the dream, then I'd have it made. And that's why I've been thinking, *This is a dream? Who's dream is this?*

Lester: Right! Discover the dreamer. To make it more intimate: I, the infinite Being, am dreaming that I am a limited body. While you are in a night dream, and you think you are a limited body in that night dream, it persists so long as you don't wake up. It's the same thing with this waking state. We're dreaming we're limited bodies. We have to wake up to the fact that we are infinite. We have to stop thinking that we're limited bodies, that's all. Stop thinking. Let go. Let be. Surrender is the word.

If we would surrender this moment, that would be it. Not I, but thou. Not my will, but Thy will. This is surrender. We could do that right now and that would be it. But no, we've got to be a busy ego-body, doing something. We must be a doer.

Q: Some of the people at the motel were discussing robots. Actually, I guess we could consider the body a robot. We're using this physical body, and when we're through with it, we drop the physical body, but what we have is still there.

Lester: That's an excellent way to look upon the body. All right, now I'll tell you something more. If you were really convinced of what I've said so far, you'd go home. You'd forget everything else, and you'd sit down until you saw this, because this would give you everything, just for the thought. If you were really convinced, you'd go home determined to sit until you see this; and if you did that, you'd see it! Just like Buddha did, when he left his throne and sat under a tree, determined not to leave until he saw the answer; and he saw the answer.

Q: Well, I think one thing that may be bogging some of us down, and I know to a certain extent it has to me, is that I have felt for a long time that I had to take something piecemeal and get each thing out of my system. Now, I'm finally beginning to realize that if I get above it, then none of it makes any difference.

Lester: Yes. We all start that way by undoing single things at first. It begins to show us our mastership. Then we master our tendencies or predispositions. This undoes all the numerous multitudes of thoughts that made up that tendency or predisposition. You should not keep undoing these single things piecemeal. That was all right for the beginning; you don't need it anymore. Drop a tendency or predisposition, and you drop the millions of subconscious thoughts underlying it.

Q: When you first started to tell us that there's nobody out there but you, some of us just couldn't understand that, me included. I have discovered why there's nobody out there but me: because it is I who creates that out there, and it is in me.

Lester: Yes, that's true!

Q: So, I really know. I had a realization that was as clear as crystal.

Lester: Okay, why not clean up that "out there" until you do not waver from seeing it all as in you?

Q: That's what I'm doing now.

Lester: You don't take enough time at it.

Q: That's true.

Lester: It should be all the time, regardless of what you're doing. While you're driving, talking to people, you can remain with it, and you would if you wanted it that much. If you really get with it, the joy of doing it is so great that you won't let go until you go all the way. It becomes the only thing you want. You begin to see the light, and then nothing in this world can interest you more than it. You just stay with it and you ride it all the way. Misery starts you in the direction, gets you to reverse your wrong direction. Then the desire for the wonderfulness of it takes you all the way to the top.

Q: Then you know you can play any game you want, because that mind is under your control.

Lester: Yes. However, the game played is after reaching the top is usually the same game for everyone, although it will express differently; it's the game of helping others, which is really a great game.

Q: It becomes an interesting game.

Lester: It's the nicest game there is; it's the most rewarding game there is.

Q: What you are teaching me is really helping me.

Lester: That which I'm offering you is more than a million dollars. What I'm offering is the whole universe. If you wanted gold, you could pile it up by the tons. Of course, when you can create unlimited tons of gold, do you want to pile it up? No, you take only that which you can use.

Q: Of all the different ways that you've offered, it seems like there ought to be one that I could be successful with.

Lester: Take any one of my many sayings and, if you carry it out until the end, that would be it. Take the good one mentioned before: Get to the place where no one and nothing can disturb you. Every time you are disturbed, look for the ego-motivation wherein you wanted it to be other than it was. On recognizing it, say, "Oh, I see," and let go of your ego-motivation of wanting it to be the way you want it to be. Every reaction or tendency is based on a selfish thing. We wanted it to be the way we wanted it to be. Keep dropping these reactive tendencies. Every time a reaction comes, look at it; see the selfish ego-motivation and drop it. You'll soon reach a place where there is no more, and you're there—all the way.

Q: Every time you feel offended or jealous or angry or hurt or anything like that, that's your ego, and that's your mind.

Lester: Right. Rid yourself of all your feelings, and you will go all the way. So, have we gained anything new?

Q: You have presented us with more of a challenge to understand what you're saying; you make it sound so darn easy, and it affronts me to think that anything that easy could elude me.

Lester: When you do it, it is easy. When you don't do it, it's impossible. That's the way it really is. When you do it, it's easy. When you don't do it, it's impossible.

Q: Oh, lord, wait a minute. When you do it, it's easy. When you don't do it, it's impossible.

Lester: It takes no effort to be what you really are: infinite. It takes tremendous effort to be extremely limited as you now choose to be. I feel as though I've given what I could on going all the way. If there's any further question, I'll be happy to do what I can to answer it. If not, this is it.

Q: I keep looking at you, and I see that there's hope. If you've made it, somebody has. It isn't impossible, and I can do it.

Lester: Yes, do it. Go all the way. Everyone was moving rapidly upward and then leveled off; some came down just a little bit and leveled off there. If you don't use what you've seen, you'll lose it. You have got to keep using it, otherwise the remaining subconscious habits will overwhelm you, and you will lose your direction.

Q: When we go all the way, we still go on doing the same things: we still go on laughing, we still go to the ballet, do all these things. There's nothing denied.

Lester: Yes. The only difference is that you're free to do or not to do whatever you want; you're no longer compelled in any direction whatsoever. I strongly recommend taking time out for thinking on these things every day, twice a day. In the morning before going to work and at night before going to bed. Never should a day go by without doing this. Get with it, totally in a quiet spot, until it sucks you in more and more, until you let go of the world pull. Getting quiet enough, the infinite part of you just takes over, and you go all the way. You reach a place where you feel helpless, because it's effortless. Keep that up, and you'll effortlessly be sucked right into your infinity.

Q: Well, I know. Sometimes it seems that I'm getting so tall.

Lester: There's a sense of surrender in that.

Q: There's that famous statement of yours: "Let go and let God." It finally struck me that that means let go of your mind and let God.

Lester: Yes, another way to say that is, "surrender." Even if you surrender to a mountain, you will get it, because surrender is "not my will."

Q: Ego, mind, and will are all the same thing. So, if you let it, that means letting go of your mind, ego, and all the other things.

Lester: Yes.

Q: Sometimes when something happens, I can be very irritated, but then I catch myself giggling to myself while I'm doing it. It really isn't affecting me.

Lester: Yes, get free, and then you may act irritated.

Q: So you can act any part? And you're aware of the fact that you're an actor?

Lester: Right. Go all the way and there is only fun.

Q: You can even keep your humor too?

Lester: Right. But the motivation for the humor is to make others happy, not for ego-approval. That's the difference.

When I say you people leveled off and are on a plateau, it's not exactly correct. You leveled off into a slow, gradual, upward direction. It could be much faster, even immediate, rather than a slow, gradual, upward trend. Go all the way, and then life from that point on is just a ball. You don't have to work. If you want to, you can. You can always be successful—or you can even choose to be unsuccessful, just to make a game out of it. If you can succeed in failing, you can also succeed in succeeding.

Q: Would helping others really be a fast way?

Lester: Not so if your purpose is ego-motivated. However, when you live only for others, it's a very fast way. Paradoxically, the most selfish thing you can do is to be totally selfless. When we are totally selfless, we have the All, the infinity. It's a seeming paradox.

Q: That's it. You offer me the All!

Lester: Yes. We've all had glimpses of it. The thing to do is to establish that permanently, for all time. So, again I say, take time out every day and effect it. Go all the way. You've got infinite power behind you; there's nothing to stop you but you. Make it part of your everyday life, and stay with it until it's established for all time. You can do it!

Releasing Explorations by Hale Dwoskin

What do you believe you must give up in order to be free? If we were honest with ourselves, most of us would have quite a long list. But what if what Lester said is correct? "There is no giving up on the path to freedom; there is only a taking on of more and more until you recognize you are the All." You can have a direct experience of being the All, if you will it or are completely open to it. As Lester used to say, "Try it, you'll like it."

Most of us do not let ourselves discover our true nature because of fear. But there is a secret about fear. Once you learn it, you can use it to help you let go of all fear, including whatever fear you have about recognizing your true nature—your freedom. Here it is: Anything that we are afraid of we subconsciously want to happen or expect to happen—and often we get to be right.

We may see or hear about something that has happened to someone else. Or we may experience something directly that we don't like. We want to avoid these things. So we think, *I hope this does not happen to me,* or *I hope this never happens again.* But, because the mind thinks and creates in pictures, it is not able to visualize a negation. By holding a picture in our minds of what we fear happening, we create it.

You can use the above information to let go of any fear including the fears associated with being fully awake. Ask yourself, "What am I afraid will happen if I wake up or I am totally free?" No matter how you respond to that question, ask yourself, "Could I welcome that?" "Could I let go of wanting or expecting that to happen?" "Would I?" and "When?" As you do let go, you will be letting go of your artificial obstacles to freedom and will feel more and more open to waking up to your true nature.

Thou Art That

Lester Levenson

Everyone is aware of the infinite Being that he is. Are you aware of the "I" that you are? The word "I" is the Beingness part of you. But it's only the Beingness part. If you experience "I am," that's it. That part of you is infinite, and you are experiencing it all the time. There's no time when you are not experiencing it—otherwise you'd go out of existence. However, you override it and hide it from yourself by saying, "I am a body." And what you're doing is saying, "I, the infinite Being, am this body."

So, if you use the word "I," you're talking of the infinite Being that you are. Every time you say, "I am something," you're saying, "I, the infinite Being, am a limited something." And being infinite, it allows you to assume limitation as much as you want. That's why you can do such a good job of limiting yourself. Does that make sense?

Q: Yes.

Lester: We can drive ourselves into such extreme limitation that we think we are a victim of our environment and subject to it. And it is an infinite Being doing that!

Q: Why do we not realize our unlimited Being?

Lester: We have the conviction that we can't do it. If we were not convinced that we couldn't do it, we could do it quickly, even in a moment. How long should it take one with all knowledge, all power to recognize that he is all knowledge, all power? No time! And each one of us is that all-powerful, all-knowing individual. It seems so hard, almost impossible, only because we won't do it. That's why it's so difficult, because we won't do it! You hold the concept that you are a body rather than that you are an infinite, unlimited Being. As long as you hold to that concept, you're stuck with it. You don't look at the other, the opposite side of you, which is unlimited.

Q: Well then, could you say that the only thing between us and realization is a thought, really?

Lester: Yes, that's it. It is a thought that is the culmination of much thought. If you would just examine how your thoughts flow after I tell you that you are unlimited, you would discover that immediately you dive right into the thoughts of being a limited body.

When I say that each one of you is infinite, unlimited—right now—at that moment you get a feel of it. Are you aware of the feeling that you get as I say it? Right now, everyone here is infinite, unlimited, omnipotent, omniscient, omnipresent. When I say that to you, for that instant you feel it; but the next moment you think you are the body and immediately take your full attention off what you really want and put it on the concept of being only the body with all its affiliations.

All right, now that you have heard this, why don't you stop doing this to yourselves? [Interruption: Two people arrive and enter the room, causing much conversation.] You have an example right now of what I've been talking about. Can you see what just happened? If what I said had been held on to, you would not have been distracted by the newcomers; the people would have come in and quietly sat down, and nothing would have been said. But we're so interested in bodies that we immediately gravitate toward them. This is the problem, our persistence in being bodies. Every moment we hold that, we are limited bodies.

What you need to do is stop doing just that. Will you do it? If you do, you will see the infinite Being that you are. It's really simple but seems extremely difficult. Not only difficult but impossible, doesn't it? It is, only because we just don't do it, and that makes it impossible. We've heard these things again and again and again. But what use is it listening to this if we don't do it? And, as I said, being infinite, there isn't anyone here who couldn't be the infinite Being he is right here and now, if only he would do it.

So, what you need to do is to get with yourself, look at yourself, and do it. And it's that simple. How many of you women go about every day trying to discover that you're a female? None. Who of you men go about every day trying to discover that you are a male? Why don't you? Why don't you people want to be told that? Because you accept it without any doubt whatsoever. But you do not accept that you are infinite. Why not? Why play the game of limitation and be miserable? Why? I'm asking you the questions now instead of you asking me.

You believe you're infinite. Why don't you be what you are, instead of this constant trying to be the limited body? The body is a very cramped thing to be, and it hurts, lifetime in and lifetime out. Why do you insist on being so cramped and incapacitated, as everyone is if one is a physical body? Compared to what one really is—infinite, unlimited, and totally free—it is ridiculous, isn't it? Maybe someone might want to answer the question, "Why don't you be what you are: infinite?"

Q: What does it feel like to be infinite?

Lester: Absolutely no limitation in any direction whatsoever. No limitations: total freedom from everything, needing no food, no oxygen, no job. Instantly materializing anything you want. Being anywhere in the universe. Being as tall as you want, or the size of an atom. Being at perfect peace and contentment. Being in the most delightful state possible.

Q: What happens to this body when that happens?

Lester: To really know that you should experience what you are. Otherwise, the reality of the body can't be understood. When you see what you are, only then do you know what the body is. It turns out to be a thought, a thought just like in a night dream when you dreamed about being a body in a situation. And when you awoke, you said, "Oh, my gosh, that was all in my mind."

The same thing happens to this body when you wake up from

this dream called the waking state. You see the body, but you know it to be the dream nature that it is. Do you see how much you're concerned about the body? And this point I make: Be as concerned about your infinite Being as you are about your body; if you are, you will discover that you are infinite.

Q: What I really meant was, when you are away doing these things, how does this body function?

Lester: Automatically. However, you can't be away from the "I" that you are. You're right where your "I" is. When you say "I," that's where you are. You can't get away from it, ever. The individuality never leaves you, and you never leave it. The "I" that you are always is. It's eternal. That's the real Being that you are.

All right now, if you will be that "I," and only that "I," then everything will turn out to be like a dream. And when you see it full, a dream that never really was, it's the same as when you wake up from a nightmare. A good allusion to what we are going through now is the nightmare. As long as you remain in it, it's a horrible thing, and it's very real. It only becomes unreal to you after you awaken. Right? The exact same thing happens to this waking state dream when we wake up from it. We first say, "Oh, my gosh, it was all a dream," and then we add, "That never really was."

And that's what happens to your body. You then see it as a dream body. Your body will change, but you never will change. You don't disappear; you don't lose anything. You just take on more and more until you see yourself first, as every Being, as every body, and then as every atom in the universe. There's no reason to fear losing your body or losing anything. You gain more and more until you become infinite. Yet, most of us are fearful lest we're going to lose our body and be nothing. That's a serious error. You could be a hundred bodies!

Q: If you think of the body in terms of Beingness—

Lester: If you do, you're committing a gross crime against the word *Beingness*. Beingness is the infinity that you are. Your Beingness is infinite. Your being a body is an extreme limitation in your Beingness.

Q: We think of body in terms of limitation; that's the ordinary concept of body.

Lester: Right, which means we have to let go of the concept: The body is I. As long as we hold that, we are holding the concept: I am an extreme limitation, a physical body. Any slight maladjustment in it, and it dies. And everyone knows that it does, sooner or later. What's this great thing called a body? It's a very disposable thing, and everyone knows that sooner or later he will dispose of it, right? But gosh, how we hold on to this limitation! And keep ourselves in extreme confinement! We are like a bird in a cage, with the door open, refusing to fly free!

Q: Well, this sense of Beingness, infinite Beingness, is far more concrete than our present sense of body, is it not?

Lester: It should be. This is what, in effect, I'm saying. If you just hold on to your sense of Beingness and just hold that, and not add "This body is I," just hold on to your Beingness only—and hold it and hold it—you'll be letting go of the feeling that the body is I. And you'll get an insight into this Beingness, as to what it is, and then you will remain in it. Then your Beingness is very concrete to you, and your body is like a dream body. When you are only Beingness, you recognize that your Beingness is all Beingness. I say that everyone here is, right now, that infinite Beingness. And the infinite part of you is the "I," the Beingness of the "I," the, "I am." And if you would hold that, that would become real and concrete to you, and all the limitation, misery, and trouble of the body would automatically be gone.

Q: I've had a few glimpses of that, but holding it is a different thing.

Lester: The reason why you don't hold it is because you are holding on to the body being you.

Q: The thing is that this Beingness cannot be conceived of with the mind, can it?

Lester: Right. However, you don't have to conceive of it if you are it. Do you have to conceive of being a male? Just only be it.

Q: But this metamorphosis, this change that must take place within the individual, requires some intellectualization at first?

Lester: The intellect directs you toward looking away from what you are not and looking at what you are. In that sense, you're right. We ask, "What am I?" and that's intellectual. However, the answer is an experience.

Q: Now this is what I was getting at. When does this intellectualization of the infinite stop, and you realize it as it is?

Lester: When your thinking quiets enough, you then see what you are, and it becomes real to you.

Q: But you're not conscious of that transition?

Lester: You're conscious of letting go of the concepts of limitation. Discovering the infinite Being that you are is no transition, because you are that now; you always have been and always will be that. So there can't be any transition there. It's the letting go of the thoughts of limitation that is a transition.

Q: Isn't it difficult for one to think of his inner Being as infinite?

Lester: In your thinking, it's impossible. You can only experience it.

Q: And yet it's real; you do come into it. There's no doubt about it.

Lester: Yes, sooner or later. When you get so fed up with torturing yourself, you then let go of all the nonsense, and you'll be what you really are—infinite. Now, most people on earth will take millions of years to do this, and you can see why. When we take into account all people, you're very advanced. And look how much you are holding on to being only that body! Your questions and talk relate mostly to the body, its transition, and what happens to the body. I'm hoping to provoke you into letting go of identifying with the body, by telling you it's impossible to be infinite, because you insist upon being the body. And so long as you persist in being the body, it is impossible. You're stuck. And you could remain this way for millions of years. Have you ever accepted the concept that you have no limitations?

Q: I've accepted the idea intellectually, but obviously not in practice.

Lester: Yes, and because you believe you are a body, it is impossible to be infinite. These bodies are very frail things, and they don't last very long, either. And we insist and persist in being the body. Now any time anyone decides—really decides—not to be it, then he will allow himself to see his infinite Beingness.

What do we do twenty-four hours a day? We cater to the body; we think we are it! We wake it up in the morning, we wash it, we dress it, we beautify it. We send it off to work so it can earn some money, so that we can put some other life (food) into it so it can rot (digest) that life inside so that it can persist. And then we go home, and we park it for the evening. It is such a wonderful life that we have to escape from it; every night we have to go unconscious, that is, go to sleep. And this we repeat day in and day out, life in and life out, until we decide that we are not the body, that we are more than the body, that we are infinite Beingness. It is really simple. The difficulty of it is the holding on to wanting to be the body. We are constantly saying, "I am the body; I am not infinite." And, of course, we can't feel the unlimited joy or happiness that we're seeking by cramping ourselves into a little body that's frail and perishable.

Q: What do you mean when you say we have such a wonderful life that we have to go unconscious?

Lester: This life that we think is so great, we cannot take twenty-four hours a day. For about eight hours every day, we have to escape it through the unconscious state of being asleep.

Q: While asleep, where am I? Why can't I remember?

Lester: Because you believe you can't. The reason is that you don't want to, because, unless you relate to the physical body and world, you believe you are a void. However, notice the fact that, although you drop the physical body and world in sleep, you still exist, don't you? Sleep is an escape from this wonderful world of ours. As we go up into higher states of Beingness, we all reach a place where we don't sleep anymore. When we do not dislike the world, there's no need to go to sleep. I want to point out how wonderful this world is. How wonderful is it if we have to escape from it every night? So, let go of it and be what you are. Be infinite. Stop looking at the world and look at the "I that I am," and keep your attention on the "I that I am" until you see it fully, and you'll drop being only a physical body with all the limitation associated with it.

Q: We keep imagining that this little limited life brings us happiness, and that helps keep us bound, doesn't it?

Lester: Yes, so why do it? Everyone is seeking the infinite Being that he is. You call it happiness, happiness with no sorrow. It is your Self, your Beingness. Why not just be it? Why don't you do it?

Q: Well, I guess we don't want it badly enough; we're afraid to go all out.

Lester: That's it, you don't want it enough. You want to be the limited body with all its adjuncts of limitation—sickness, trouble, and finally death. Ridiculous, isn't it?

Q: Actually, if this were the most important thing in your life, it wouldn't take long to become that. But we all have our side tracks that keep us going in all directions.

Lester: That's it. We really don't want this knowledge of our unlimited state, right? Therefore, our attention is in the other directions.

Q: It's unlimited, we know this intellectually, but do you think we have a resistance, not knowing exactly what is there for us?

Lester: Yes, and no. You know you're infinite, and you're seeking it. In your every act, every day, you're seeking this infinite Being that you are. You call it happiness. If you would trace happiness down to its source, you would discover that there is no happiness in external things or people. Happiness is something you experience within.

And it's there all the time if you just don't cut it off by making it dependent on someone liking you, or on your getting gold.

Once I say, "In order for my inner happiness to be, I must have gold," I cut off that happiness unless I get gold. So we're cutting off that unlimited happiness and saying it's in the world, in tiny bits, while all the time it's unlimited right within us, not out there in the world. But, as you said, we're so convinced that it's in the world that our attention is in directions other than on the infinite Being that we are. If we really wanted to see this infinite Being that we are, our attention would be there all the time.

Q: And we could be that right at that moment!

Lester: Right. At that moment, or soon, or in a month or two. But I say you are condemned to millions of years of misery if you persist in being the body.

Q: If one experiences very intense misery where everything seems to be cut off, an awakening can come out of this sometimes, can't it?

Lester: Oh, yes. That's the way we usually do it. When we are in the direction of limitation, we keep making ourselves more and more limited until we go to extremes and think we are in danger of becoming incapacitated with something severe, with sickness or death. Then, with our determination, which everyone has, we say, "To hell with this!" and we go in the right direction. However, we could and should go in the right direction because of the wonderfulness of it.

Q: I think the tendency often is to try to contact the infinite and then use it to make this finite life comfortable, pleasant, prosperous, and things like that.

Lester: Right. We try to contact our unlimited power and then use it to make a better body and world. We can make the body and world better, but we cannot achieve sustained happiness, because being subject to this body and world is being subject to limitation and non-freedom.

Q: But getting rid of your body isn't going to help much, though, is it?

Lester: I'm not suggesting you do. Until you can consciously leave your body, if you forcibly got rid of your body, you would just come back again through the womb and wait twenty years while growing up before starting again to learn that you're not the body. So, forcibly dropping the body would be a very wrong thing to do. But to show you how much you think you are the body, just ask yourself how close could you come to throwing your body out on the highway and letting cars run over it. This will show you how convinced you are that your body is you.

Q: Is it our unconscious mind that prevents us from being our infinity?

Lester: It's you, making your thoughts unconscious. I say it's you; it's not your mind. Or, if you want to argue it, show me this mind you are talking about. Where is it? And how is it holding you back? Does it have a life other than you? Is it other than you? What is this thing? You're preventing yourself, whether via the mind, the body, anything. You are doing it. It's important that you take full responsibility, because, if you don't, you will never get out of this trap.

Q: I understand that it is something that we have created ourselves, but it has reached such a proportion!

Lester: Not it, it is you who have reached such a proportion. So long as you blame something else, you'll never get out of it. You're doing it. Can't you see that you cannot undo your limitation as long as you'll not take responsibility for it? No matter what you call it, whether you call it mind, or body, you are doing it.

Q: I am taking responsibility for it, because I'm trying to do something about it.

Lester: Okay. As long as you say, "I'm taking responsibility," that's all right. But when you say, "It is the mind," you are not taking responsibility for it. Then the mind is responsible, not you. Do you see that?

Q: Well, I'm responsible for it; it's my creation.

Lester: Right. Whose mind is it? It's yours.

Q: But, still, it has become a sort of Frankenstein's monster that's gotten out of hand. And isn't that what stands in the way?

Lester: No, you do. As long as you think it's something other than you, you have no chance. As you speak now, you are convinced that the mind is doing it, and not you.

Q: So we make the mistake that the mind is going to see, and the mind will never see it.

Lester: Right!

Q: And we're so conditioned to function as mind that that seems to be the only tool we know we have, and so we're using the wrong tool.

Lester: Right.

Q: So, what we need to do is just throw the tool out.

Lester: Right. Then what's left over is the infinite you. Throw the tool out. It takes no tools to be what you are!

Q: That's the mistake; we keep trying to do it with the mind, because that's the only thing we're familiar with.

Lester: It's not the only thing you're familiar with; you are also familiar with the "I" that you are. Just the word "I," and that's you, that's not your mind. You have the mind. You are always experiencing this infinite Being that you are, and it's the "I." You lose sight of this infinite "I" by identifying the mind and body as you. Let go of identifying with your body and mind, and what is right there in the pure "I" is an infinite Being—you. Simple enough?

Q: You say the "I" has been for billions of years. Is the "I" always the same?

Lester: The "I" that you really are is always the same: changeless, eternal, and perfect.

Q: It has always been the way it is, and the way it will be?

Lester: It has always been that way: perfect, changeless, immortal. And that's why we have the tendency to think of the body that way. We try to make it perfect and immortal, even though we know we can't.

Q: Does the body serve a purpose?

Lester: Yes, it hurts; it confines. This serves to redirect you back to seeing that you are infinite. The purpose of having the body is to help you learn that you have no limitation. So, you conjured up the extreme limitation called the physical body in order to learn that you have no limitation. That body is going to hurt more and more the more you think that you are it, until someday you say, "The heck with it!" Then, with full determination to see what you really are, you suddenly awaken to what has always been—that you are infinite.

Q: Has the "I" always used the body?

Lester: No, the "I" never used the body. The "I" is changeless and perfect. The "I" imagined, dreamed, it used the body. It's an illusion; it's a dream, but while you're in the dream, it seems real. Wake up out of this dream. See what you are. That is the thing to do. Notice how much you ask me questions about the body. Are you aware of that?

Q: In order, I guess, to define it.

Lester: No, you are trying to express your infinity in terms of this extreme limitation. And this is why you're stuck. Reverse it. Let go of the body. Put all your attention on the infinite "I" that you are, and only then will you have a possibility of seeing the infinite "I" that you are. You must let go of the concept of that body being you.

Q: Pain is a great awakener, then, isn't it?

Lester: Yes. However, we're not aware of how much pain there is, because we have accustomed ourselves to it and made ourselves immune to the real amount. Because we're infinite Beings, and we're trying to be this limited body. It's very painful. And when you awaken from this dream, you'll see how much pain there was. It's almost infinite pain compared to what you really are, which is infinite joy. I'm emphasizing that you should be not the body and be not the mind, but just be.

Q: In meditation, doesn't one use the mind to a certain extent?

Lester: Yes, however meditation is used for quieting the mind. You use the mind to quiet the mind. When the mind is quiet enough, this infinite Being that you are becomes obvious. That is the whole purpose of meditation. If anyone gets his mind quiet enough, he cannot help but see this infinite Being that he is, because it's only the thoughts that cover it. And the mind is nothing but thoughts. So, meditation is used to get the mind quieter, until you get it so quiet that you see your Self, your real Self.

Q: Would directing the thought toward the infinite be a step toward getting there?

Lester: Yes. However, it is another thought.

Q: It's another thought, but some thoughts are more God-revealing than others, are they not?

Lester: No thought can reveal God. Every thought hides or covers God, your Self. Every thought is a chain; nice thoughts are golden chains. A golden chain will keep you imprisoned just as much as an iron chain. You must undo all thinking. Get the mind quiet, and then quiet enough so the infinite Being that you are is self-obvious. It's there all the time; the thoughts are the noise that's covering it. However, if you must have thoughts, a thought in the direction of God is much better than a thought in other directions, as it points you toward God.

Q: But if the infinite is non-mind, how can you speak of it as infinite, because infinite is a mental concept?

Lester: No. No mental thought can be infinite. Every thought is a limitation.

Q: Then how can you know that you are infinite? How can you vocalize it?

Lester: You cannot mentally conceive of infinity, nor can you vocalize it. That is impossible. Try it when you're home. It's impossible to conceive of unlimitedness.

Q: Well, it's an experience.

Lester: Right, it's not a thought; it's an experience, an experience of being infinite. The mind can allude to it but cannot describe it. Any description is necessarily a limitation.

Q: Where does the mind begin, and where does the mind end? Where does God begin, and where does God end? And where does the infinite begin, and where does the infinite end?

Lester: God, the infinite, the Self, has no beginning and no end. The mind has a beginning when you create it. It has an end when you let it go.

Q: It seems to be a painful struggle to let it go.

Lester: You're holding on to it while trying to let go of it. The holding on to it is the pain. Why don't you just be what you are? Why question me on the opposite side, on the struggle? Why do you talk about it? Because you're interested in it, and you would like me to relate the infinite to it.

Q: Well then, if, when you think, you just know who is thinking— that takes care of it?

Lester: Right! Discover who the thinker is, and you'll have the answer. When you discover who the one is that has the mind and has the body and does the thinking, you discover the real you, an infinite Being. So, look away from the body! Look away from the mind, and look toward the Beingness that you are and never stop until you fully discover that thou art that!

Releasing Explorations by Hale Dwoskin

A quote from this session is a key for your awakening: "God, the infinite, the Self, has no beginning and no end. The mind has a beginning when you create it. It has an end when you let it go." We actually recreate the illusion of the mind every day after we wake up and every time we refer to "I" as anything but the infinite Being that we are. But the mind does not ever exist. It only appears to exist when we refer to it as previously mentioned. We also let the mind go between our days in order to sleep. And we let go of the mind whenever we are fully present and engaged with what is now without saying this is "me" or "this is mine."

So you are picking up and recreating the illusion of mind all the time. Yet it is never ever real.

Allow yourself to become aware of how you are recreating the illusion of "me" or of "mine." As you catch yourself appearing to create limitation, switch your attention to becoming aware of that which never changes and is always present as Beingness. "I" all alone. You can do this throughout your day.

It is especially helpful when you awaken first thing in the morning to notice that all there is, is the "I." After we awaken, we attach the "I" to person, place, or thing. You can also become aware of how you automatically let go of "me" or "mine" when you fall asleep. In fact, if you did not let it go, there would be no sleep. As you do this exploration, you will become less and less attached to what you are not and much more aware of what you always already are.

You may also want to explore the following question: "If I am not the body and I am not the mind, then what am I?"

The Self (Your Self)

Lester Levenson

This session is composed of aphorisms collected from various talks by Lester. Please allow yourself to ponder each one individually before going on to the next in order to get the maximum benefit.

The Self, which is only your real Self, is the real "I" of you, knowing which, you know all there is to know.

Knowing your Self is being your Self.

The ultimate goal of every Being in the universe is total freedom, and that is when you are only your Self.

The only reason why you are not aware of your Self is simply because you want to be only a single body in the world.

Everyone will someday wake up to the fact that he is the Self.

To see your Self, you have to quiet the mind enough. When the mind is being stimulated by the thousands of thoughts in the subconscious, there's little chance of seeing your Self. The thousands of thoughts culminate in tendencies. Drop a tendency and you eliminate the thousands of thoughts under it.

The only things preventing you from being your Self are your mental habits, called tendencies or predispositions. Will them out!

If you discover that the source of the tendencies or predispositions is the Self, your Self, you will drop them, then and there.

When the mind gets free enough, then the Self of you takes over, and you are from then on Self-propelled.

To be the non-Self requires much effort; it is the effort we feel in life.

It requires no effort to be your Self!

The effort that you think you use to try to be your Self is the effort you use in trying to resist being the non-Self ego.

Your wishes to be the ego and, at the same time, not to be it, double the effort.

All the effort you're involved in is the effort to be an ego, or to resist being an ego.

Do you see what the problem is? It is your constant effort. You must become effortless.

There is only one real killing, and that's the killing of the Self. Kill the Self, and you've got ego and troubles. So everyone is a murderer of the Self who thinks he is an ego.

The only reason why anyone isn't aware of the Self is because he wants other than that.

If one wanted the Self as much as he wanted the world, he would soon have it.

When you find more joy within yourself than in anything else, then you're really moving in the right direction. If you find any joy in

392

life, you're in the wrong direction. Enjoying anything is wrong. Seek joy within. Be joy. There's nothing needed to enjoy if you are all joyous. If we are enjoying anything, we are in duality.

If I enjoy this, there's "I" and "this." If there's God (Self) alone, there can't be any "I" and "this." The basic Truth is that you are all joy. Enjoying something will impose an extreme limitation upon your natural state of all joy. To enjoy something, you're recognizing something other than you. So, I repeat, we should never enjoy anything. Seek joy only within, and then the natural state of infinite joy is discovered.

There is really only one happiness: it is being our very own Self. The happier we are, the more we are dwelling in our Self.

Every time you're high, you're only being your Self, and it feels terrific.

Living in your Self is living in ecstasy. Living in worldly desires is living in misery.

Everyone, in every moment, is experiencing his Self and, in every moment, saying otherwise.

It's only without thought that you can be the Self.

Discovering and being your Self is either easy or impossible.

Finding the Self is the easiest thing in the universe when you do it. When you don't do it, when you continuously keep looking away from it, you can never see it. And then it is the most difficult thing in the universe.

Being your Self is easy; being an ego is difficult.

When you realize what you are, it's the dropping of what you are *not* that is the growth. Each time you see what you are, you should drop that which you are not.

Everyone is seeking the Self, calling it by different names.

Anyone who's seeking happiness is seeking the Self. There are two kinds of people in the world: those who are consciously seeking God, happiness, and the Self, and those who are unconsciously seeking them.

In the consciousness of materiality (mammon), there is no God (Self).

You cannot see God in the world until you see God in yourself.

God is All and God is perfect. Therefore, anything that we see as imperfect is in us.

If you see separation, you see not the Self.

When the world is real, it is heavy. When the Self is real, the world is light.

When our false identity as a body-mind disappears, our real identity as Self appears.

We are the Self now. All that we have to do is to let go of the concept that we are not.

The Self is God. The ego is the devil.

God (your Self) is infinitely individual and individually infinite.

The most beautiful beautiful is God.

There is something far more beautiful than nature, it is the source of nature, the ultimate beauty—God.

No matter how much trouble man can get himself into, God is more resourceful in getting him out of it.

When we behave like God, we have Godlike powers.

God (Self) can materialize anything instantly.

The All that is God is not every little thing; it is the singular same essence behind all the little things.

God and good are sometimes used synonymously. Because everyone wants good, they make God good. God is above good and bad. However, good leads us to God.

If God is All, that leaves no room for the devil.

In reality, there is only God (your Self).

It's better to think of Self rather than God, because you generally think of God as other than you, and you generally think of Self as you.

There's no such thing as an external called God. There is a God, but it is the internal Beingness of each one.

Everything that is, is the Self, has its isness, its Beingness, in your Self, in God.

God is this world, the way this world is, and not the apparency that we see.

God—Truth, the Self—is changeless. If God knew change, he wouldn't be changeless. There is no action in God. God knows nothing of this world as we see it. God is only the changeless Beingness behind the world.

Everyone experiences his Self every moment of his life.

Self is the nearest of the near and the dearest of the dear.

Look to the Self for everything!

If you want to get more comforts, know thy Self.

The only answer to all problems is knowing your Self.

We will never be completely satisfied until we are completely being the Self.

To discover your Self is the reason why you came into this world.

Everyone is seeking his Self in his every act. The ultimate happiness is the Self. Any other happiness is only a bit of the Self.

When you know that the only joy there is is of the Self, you take it directly and, in its fullness, rather than meagerly, as you formerly took it.

The only one needed to know your Self is yourself.

This feeling of needing someone else to be your Self is ridiculous. It limits your being your Self.

Everyone is actually the Self-expressing the Self as extreme limitation, identifying as a limited body-mind. When you say "I" and add nothing to it, that's it.

When you are not identifying with the ego, you are the Self.

The only direct knowledge is of the Self. All other knowledge, needing something external to ourselves, is indirect.

If, at this moment, you identify with your Self, you are infinite.

That part of you that really is, your Beingness, is eternal. It's the I that you really are.

The little self, the ego, is nothing but the innate, infinite Self assuming that it is limited. There are no two selves, one higher, the other lower; there are no two "I's." There is only one Self. It is perfect and always will be perfect, even though you make the false assumption that it is imperfect and limited. You are now, always were, and always will be your Self.

Although one always experiences his Self, he usually needs to be directed to it before he becomes aware of it.

It is the Self that is the source of the ego, the source of everything.

You are every moment the unlimited Self, every moment saying, "I am limited." When you drop into the Self, you stop saying, "I am a limited body-mind." Look only at the Self; then the ego is eliminated.

When you dwell in your Self, you have no desire to be liberated. It is only when you are in the ego that you desire liberation.

The Self is not aware of the ego, and the ego is not aware of the Self.

When I, the infinite Being, feel like a body, it's the infinite Being imagining it is feeling like a body.

When the Self is real, the body is not real, and vice versa.

Identify with your body, and the extreme limitations of a body are yours. Identify with your Self, and you are all things: all knowledge and power, with no limitations.

There isn't anyone who couldn't materialize anything right now if he or she would just let go of identifying as the limited body.

If you will discover your Self, you'll see that the body and mind are servant to you.

Obtain and maintain direct experience of the Self. It is easier to obtain than to maintain direct experience.

Every time you say "I," it's everything, it's all the power in the universe. Every time you add something to it, you pull it down into limitation.

When you see the perfection, you see the other one as the other one really is, which is the real thing, the perfect Self.

There's not a higher Self and a lower Self. There's only you identifying with your limitless Being or identifying with your limited being.

You're never satisfied until you go all the way.

There's only one thing that satisfies fully and eternally, and that's total awareness of your Self.

Everyone is aware of a selfhood. It is the Self being wrongly identified as only a body.

If you would just be aware only, you would be your Self. If you would be only, you would be your Self.

This infinite glorious Being that we are, being absolutely perfect, can never change. It's always there.

The greatest of all teachers is your Self.

Look to your Self until you see it completely.

All Beingness is God, your Self.

In the Self, there is no haver, having or thing had. There is no doer, doing or thing done. There's no knower, knowing or thing known. There is only Being, being all Beingness.

When man seeks and discovers the seeker, he discovers that
In the Self:
God is not being something, God is Beingness.
God is not conscious of anything, God is consciousness.
God does not enjoy anything, God is joy.
God does not love anything or anyone, God is love.

In man:
His Beingness is God.
His consciousness is God.
His joy is God.
His love is God.

Act as though you are the Self. This will lead you to seeing it.

The reality of you (Self) is perfect: all joyous, all glorious, all happy.

The higher you go, the more you realize your Self, and the more you treat others as your own Self.

Being the Self is being selfless. In that state, you are interested only in serving others, in serving them as your Self.

The Self is absolute, profound, indescribable peace.

The only requisite for the realization of the Self, your Self, is stillness.

When one realizes his Self, all his actions and possessions are not perceived as his. He has given up "me" and "mine." Everything is the Self.

When you experience the Self, you can't tell about it. Anything you can tell something about isn't it. It's the state of only being. There's no action there, there's no form there. It's isness, and that's all that it is. You can't use it, you can't know it, you can only *be* it. When you're there, there's only one, only you, and that's all there is.

Anything but the Self is wholly imagination. The ego is only an apparent actor in the imaginary story script you wrote. Thou art that, here and now. Do not delude yourself. Drop your illusory limitation.

The Self is quiescence: perfect Awareness with perfect stillness.
He who seeks God will not find God in duality.
There is no human, since God is All.
There is no time, no becoming.
There is no creating in total perfection.
Only God beholds God, there being nothing else.
Only God loves God, God being All.
Be still and know that you are God!

There is only God, nothing else. If there is only God, then I am that. At the end of the road, we discover that there is only "I," all alone.

You are the Self, saying otherwise, but that doesn't make it so. No matter how much you say otherwise, you are that infinite Being right now.

You can't become your Self, you already are!

Every time you say "I," that's the Self—if you would only stop there!

The word "I," with nothing added to it, is your Self. When you just say "I," that feeling of "I" is the Self. When you say, "I am something," that isn't it, but just pure "I" and only "I" is it. When that is all you see and all you know, that's God, your Self. That's why God is closer than flesh! Just hold on to the word "I," only "I, I, I, I." Try it when you are alone. Just "I, I" and not "I am a body," but "I, I, I, I"—that feeling of being. Hold that; experience it. Be it! It is your Godhead—your Self!

Releasing Explorations by Hale Dwoskin

To summarize: There is no growing into the ultimate Being that you are. It is you right now and has always been. Every moment you are choosing to either identify with your limitless Beingness or with the appearance of a limited you.

Choose now to be still and know what you are.

Allow yourself to explore the "I" meditation that Lester described above. Simply repeat the word "I" to yourself without adding anything to it. As you do, allow yourself to drop everything but the "I" as best you can, and rest as the feeling or the presence that you are aware of as you repeat the word. Allow yourself to feel into that presence more and more as you repeat "I," until that is all there is. Then, just rest as that which you have always been.

You can do this meditation in isolation or in action. Either way you will be supporting yourself to rediscover your true nature and make it a conscious part of your awareness in every moment.

Thank you for reading this book. We are deeply grateful and honored that you took the time and focus to explore this way of viewing Truth. You will find that the more you explore this material, the more you get out of it. It is our sincerest desire that you discover and live the Truth of who or what you are. In fact, it is our wish that everyone learns the key to living life without suffering as their natural state of happiness, peace, and joy.

The Next Steps

Congratulations on completing *Happiness Is Free*. As you apply what you've learned to your quest to have a life filled with happiness, joy and unshakable peace—including the ultimate understanding—you'll find your apparent problems dropping away and your natural freedom shining through more and more. As you incorporate releasing into your life, it will get progressively easier, as will your use of these techniques. Even what you used to consider some of your most unattainable goals will come to you with greater ease. This progression will continue until you are at rest in every moment as the Being-Awareness that you have always been, and you see the exquisite perfection of All That Is. The following suggestions are designed to help you get the maximum benefit from the material in this book on an ongoing basis.

Allow yourself to use the material in every part of your life.

If you only thought about and explored freedom and letting go for a few minutes a day, you would gain tremendous benefits. However, if you allow releasing to be in your mind and heart throughout the day, your results will increase exponentially. Like everything else, the more energy you put into the process, the more you get out of it.

Review the material often.

Every time you reread and work with the ideas in this book, you'll get more out of them. As you grow internally, you'll understand and be able to apply what you learn on deeper levels. Treat each review as though it were your first reading. Explore all the exercises with as fresh eyes as you can.

Watch free videos of Lester Levenson.

To truly appreciate the power of Lester's words the best way to experience them is through one of the rare video recordings of Lester, which we are sharing free on Sedona.com. We also have many audio recordings of Lester available for download on Sedona.com at reasonable prices.

Watch our movie and other video resources.

In one hour and eight minutes, you can learn how to let go of stress, tension, and anxiety using one of our most powerful techniques called Triple Welcoming. It is absolutely free to watch *Letting Go: The Sedona Method Movie* on the Sedona Method channel on YouTube. If you have Amazon Prime in the US or the UK, you can stream it for free. Otherwise, there is a rental charge. Search movies for *Letting Go: The Sedona Method Movie*. There are also over 200 releasing videos on the Sedona Method channel on YouTube at youtube.com/TheSedonaMethod.

Join our Facebook community.

Follow and like the Sedona Method Facebook page, which has new quotes from Lester and me every day. Plus, we post videos there often. It is a great way to stay in touch with the releasing community. And join the Sedona Method community on Facebook and find like-minded people who are as focused on freedom as you are. It is a great place to find a releasing partner. Visit facebook.com/TheSedonaMethod.

Deepen your understanding of the Sedona Method.

By attending a retreat, one of our other releasing events, which are offered online or in person, or exploring one of our many powerful audio and online programs, your understanding of Truth and your ability to master all of life's challenges will expand exponentially. In this book, I have done my best to impart some of the key parts of the Sedona Method in an accessible and easy-to-apply way. For many people, however, reading a book is not an adequate substitute for the experiential understanding that comes from learning the Sedona Method in a more interactive way. All these learning approaches support the others.

Read *The Sedona Method.*

This book is an in-depth exploration of what Lester believed was his true gift to the world: releasing or letting go. It is filled with insight, clear and concise explanations, and powerful ways of incorporating releasing into your life.

Share what you have learned.

Communicating these ideas and practices with your friends, relatives, and acquaintances should stretch you and deepen your own understanding. Additional benefits come from surrounding yourself with like-minded people who are also interested in deepening their freedom and letting go of their pain and suffering. However, please share this material only with those who are truly interested in hearing about it. Grant those you know their Beingness—see them as already perfect—whether or not they share your interest.

Sedona Training Associates
2000 Plymouth Road
Suite 300
Minnetonka, MN 55305
1-844-978-2072 (toll-free in the US and Canada)
1-952-767-9822
Mail@Sedona.com
www.Sedona.com

You are the key to your own happiness, health, well-being, and success. All you need to do is use this key to unlock the secrets of freedom and happiness that are waiting to be discovered right within your own heart.

About the Authors

Lester Levenson

Lester Levenson was a man who mastered life's greatest challenge. In 1952 at age forty-two, Lester, a physicist and successful entrepreneur, was at the pinnacle of worldly success, yet he was an unhappy and very unhealthy man. So unhealthy that after having a second coronary, his doctors sent him home to his Central Park South penthouse apartment in New York City to die. Lester was a man who loved challenges, so instead of giving up, he decided to go back to the lab within himself and find some answers.

Because of Lester's determination and concentration, he was able to cut through his conscious mind to find all the answers. What he found first was a way of letting go of all inner limitations. Lester was so excited by his discovery that he used it intensively on himself for a period of three months. He then discovered the ultimate Truth of who and what we all are. At the end of that period, his body became totally healthy again, and he entered a state of profound peace that he never left through the day he died on January 18, 1994.

After Lester's awakening, he dedicated the remaining forty-two years of his life to helping others discover what he had discovered, including inspiring the creation of the world-renowned Sedona Method course. He is also a featured teacher in Rhonda Byrne's *The Greatest Secret* book. Several of the other featured teachers, including Rhonda's anonymous teacher, are students of Lester's teachings.

Hale Dwoskin

As part of being the designated heir to all of Lester Levenson's teachings, Hale Dwoskin has dedicated more than four decades to teaching and sharing the Sedona Method all over the world. His life has been focused on helping people alleviate their suffering and discover the Truth of who or what they are. Hale is the *New York Times* best-selling author of *The Sedona Method*. He is one of the featured teachers of the book and movie phenomenon *The Secret* as well as a featured teacher in *The Greatest Secret*. He is also featured in the movie *Letting Go*.

He is the cofounder of Sedona Training Associates, an organization created to promote the emotional releasing techniques inspired by his friend, mentor, and teacher Lester Levenson. He is also as a founding member of the Transformational Leadership Council.

Printed in Great Britain
by Amazon

24354239R00235